A Great Cloud of Witnessing

A Great Cloud of Witnessing

Arts Journalism of
Nancy Bauer

Edited by
Ian LeTourneau

Chapel Street Editions

Appreciation of Place

Chapel Street Editions exists within the unceded and unsurrendered territories of the Wolastoqiyik, Mi'kmaq, and Peskotomuhkati people. The work we do is born from the stories carried by this land and its inhabitants. The animals, plants, soil, water, and air make this place home for the Indigenous people who belong to this land, for the descendants of those who took this land and made it a belonging, and for those who have since come from away. Chapel Street Editions holds a deep appreciation for our place within this land and the stories it tells. We honour the land's Indigenous caretakers and are grateful for their wisdom and guidance.

Copyright © 2025 by Nancy Bauer
All rights reserved

Published by
Chapel Street Editions
150 Chapel Street
Woodstock, NB E7M 1H4
chapelstreeteditions@gmail.com
www.chapelstreeteditions.com

ISBN 978-1-988299-55-6

Library and Archives Canada Cataloguing in Publication

Title: A great cloud of witnessing : arts journalism of Nancy Bauer / edited by Ian LeTourneau.
Names: Bauer, Nancy, 1934- author. | LeTourneau, Ian, 1975- editor.
Description: Includes index.
Identifiers: Canadiana 20240524063 | ISBN 9781988299556 (softcover)
Subjects: LCSH: Arts, Canadian—New Brunswick—20th century. | LCSH: Arts, Canadian—New Brunswick—21st century. | LCSH: New Brunswick—Intellectual life—20th century. | LCSH: New Brunswick—Intellectual life—21st century.
Classification: LCC NX513.A3 N443 2024 | DDC 700.9715/1—dc23

Cover painting by Stephen May
"Nancy's Living Room with Nancy"
Oil on canvas, 2022

Author photo by Grace Bauer

Book design by Brendan Helmuth

Table of Contents

"Everything reminds me of an arts column": An Introduction . . i

Introduction to Kent Thompson's *Shotgun and Other Stories* (New Brunswick Chapbooks) 1

The Long Distance Running of David Adams Richards (*ArtsAtlantic*) 3

Fred Cogswell: Creating Space and Time (*ArtsAtlantic*) 10

Oberon Press: The Other Ottawa Connection (*ArtsAtlantic*) . . 17

Alfred Bailey and the Creative Moment (*ArtsAtlantic*) 20

Remembering the Ice House Gang (*ArtsAtlantic*) 26

The Report of the New Brunswick Arts Policy Advisory Committee, Fredericton (*ArtsAtlantic*) 34

Premier's Advisory Committee on the Arts (PACA) Board Meetings (*ArtsAtlantic*) 38

Renaissance Man (*The New Brunswick Reader*) 42

Bill's World (*The New Brunswick Reader*) 48

Robert Gibbs: A Sharp Selfhood (*ArtsAtlantic*) 53

Local poetry has the power to broaden our community (*Salon*) 61

Mixing cultures promises to stimulate the fruit of our literary labours (*Salon*) 64

Provincial writers' federation falls short (*Salon*) 67

In the arts, one person can make a difference (*Salon*) 70

Written accounts do more to support the arts (*Salon*) 73

The fine and often thankless art of book reviews (*Salon*) 76

Many heads are better than one (*Salon*) 79

A man who embraced us all (*Salon*) 82

The uncertain future of books (*Salon*) 85

Artists need cash to create (*Salon*) 88

You can't browse at online bookstores (*Salon*) 91

Books in the hands of the writers (*Salon*) 94
Into the inner lives of poets (*Salon*) 97
A world that arises from a sentence (*Salon*) 100
Alden Nowlan, the great energizer (*Salon*). 103
The manuscripts in my attic (*Salon*) 106
Extracting emotions from rocks (*Salon*) 109
A personal rapport with an artist one hasn't met (*Salon*) . . . 112
A brain conducive to creativity (*Salon*). 115
Portraits that capture the essence of a persona (*Salon*). 118
Support for a land of scribblers (*Salon*) 121
Renewed life for two arts groups (*Salon*). 124
Power in one's talent being recognized (*Salon*). 127
Reflecting on endings and beginnings (*Salon*) 130
Framework of hope is built on past successes (*Salon*) 133
Finding a pattern with soothing words (*Salon*) 136
In memory of Helen Weinzweig (*Salon*). 139
Recollections of artists, life lessons (*Salon*). 142
Making it strange in Odell Park (*Salon*). 145
Reflections on journeying the road less travelled (*Salon*) . . . 148
Memories of Molly (*Salon*) 151
Falling for a federation (*Salon*). 154
Casting a vote for the arts (*Salon*) 157
Inky poetry (*Salon*). 160
Not for ourselves alone, but for all (*Salon*) 163
Your last and final 400 words (*Salon*) 166
The theatre of real life (*Salon*) 169
Rabbit in your headlights (*Salon*) 172
When someone great is gone (*Salon*) 175
The Eclectic Reading Club (*Salon*) 178
Workshop wake up (*Salon*). 181

Of Goodridge and graves (*Salon*) 184
Writing waypoints (*Salon*) 187
Footnotes to the book (*Salon*) 190
Doting on Davies (*Salon*) 193
A richly creative life (*Salon*) 196
I shouldn't complain (*Salon*) 199
Odd Fellows (*Salon*) 202
Chapter and Verse (*Salon*) 205
The new *Fiddlehead* is full of New Brunswick content (*Salon*) 208
Changing the way we think about beauty (*Salon*) 211
The Prat sisters' bindery (*Salon*) 214
A Sunday of rich music and saying farewell to a poetry-reading host (*Salon*) 217
Introducing our cultural laureate (*Salon*). 221
Why is it that our province is the last to have a provincial book awards? (*Salon*). 224
Large crowd of writers honoured (*Salon*) 227
The literary life (*Salon*). 230
A bolt of poetry among grey clouds (*Salon*) 233

About the Cover Painting 237
About the Author 239
About the Editor. 241
Index 243

"Everything reminds me of an arts column": An Introduction

Nancy (Luke) Bauer was born in Chelmsford, Massachusetts in 1934. In 1956, she graduated with her BA from Mount Holyoke College and married Bill Bauer. They moved to Fredericton in 1965, where Bill was hired to teach in the English Department at the University of New Brunswick. While raising 3 children, she became active in the writing community, attending the fabled Tuesday Night group, a gathering of professors, students and local writers who met at McCord Hall, the refurbished 1851 ice house on UNB Fredericton's campus. She was the editor and publisher of the New Brunswick Chapbook series, which grew out of the ice house group and featured many established writers such as Robert Gibbs and M. Travis Lane but also published early work by David Adams Richards, Brian Bartlett, and Michael Pacey. She was a founding member of the Writers' Federation of New Brunswick and founder/organizer of the Maritime Writers' Workshop (WFNB and MWW, she tells us in one of her columns, began their lives without the apostrophe!). She has published 5 novels, including *Flora, Write this Down*, the first fiction title published by Goose Lane Editions in 1983. She has also served as Writer-in-Residence at two universities, at Bemidji State University, Minnesota in spring 1987, and at the University of New Brunswick for the 1989-90 academic year.

Nancy Bauer's career as an arts journalist began in 1980 when Joseph Sherman, the editor of *ArtsAtlantic*, the "arts journal of record," asked if she could be their New Brunswick-based writer. Over almost twenty years, she contributed 18 articles as well as reviews of books, plays, exhibits, and even one lecture (John Ralston Saul's Christina Sabat Memorial Lecture Series), as well as providing notes and updates from important happenings in the province, such as the foundational meetings of the New Brunswick Arts Board.

In 1993, *Telegraph-Journal* editor Neil Reynolds conceived of a new Saturday magazine insert for the paper, *The New Brunswick Reader*, focused on arts and crafts, and he invited Nancy to contribute profiles of artists and craftspeople living province-wide. Not only did she write 44 such profiles over a year and a half, but for the first year of its existence, she also supplied the photographs for the cover.

If that was the extent of her output, then it would be an impressive body of work and a valuable contribution to the documentation of arts in the province, but in 2007, she signed on to write a weekly column for the brand-new *Salon* section (which replaced *The New Brunswick Reader* that year). "State of the Art," the name of this column, is what I suspect most readers of this book think of when they think of Nancy Bauer. Over the next 11 years (2007-2017), she wrote a total of 531 columns (by my count), 800 words per week. Anchored on page 2 of the section, this weekly column was a must-read for anyone interested in New Brunswick arts; it encapsulated what was happening in New Brunswick's arts and culture scene. As it delivered the scoop on the present moment—book launches, gallery openings, theatre productions, award ceremonies, etc.—it also documented significant developments of the past, like the formation of Fredericton's Gallery Connexion. Filled with curiosity, passion, and insight, these columns grappled with pertinent issues of the day like arts funding and the rise of the e-reader; they paid homage to the people that were making things happen in New Brunswick's arts and culture scene and commemorating significant figures on their passing. All of this makes her columns, and the body of work in whole, a necessary starting point for anyone who plans to research or write about New Brunswick arts and culture.

This book collects only a fraction of the over 500,000 words of arts journalism and that selection mostly focuses on the literary side of New Brunswick arts and culture, a side I thought I knew well, but for which I now have a deeper appreciation. Nancy has the skills of a great chronicler: she captures the moment with a mixture of personal and historical. As we learn about the events she attends or the subjects she contemplates, bit by bit we learn more about Nancy, her family, her creative practice, and her place at the centre of New Brunswick cultural life. For instance, we learn that her grandfather was a paving stone cutter and that she has five rocks in her bureau, one of which is from the moor of Wuthering Heights. In one column where she lists all the events and writers who have passed through her house, we are told that one guest, Michael Ondaatje, taught her daughter chopsticks on the piano. And we learn about important arts figures, like Elizabeth Brewster, Alden Nowlan, and Molly Bobak, to name just a few. We see the development of literary history from someone who played a central role in its creation but we also witness as it continuously unfolds: the Writing on the Wall series of exhibits at the Beaverbrook Art Gallery that paired poets with artwork (which she curated after its creator Joe Sherman died), the flourishing of book festivals in the major cities, and the establishment of the New Brunswick Book Awards. Reading "State of the Art" every weekend in particular was like sitting in Nancy's living room, picking up the conversation from the last visit, hearing about what she has been doing since last week while also being regaled with stories. The writing creates an inviting atmosphere, just as depicted in Stephen May's painting of her living room that graces the cover.

The title of this book, by the way, comes from a line in Nancy's keynote address at the 7th annual New Brunswick Book Awards, given on June 4, 2022: "We as writers are delighted when we have a book in our hands with our name under the title, but I have to believe that in the grand scheme of things that is not important. What is important is that a great cloud of witnesses has been pondering our human condition." That struck me as a profound statement when I heard it at the event, and it resonated time and again as I read through Nancy's extensive nonfiction. She has so expertly, sensitively, knowledgeably pondered the role the arts play in our human condition. A great cloud of witnessing, indeed.

Ian LeTourneau

Introduction to Kent Thompson's *Shotgun and Other Stories*

Kent Thompson writes about the end of things: the end of life, marriage, home; he also writes about people in passage: from one love to another, from one home to another, in the process of dying. The result of such preoccupations is that the reader is able to watch naturalistic characters becoming allegorical figures. The narrator in "I Live in Canada" introduces himself in a dream, "Coming up out of the dark—waking." He has dreamed about the allegorical Political Figure (who appears also in "What Costume Shall the New Man Wear"); he himself is the allegorical Hunted. The Political Figure, the Hunted, the Hunter, become real; the Hunted becomes the Hunter and Barbara becomes the Hunter with T. J. Clark the ridiculous Political Figure. The story functions equally well on the realistic level and the allegorical level, and each level illuminates the other.

In fact, this collection could serve as a manual for the craft of the short story, because for Thompson the technique is the story. In an essay in John Metcalf's *The Narrative Voice*, Thompson says, "I think of my stories as consisting of a series of 'weights'…I am attempting to structure the story by means of emotional weights." Pace and syntax, he says, contribute to weight: "The release of emotion is indicated by the turned-loose sentence structure." The emotional effect of short sentences can be illustrated by the beginning of "Among Women." "Fredericton was a sad place then. The soldiers were leaving. She did not know much about me."

These short sentences not only carry emotional weight; they characterize the simple nature of the narrator. Although Thompson uses a wide range of narrative voices and tones, his narrators are always on their best behaviour. Their language is rarely chatty; it is almost always the formal language used to tell an important story—to try to make sense of what has happened to them. This tone is most successful where it more exactly defines the character of the narrator: an old man trying to retain dignity in "Shotgun," a drunk in "Because I am Drunk" who realizes well enough his own degradation, a woman with a slim hold on respectability in "Among Women." In "Perhaps the Church Building Itself," the narrator, Benjamin Wilson, uses a language that does not imitate the way such a man would talk to himself or even talk to a stranger, but rather that imitates the language of the man of substance he would like to be. "But I was led astray," he says. Or, "Indeed, I thought I was in exactly that state when Rev. Williams found me." When he uses foul language, "Lying there weeping while my shit and piss poured from me," we are ashamed with him; we know to what depths he has sunk. And, in "Shotgun," when the same narrator uses a periodic sentence, "And senility, I surely believe, is nothing more nor less than the slipping into one's alternative life…" we understand that he is trying to overcome this senility.

Such formal diction — the use of "of course" and "therefore" and the pronoun "one," an opening such as "They speak a jargon all their own," or an ending such as "But portents, you see. Portents. What's on the other side?" — has a similar effect to the rhetorical "Once Upon a Time." The diction enables the stories to function on two levels, as John Mills has pointed out in a review of "Perhaps the Church Building Itself." They function on the literal level of an authentic voice telling a believable story and on the level of a metaphor with its resemblances and reverberations.

The use of the weight of words and of sentence and paragraph structure: is the word light or heavy? Anglo-Saxon or Latinate? are the sentences simple or periodic? does the paragraph move swiftly or slowly? — constitutes the use of prose as a man who is a poet might use it. And indeed, Kent Thompson is a poet of economy and lucidity. The New Brunswick Chapbooks has published two collections of his poems. We are very happy to introduce our new series of prose chapbooks with this collection of his stories.

New Brunswick Chapbooks, 1979.

The Long Distance Running of David Adams Richards

One Tuesday night in the fall of 1971 a group of writers meeting in McCord Hall listened to David Adams Richards read the beginning of his first novel: "Blood had dried to his hands by mid-morning, thin streaks of blood on his fingers and knuckles. He cradled his rifle, walking slowly over wet gully leaves, his jacket opened, his blond hair in sweaty knots."

McCord, a restored ice house on the Fredericton campus of the University of New Brunswick, had been for four years the scene of an informal writer's workshop; those of us attending had heard many pages of prose and poetry read there around the huge oak table. Much had been Richards' work; we had been enthusiastic over it, and we were especially impressed with the first chapter of his novel. But it was only as chapter followed chapter, week after week, that we began to realize what we were hearing. The abundance of Richards' prose, the way the words flowed out of him, 45 pages at a time, the instinctive way he moved towards an end rather than floundering about, and above all, his breathtaking handling of the scenes between the father and the mother—all convinced us that here was a born novelist. Nine months later he read us the final chapter.

The Coming of Winter did not wait long for public recognition. It was accepted quickly by Oberon Press, the first publisher that had a crack at the manuscript. Richards at 22 had published what was essentially the first draft of the first novel he had ever written. Once those first chapters had started to come, he realized that the novel was his form: "I'm a long-distance runner; even my short stories run to 40 pages." *The Coming of Winter* was widely reviewed, most often favourably, went through several printings, was adopted by many Canadian literature courses, and became the favourite underground novel for high school students over the Maritimes. Fred Cogswell called it the best first novel ever to come out of New Brunswick. John Metcalf said of it, "— one of the most important Canadian novels I have read in a long time—a powerful and important debut and the beginning of what I am convinced will be a major literary career."

When Oberon announced last summer that the translation rights to *The Coming of Winter* had been sold to the USSR, a circle had been completed. Richards says that the book that most influenced him was one he read as a teenager, *Six Great Russian Novels*, especially Dostoevsky's *The Gambler* and Pushkin's *The Queen of Spades*. Now, publisher Michael Macklem estimates that a quarter of a million Russians will read *The Coming of Winter*. "The Russians print big runs of a few books and these are widely circulated. When you realize that 2400 copies of the book were sold in Canada, you can appreciate the size of the audience. More people will probably read *The Coming of Winter* than have read all the books we've published."

David Adams Richards' first publication was *One Step Inside*, a privately-printed pamphlet of poems and stories. In it, the young Richards announced his *ars poetica*: "Rather a poet should take one step inside, to 'begin at the beginning,' and dedicate his work to revealing man's emotions, humanity, or the lack of both." No one reading this volume would say, "Here is a major talent." Still, there are in that volume themes that Richards develops later: "And how can I love you? / With years of lice between us."

In December of 1971, *The Atlantic Advocate* published a story, "The Child and the Boy." It was not a very good story, Richards admits, but the prose style is one he will use in his later and better work, a style that delights but discomforts some. The story begins, "As they walked, they were cold and would stamp their feet for warmth and walk faster for warmth and wave their arms like wings of wounded birds for warmth." The technique of repetition at the beginning of stories is one the Russians love: Gogol's use of the repetition of "department" in "Overcoat," for example.

During the years 1972 and 1973 Richards continued to read new work to his Fredericton friends, once holding them spellbound as they insisted he go on reading by candlelight during a power failure. For most of that time he was a student at St. Thomas University, but he left before graduating. *The Coming of Winter* had been accepted by Oberon Press; a section of it had won the Norma Epstein Award; he had been given an Ontario Arts Council grant (and a little later two Canada Council grants) — a B.A. didn't seem necessary.

By late 1974 Richards began reading chapters of *Blood Ties* to the Ice House Gang. They were not disappointed: *Blood Ties* is a more complex, much richer work than *The Coming of Winter* — a real advance. In 1976 it was selected to be Oberon's 100th title, the cover done in gold, the publisher and Richards both announcing to the world that although they had done great things in the past, even greater things were to come. "*Blood Ties* is Oberon's hundredth title and as such it represents a major achievement for both writer and publisher."

Richards' next book was *Dancers at Night*, a collection of six stories, of which the reviewer in *The Canadian Forum* said, "Richards has, in *Dancers at Night*, written five exciting stories and that excitement is the product, quite simply, of consistently good writing."

David Adams Richards was born October 17, 1950, the third child of six brothers and sisters. His grandfather Richards had been a traveling musician from Wales who settled down when he met David's grandmother, the violinist at the Newcastle Opera House. After they married, they purchased the Opera House and together played music to accompany silent movies. Left a widow, Grandmother Richards not only coped, she couped, by securing a five-year monopoly for talking movies in that area. The events surrounding Richards' birth most certainly predisposed him to be a writer, Richards thinks. His mother, seven months pregnant, fell while hanging out the clothes; David was born prematurely with a brain hemorrhage. His left side was damaged; he didn't walk until late; they feared he was developmentally delayed. "I'm convinced that helped me to an essential understanding of cruelty," he says. One of his first memories is of the train ride to Montreal when he was two to see a brain specialist. His mother was determined to place him under the best possible care. The doctor handed David a ball, asking him to give it back. "Faster, faster," the doctor kept saying as the ball went back and forth, until David took it and threw it at the doctor, hitting him on the head. "There's nothing wrong with his intelligence," the doctor said.

David grew up in Newcastle, graduated from Harkins High School, fell in love with the elegant Newcastle Library, the scene of his story, "The Age of Chess"; he hung around the pretty little park in the centre of town (many scenes from *The Coming of Winter* are set there), went fishing in the Big Sevogle, hunted, escaped death in a bad car accident, worked at the Heath Steele Mines (where Cecil of *Blood Ties* works), and socialized at the Black Horse Tavern ("He was crossing the park to the tavern now but crossing it slowly because he wished to avoid where he was going, at least for a time").

He went to Europe, returned, and in 1970 enrolled in Saint Thomas University. He married Peggy McIntyre from Bartibog and after *Blood Ties* was finished they traveled around a bit — out to Vancouver, over to Spain. But in March of 1976 they went back to the Miramichi. For a while they lived in an enclave of writers at Black River Bridge on the Bay du Vin: Richards, the poet John Stewart and the novelist Ray Fraser had met in Alden Nowlan's living room and along with Leo Ferrari and Al Pittman had planned practical jokes to play on the world — The Flat Earth Society and the Restoration of the Scottish Pretender, Stewart himself.

Richards' Peggy is his Beatrice. "To Peggy" is the dedication of his first three books. Richards says, "my dependence on her is almost frightening." Peggy looks like a Beatrice; she is beautiful in a sweet Pre-Raphaelite way. A patient, intelligent, and lively woman who is not only an inspiration but, more practically, a patron.

Russian readers can find in Richards' novel many of the devices diagnosed by their own theoretical critics, but Richards' art is quite unconscious. "I love talking about literature and writing it, but to tell

The Death of Little Simon will be Book I of a projected longer work, *Lives of Short Duration*, one that has been rumbling around in Richards' head for quite a while. Book I deals with the life, and death at 28, of one of a large group of people on the Miramichi, all related in a clan-like way. "One woman asked me why didn't I deal with incest in my novels," Richards says. "When I started to trace all of the characters back, I found out they were all related somehow, so maybe this work is about incest. We're not a pure race up here on the Miramichi."

These days Richards lives a life in Newcastle far away in truth and spirit from other writers. His friends are his boyhood friends. He says, "I think Dylan Thomas was right when he said the boyhood friends are your only true friends." He curls, "I'm the best curling writer in the world!", has a beer with his buddies at the tavern, writes. Occasionally he and Peggy come to Fredericton to visit his brothers and sisters, to see Alden Nowlan. When he finishes this book, he would like to go to England, look up Alan Sillitoe and have beer with him ("I really admire his work—especially *Loneliness of the Long Distance Runner*"), and visit Malcolm Lowry's grave ("I think Lowry's the greatest writer of the 20th century").

His readers can only hope that after that, Richards will start Book II of *Lives of Short Duration*, that it will be the volume dealing with the 19th century history of the clan, that it will live up to the promise of "Kopochus", the story of the 1825 Miramichi forest fire in *Dancers at Night*, and that we can say of *Lives* what old Patrick says as he flees the fire, "if I last through this 'ere I'll live a long time yet."

ArtsAtlantic 2.4 (Summer 1980)

Fred Cogswell: Creating Space and Time

East Centreville, New Brunswick is the result of a geometrically tidy crossroad from where you can look out over an unobstructed view of rolling farmland and the larger hills beyond. On the lesser road, running along a ridge, is the farm where poet Fred Cogswell was born. The architecture of the house, repeated many times in the area, is of a severe geometric simplicity: two-storied, perfectly square, with its roof formed by four equal triangles. Geometry, direction, perspective, and space are important in Cogswell's poetry both for imagery and for philosophical analogies. In his poem "Direction" Cogswell writes:

> by the black lines
> of a street-map
> I travel this city,
> recalling no north
> south east or west
> in its fragmented sky
>
> but when I go
> back to the place
> where my heart grew
> the sky inside my head
> I move as birds move
> when they fly

In East Centreville, you can see the influence of place on the making of a poet; you can understand better the tension in Cogswell's poetry between his geometrically tidy mind and his tolerant and eclectic heart.

As a boy, he was interested in everything: collecting butterflies, fishing, hurt people, baseball, basketball, birds, books. "I was precocious and my mother encouraged me in my many interests because she could see I wouldn't make a very good farmer." That a butterfly could be both real and image, both literal and symbolic, fascinated him even as a boy. That a caterpillar could change into a butterfly seemed wonderful enough, he says, but that the change could symbolize death for the Greeks or that a butterfly could be an image for Psyche seemed more wonderful still. "I've always tried to reconcile the dualism of the world of the senses with the world of words and symbols," he says. The poem "Phaeton" is at once the recounting of a childhood experience, "All the years I hunted butterflies / In field and wood and lane / I saw but once a phaeton / Perched on a blue vervain," and the synthesizing of that experience into a larger symbol.

Of the many poems using fish as images, he says, "I spent a lot of time fishing as a boy." In "Fish-Dinner" he uses the myths and rituals developed over centuries to invest the simple eating of fish with its forgotten, larger meaning, "though fish-knives keep/ceremonial shape/fish bring no fear/ to eaters here."

Fred Cogswell is well-known as a champion of the underdog and the unfortunate. When he was ten, he even defended the devil in his Sunday School class. But when he was twelve, he came to appreciate the plight of the unfortunate even more deeply when he overheard girls making fun of his appearance and his speech impediment. Not only the concern for others but the synthesis of poet and lover that forms a major part of Cogswell's poetry must stem from that moment vividly remembered: "We were writing exams; the girls were standing in back of me." In reaction to the hurt, he began to write poetry, imitating poems from Palgrave's *Golden Treasury*.

Eclectic is a word that is often used to describe Cogswell in all of his many capacities: as publisher, as editor, as scholar, as teacher, as translator, or as poet. This eclecticism must have come in part from his experience in the Centreville schools. With many grades in one room, the teacher had to leave the students to their own devices. Fred read everything the school library had to offer—the encyclopedia, the dictionary, William Langland's *The Vision of Piers Plowman*, Sir Edward Creasy's *Fifteen Decisive Battles of the World*, R. D. Blackmore's

Springhaven, the *Campfire Girls* books, Grace Livingston Hill, a volume of Burke's speeches. What he liked about high school was that there were a lot more books in the library—Dickens, Scott, and Jeffrey Farnon's books about medieval chivalry. The Farnon books influenced his attitude to women and gave him the conviction that magnanimity is the greatest of all the virtues. "I can remember reading Hardy's *Under the Greenwood Tree* while standing up grain. I'd read a bit and then go back to work and then read a bit more."

Another book he read was the Bible. "I liked the Old Testament best because that was where the action was." The Baptist Church claimed his attention Sunday morning and evening and sometimes during the week for prayer meetings and hymn sings. The church played a part in the making of many New Brunswick writers, he says, because, "There is little for the mind in rural New Brunswick. At church we came upon our first abstract ideas. The nearest thing to a sustained intellectual address we heard was the sermon. My idea of Nirvana is to be immersed in religion. I've gone to Mass for 37 years."

In 1940, he went into the Army, serving in the infantry and the Canadian Forestry corps, first in New Brunswick, then in Québec City, and finally in Scotland. In the army he first read the poetry of Stephen Crane in an anthology edited by Richard Legalian. Crane's brevity and the formality of his language influenced Cogswell deeply. The same anthology contained some sonnets by E.A. Robinson, but Fred says that although it might seem as if he had been influenced by Robinson when he wrote the sonnets in *The Stunted Strong*, he doesn't believe he had been. He thinks these sonnets about the people of rural New Brunswick must have sprung up of their own accord.

In a recent introduction to his poetry he writes, "I must confess, however, that how and why such a poem came to me in the form that it did—free verse, couplet, epigram, sonnet, etc.—is more of a mystery today than it was when I began to write at least 45 years ago…I am convinced that analytical tools cannot cope with the mystery of synthesis beyond the most rudimentary examination." When he began to translate DesRochers, he was surprised to find that DesRochers' sonnets were like his own, in the French *terroir* tradition. Why the poems were alike, even though there had been no direct influence, is "an unsolved mystery."

Before he writes a poem, he says, "I get an idea in my head, walk around and let it stew. Then the poem comes. Sometimes it takes 40 seconds to write it down, and sometimes it takes years to get it right. The form it comes in determines the selection of details, so I'm not my own man. I find free verse too easy—it seems like notes for a form instead of the form itself."

After the war was over, he enrolled in the University of New Brunswick. There he encountered the poetry of Alfred deVigny. What impressed him was deVigny's theory, illustrated in "Le Cor" and "Möise," that you could describe an action or incident and, through the choice of details, make that action symbolic. At UNB he also met Latin epigrams which reminded him of Crane's epigrams and the haikus he had read in a book by Lin Yutang. These epigrams and haikus reinforced Cogswell's natural bent toward short forms. "I don't like to write long things, even long essays."

When he had received his Ph.D. from the University of Edinburgh, he returned to UNB to teach. He became editor of *The Fiddlehead*, transforming it from a student publication into an international literary magazine, publishing many young poets who were later to become famous. After 14 years, he retired from the editorship to expand the Fiddlehead Press, turning it into the most amazing publishing house of poetry in Canada, with over 300 titles. His scholarship, especially in the field of Canadian literature, has been seminal and important. Very few studies of Maritime literature fail to quote his perceptive survey in the *Literary History of Canada* (General Editor, Carl F. Klinck).

His activities did not get in the way of his teaching though, for he has always been a popular and influential professor. He says that, because of his speech impediment, the students have to concentrate hard to be able to understand what he says. "They learn well that way."

How does he have the energy for this prodigious schedule? "When I'm tired, I feel better. I go around in a constant state of euphoria." Euphoria is a good state to be in when you are writing poetry.

The difficulty of communicating the nature of reality as he sees it is the subject of many of Cogswell's poems. But some reality, he says, can only be sublimated. "The intense kinesthetic experience of love doesn't demand expression and can't be expressed." In "A Lover's Catechism," a successful experiment with form, he writes, "What then are painting, sculpture, music, and / poems in relation to love? / These things are the masks that memory / creates to hide the failure of love. Its / success requires neither shape nor sound."

In many poems, "Like Two Slant Trees," for example, he portrays a crippling emotional dependence in marriage. He says, "I don't like the idea of marriage as a crutch. I've always insisted on the rights of each individual." His own family demonstrates this principle. His wife Pat has a strength of character that is now legendary, and his daughters Carmen and Kathleen both have impressive careers of their own.

In the last few years, a new, more complex metaphysics has developed out of Cogswell's imagery of space and time. In poems like "Act of Love," "There are Two Worlds in Time" and "When Mind Jumped the Void" he explores a metaphysics that has its roots in Vico and in Blake. Cogswell develops Vico's idea that the word-world of the mind is closer to us than the physical world of the senses, because Man has created the world of words and symbols, whereas God has created the physical world. In "Act of Love" he writes:

> Although the space between us lies immense,
> There floats across the void from him to me
> The fine-spun gossamer of poetry
> Drawn from the entrails of experience.

If words and symbols can transcend time and space, so can memory. In "Above the Purple Heather," this idea is compressed into sixteen lines and a beautifully simple image:

> Above the purple heather
> A bird sang in the sky.
> It is more than thirty years
> Since last I saw it fly
>
> . . . .
>
> Above the Scottish heather
> A lark its song set free:
> All of it that lives is now
> In Canada with me.

Cogswell's imagery of perspective, of space, and of direction has modulated into the more complex imagery of void, stasis, and quasar: "When mind jumped the void / Between sounds and found symbols / A new arc-light blazed." Eternity is not of duration because the world of thought and of symbols defies the battle of energy and entropy in the physical universe. He says, "There is less sadness and concern in my later poems, because I've come to see that epiphany and eternity are what really matter, not accidents of time and space."

In "Against Perspective," he expresses the artist's hope of entering that world of epiphany and eternity:

> Watch that man
> on the runway there
> He dwindles as your plane
> noses upper air
> and vanishes even
> as you scan
>
> Time, too,
> is such a plane
> What space can do
> time can as well
> even to me
> even to you

A Great Cloud of Witnessing

        Time and space
        are false compasses
        and kill all hope
        Art is the true pole
        in a kaleidoscope
        Art lies within

        Watch that man
        then close your eyes
        and keep them closed
        until your plane
        has reached the skies
        He will not disappear

        Then draw his face
        each telling line
        in due proportion
        and in proper place
        You may have cheated time
        as you have cheated space.

ArtsAtlantic 12 (3.4: 1981)

Oberon Press: The Other Ottawa Connection

In the last eight years, Oberon Press has published twenty-four books by fourteen Maritime writers. That's no accident. When Michael Macklem, his wife Anne Hardy and their sons Timothy and Nicholas, founded Oberon in 1966, their intention was, in Hardy's words, "to become a truly national publisher with interest in the various regions." And, says Hardy, "even though, or perhaps because the Maritimes has a strong regional feeling, it has a strong Canadian feeling. Fifteen years ago the two most Canadian parts of the country were Saskatchewan and the Maritimes. And because the Maritimes has always been a literary society, they were in on the beginning of Canadian nationalism's literary movement."

It was in 1974 that Oberon's interest in the regions and this Maritime literary society came together. Oberon accepted books by three New Brunswick writers, David Adams Richards, Joseph Sherman and Elizabeth Brewster, and because a surprisingly high percentage of its new list was by New Brunswickers, Macklem decided to try an experiment, to hold his fall launching party in Fredericton. The October weekend that the League of Canadian Poets was holding its annual meeting in Fredericton seemed like a good time for the party, hitting the local literati as well as writers from across the country. What sealed the Oberon-Maritime association was the success of the venture. As Macklem summed it up, "A lot of people came and came with dry feet. They drank all the wine and ate all the cheese. They bought all the books. They got to know the local writers and the writers met the press and media. Oberon made itself known in Fredericton. What more could one ask?"

Some one hundred and fifty people had turned out, proving that New Brunswick could back its writers. As Macklem told an interviewer two years later, "There is no place else where the literary community is so cohesive and the general public so supportive of its writers." The New Brunswick literary scene, he said, is the most exciting in Canada.

Since 1974, Oberon has held three other parties in Fredericton to launch books by such Maritime writers as Marjory Whitelaw, Susan Kerslake, Ann Copeland, Terry Crawford, and William Bauer. This year Oberon returns to its "original" writers, publishing Richards' fourth book, *Lives of Short Duration*, Sherman's second, *Lords of Shouting* and Brewster's *The Way Home*.

Oberon's Maritime connection extends even further. Twice Macklem has come to the Maritime Writers' Workshop to advise students. Oberon's annual short story collection always has a liberal representation from the Maritimes; in 1977, for example, five of the ten stories. When Macklem is not visiting, he is writing his writers, exhorting them to finish what they are working on, or urging them to write their MP in support of literary publishing.

Macklem and Hardy seem at home here. At one of the launching parties, Hardy appeared with earth-stained hands. "I've been weeding Miss Hall's garden," she explained. Hall's Bookstore had been one of the first in the country to feature books by Canadian writers, she said. Oberon thrives here because it understands the region. Hardy, whose father is a Maritimer, says, "People in central Canada think of the Maritimes as a homogeneous unity, but it isn't. There are four separate audiences, centred around the four capitals. Richards' Miramichi novels will sell in Fredericton, but not in Truro. The provincial boundaries are important."

The connection, however, has not been without its problems. Oberon has had criticism hurled at it by the very writers it tries to serve. Macklem, they say, writes too tough a contract. But Kent Thompson, whose novel *Shacking Up* Oberon published in 1980, argues, "He publishes things no one else will publish. So he has a right to demand a tough contract."

One of the things no one else will publish is short fiction and certainly not first collections. Oberon has made short story collections its special interest and half of the Maritime books it has published have been of this genre. Oberon also publishes literary novels, in a time when more and more publishers are selling out to consumerism in fiction.

Another criticism writers make of Oberon is directed at its distribution, a perennial problem for small presses. But Thompson says to this, "I think distribution is Macklem's strength. He distributes the books himself. *Shacking Up* has made more money for me than either of my other two novels" (published by two larger companies, one Canadian, one American).

To effect this distribution, Macklem and Hardy crisscross the country by car, visiting bookstores and libraries and meeting with their writers. Out of these exhausting and sometimes dangerous journeys (they were involved in a serious accident on one western swing) comes Hardy's *Where to Eat in Canada*, Oberon's bread and butter book. "It's a mad, hard life, but presumably it's worth it," says Macklem.

Oberon continues to find new Maritimers to publish. Nova Scotia's Veronica Ross and New Brunswick's Joseph Green are two recent examples. As Robert Gibbs (*I've Always Felt Sorry for Decimals*) says, "Oberon's openness to Maritime writers is something to rejoice about because it gets us a national audience."

But the benefits are not all one way. Oberon's Maritime connection has helped it to earn accolades. *Books in Canada* writes, "the Oberon imprint is about as close to a name brand as there is in Canadian publishing." And Alden Nowlan calls it, "one of the country's most prestigious publishers of poetry and fiction." Writers like Gibbs, Richards, Copeland and Beth Harvor have helped to establish that reputation.

Even more important than the accolades it receives, however, is Oberon's ability to survive. Literary presses come and go, but Oberon hangs on, largely because of the energy and devotion of the whole Macklem family. Zealous Maritime readers can feel that they too have aided in that survival.

ArtsAtlantic 14 (4.2: Summer 1982)

Alfred Bailey and the Creative Moment

Dr. Alfred G. Bailey, professor emeritus of history at the University of New Brunswick, distinguished man of letters, and a senior Canadian poet, has long been interested in the patterns taken by culture in general and art in particular. In his book of essays, *Culture and Nationality*, and in many uncollected essays, memoirs and lectures, he has explored the waves, pulses and climaxes that describe the Canadian cultural tradition.

Bailey believes that, at certain periods in the development of a given society, the conditions are right for a flowering of that society's culture, an efflorescence in art and literature. What, he asks, are those conditions?

And because he is a poet as well as an historian, the answer has more than a theoretical interest. Can a society consciously foster the conditions that might lead to such an efflorescence? Bailey's actions over the last fifty years indicate that he believes so.

In its short twelve pages, Dr. Bailey's essay "Creative Moments in the Culture of the Maritime Provinces," is endlessly stimulating, both in its explanation of the moments he identifies and in its general exploration of what makes a "creative moment." Bailey writes, "At the creative moment the interacting elements out of which the society is composed are suddenly transcended, and a proliferation of forms ensues that are new and different from any that could have appeared at an earlier period in the community's course. Like metropolitan societies, which tend to be worlds-in-themselves, small communities must become as mature as their narrow limits allow before they can fulfill the purpose that is within them."

Fulfilling that purpose led to two particular efflorescences: the Haliburton-Howe era in Halifax and the Carman-Roberts years in Fredericton. In his essay, Bailey demolishes the notion that Bliss Carman and Charles G. D. Roberts had sprung full-blown out of the soil, "exemplars of Romantic individualism." They were, Bailey insists, the culmination of a long literary tradition going back to the New York of Jonathan Odell and the Concord of Carman's and Roberts' forebears, and the result of the intellectual stimulation of a long line of distinguished teachers at UNB. The Carnegie Foundation, engaged in a study of how universities could contribute to culture, was so impressed with the essay that they reprinted it for distribution to universities.

The essay does seem to hold suggestions for the present because, as M. Travis Lane has written, Bailey "does not research the past so much as he recognizes the present." When he returned to New Brunswick in 1935 from his studies in Toronto and London, he recognized the past in the present and began to contribute to the conditions that would foster the creative life of the province. Bailey was, in many ways, peculiarly suited for the task. As with Carman and Roberts, Bailey himself is the descendant of a long literary tradition, with connections to Ralph Waldo Emerson and to Carman. What is more, he is a descendant of a line of distinguished UNB professors, Marshall D'Avray and Loring Bailey.

But while tradition may provide the soil for an efflorescence, there must be more immediate stimulating causes. Charles G. D. Roberts writes, in "Reminiscences of Bliss Carman," "This sudden out flowering of the poetic impulse which, for perhaps a score of years, made the name of Fredericton conspicuous in the world of letters, is a thing which some critics have been puzzled to account for. I am inclined to ascribe it, in no small part, to the vitalizing influence of George R. Parkin, falling upon soil that was peculiarly fitted to receive it." Parkin had gone to Oxford from New Brunswick and had come back with exciting ideas. He had heard Ruskin's first Slade Lecture, he had visited Pusey, and he had memorized Pre-Raphaelite poetry. Roberts wrote of Parkin that he loved "The Blessed Damozel" so passionately "that Bliss suspected him of sometimes saying it instead of his prayers."

Bailey, too, came back from his travels with exciting new ideas. In Toronto in 1931, Roy Daniells introduced him to the poetry of T.S. Eliot. Bailey recalls Daniells reading out loud to him and his fiancée Jean, "The Hollow Men," "Prufrock" and "The Waste Land." "I experienced the greatest excitement such as I had never experienced before…We came to know all his work by heart." In London, Bailey came upon the poetry of Dylan Thomas and realized what an impact on poetry he was destined to have.

Bailey communicated his enthusiasm for these new poetic forms to his students. In 1940 he established the Bliss Carman Society, which several years later founded the periodical *The Fiddlehead*. Elizabeth Brewster, Fred Cogswell, Robert Gibbs and Desmond Pacey were at one time members of the Society, meeting together to read each other their poetry and to set themselves exercises in versification so that they would be, as Eliot advised, "like a well-oiled fire engine" for the moment of inspiration. Bailey said in his manifesto for the group, that they should bring the Fredericton literary tradition "to the point of contemporaneity."

Bailey wrote later that "…I do not conceive the goal of the individual and the goal of society as distinguishable." While fostering the cultural goals of New Brunswick, he was rewarded himself. He recalls, "The association with members of the Bliss Carman Society stimulated me to write more and better than I had ever done."

He worked in other ways to prepare the soil for a possible efflorescence. In London, Bailey had come to know the theories of Arnold Toynbee and had visited that great historian. He studied under the famous sociologist Morris Ginsberg. He even visited a cell of Trotskyites. After a brief stint at the New Brunswick Museum, Bailey went to the provincial government to see if he could get funds to start a Department of History at UNB. And although Attorney General J.B. McNair "glowered at me" while Bailey was pleading his case, he got the funds.

He was prepared for the task. His own academic background was wide, embracing the new disciplines of ethnohistory, sociology, anthropology, as well as the history of art and the history of ideas, His book, *The Conflict of European and Eastern Algonkian Culture, 1504-1700*, published in 1937, was a pioneering study in ethnohistory. He taught the first course in anthropology in Canada outside Toronto, as well as all the classes in history. There can be few UNB graduates of those years who were not influenced by Bailey in his by now legendary courses, graduates who would go on to play leading roles in the provincial government and the burgeoning university itself.

Not only did he teach some seventeen hours a week, but he was largely instrumental in establishing a good library. When he arrived at UNB in 1938, the library had 12,000 uncatalogued books. Enlisting the aid of Lord Beaverbrook, Bailey made a shopping list of 50,000 carefully-chosen books, and Beaverbrook sent his agents into the bookstores of England to obtain them. "It was like the Battle of Normandy—books poured across the Atlantic." When the two men were finished, UNB was a university in substance as well as in name.

Bailey does not think of a creative moment solely as an efflorescence in the arts. Inhibiting the spread of the creative moment to other parts of New Brunswick in the Carman and Roberts years was the "lawless and speculative spirit of the timber trade," which tended to disrupt agriculture and render impossible "an ordered social existence." A.L. Kroeber, with whose descriptions of cultural patterns Bailey agrees, writes that culture includes things so diverse as hoeing corn, singing the blues, wearing a shirt, speaking English, and being a Baptist." For Bailey, the whole social fabric must contribute to a flowering in the arts, just as that fabric will be enriched by the flowering.

In a recent poem, Bailey describes the poet making his way past "the smell of sweet hay," past the "carrots, parsnips, the tomatoes and cabbages," to the university, where he feels it his task not only to hand down the memory of former times but, in so doing, "to praise endurance and foresight, things done in mercy and grandeur."

And indeed, those who have made their way to Fredericton have found a unique combination of the civilizing aspects of a city with the humanizing activities of farming, fishing, a closeness to the land. In his collected poems, *Miramichi Lightning*, Bailey points out, over and over again, the value of this combination of a living artistic tradition with access to rivers, woods and the sea. One poem starts out, "We the People of the great North American societal provenience" and ends with the words, "a trip to the woods in spring to admire the skill of the trailing arbutus in decanting its fragrance."

Charles Roberts describes the Fredericton of his day: "She was not stagnant, and was not smug. Instead of expecting all her people to be cut of one pattern, she seemed rather to prefer them to be just a little queer...Conformity, that tyrant god of small town life, got scant tribute from her." Bailey's poems preserve the memory of many such "just a little queer" people: La Freneuse, Will Taber, Uncle Taber.

He has often quoted Whitman's dictum that to have great artists you must have great audiences too. Bailey and his wife Jean read carefully and comment fully on nearly everything that is published by Fredericton writers. They are generous in their praise. In his unpublished memoirs (a fascinating document), Bailey strives to give everyone his due, to record the names of all who fostered the climate he hoped to establish. For example, he takes particular care to record Donald Gammon's initiative in founding *The Fiddlehead*.

Both the artist and the audience should have a sense of the adventure in life, a theme Bailey treats many times in his poetry. One poem describes the young Bailey reading Frederick Burnaby's *A Ride to Khiva* in a school study period and imbibing the adventuresome spirit. The survivors of the wreck of the Angel Gabriel (including some ancestors of Bailey and Fred Cogswell) can think, "Something beyond awaited us, we did not know what to call it, but went forward to search for an answer."

In going out to search for answers the artist comes into contact with other cultures. Although there can be a terrible result to such a conflux, as happened when the European came into conflict with the Indian and "met the challenge of the aboriginal cultures by shattering them and obliterating the remnants," there is also the possibility of such a meeting having productive effects. In the essay "The Historical Setting of Sara Duncan's *The Imperialist*," Bailey describes the effects on a creative spirit of two cultures coming together. In another essay he writes, "to become fully oneself, one must first lose oneself—flood oneself in the immediate age, as Whitman puts it—in the vastness and infinite variety of the metropolitan process. Instead of trying to achieve identity by building a Chinese wall around one's home territory, one should open one's mind to all the winds that blow."

It is not easy to give a man like Bailey his due. As he writes about others, "The identity of sources of inspiration in earlier generations could, and often does, become lost, while their effects persist as anonymous increments, mingling and enriching each other until a point of conspicuous endeavour is reached and passed." Concrete evidence of his worth includes five books of poetry, the last nominated for the Governor-General's Award, two books of ethnohistory, many honours, including Officer in the Order of Canada, three honorary degrees, and words of praise from some of Canada's leading intellectuals.

In the Fredericton of the last fifteen years, many writers have found the stimulus necessary to the creative process. At the moment, some thirty-five published writers thrive in the climate that Alfred Bailey helped to create. It was inevitable that he would be named honourary president of the newly-formed Writers' Federation. He had no guarantee that his efforts would result in a flowering, but in "Journey Without Words" he writes that he "had a premonition of coming to a place where things could happen, where something was going to happen." Alfred Bailey worked hard to make sure something did.

ArtsAtlantic 18 (5.2: Winter 1984)

Remembering the Ice House Gang

For more than a year, at the request of *ArtsAtlantic*'s editor, I have been trying to write about the Tuesday Night Group, a writers' workshop that met for seventeen years in McCord Hall on the University of New Brunswick campus in Fredericton, once designated the Poet's Corner of Canada. Why has it been so difficult for me to begin? Am I reluctant to admit to myself that a golden age has passed? Do I feel "Time's winged chariot" at my back, driving me forward so that I have no time for backward glances?

Or, more likely, have I already in my fiction made use of what I discovered during the seventeen years I sat in McCord Hall listening to some 200 writers read their work? Yet I do feel some impulse to chronicle those meetings.

In 1967 the stars provided me with a fortunate concatenation of events. Dorothy Livesay was writer-in-residence and Kent Thompson arrived from the USA to be creative writing teacher at UNB. Dorothy invited students and teachers to her apartment to read their work and, when she finished her stint at UNB, Kent decided to continue the practice. In March of that year, I began to write, and no sooner had I begun than Kent invited me to join the writers group. At first, we met in each other's homes and, at my house, my husband Bill joined in and afterwards began writing poetry so that he too could come to the meetings. Bob Gibbs came, as well as a number of students, including Barbara Saunders, Joe Sherman, and Carole Spray. Eventually we settled on meeting Tuesday nights in a restored campus ice house, McCord Hall.

The charm of the building had something to do with the longevity of the group. The lower walls of its one room are fieldstone, its upper walls wood, and its peaked roof crisscrossed by beams. A long, heavy antique table, a dozen black and gold UNB chairs, a curious chest with two figures carved on it, and an eccentric heating system sounding like a jet taking off give the place character. The whole room looks like a miniature Viking banquet hall, both cozy and strange. No one else used the building at that time; it became ours, our shelter, and it gave us our identity. From it we took our informal name, "McCord Hall," although some of us called the gathering "Tuesday Night" or "Tuesday Night Group." Later, someone writing about us (I think Alden Nowlan) called us the Ice House Gang. We rarely cancelled. Sometimes Tuesday night would fall on a Christmas eve but, in the main, we must have missed no more than five nights a year, meeting during a hurricane once, and during numerous blizzards.

Anne Cheverie Forrestall completed an M.A. thesis on the group in 1984. Browsing through her essay, bibliography, and list of names, I was surprised at some of the statistics I dug out. Her list of everyone who had attended even once included 160 names. There were, in addition, at least forty more we'd missed—people we could remember only by physical description or work read. Of the 160 on the list, about eighty were regulars for at least several months. And of those eighty, fifty writers had published at least a few poems or stories.

In my mind the group's seventeen-year history divides in different ways. One of these divisions is by dominant personalities. The first period was "dominated" by Joe Sherman; the second by Alex Jablanczy and Pam Allpress, a third period by Brian Bartlett, Dave Richards, Michael Pacey and Paul Hess; a fourth period by Dale Estey, Pam Margison and Ted Colson; a fifth by Yvonne Trainer and Leona Keenan.

A second division in my mind is in two parts. The first part, until 1976 or so, was of all of us—eager, equal, unpublished—experimenting with voice and form. During the second part, Kent Thompson dropped out, and Bob Gibbs, Bill Bauer and I, aided by Ted Colson, became the guardians. The people around the table began to regard us as mentors. And somehow the excitement and the energy began to run down until, in the spring of 1983, we stopped "for a while." Kent and the Scottish exchange writer, Ron Butlin, revived the workshop for a year, in the fall of 1983, under new rules — we met on Thursdays, we xeroxed our work to pass out before the meeting, and we were a closed group.

For Tuesday Night, the fact of our openness was important to us. We welcomed everyone, made a conscious effort to make newcomers feel at home and at ease. In fact, that openness added to the interest; as Bill Bauer said, "You never know who is going to come through the door." At first those who came were university students and professors, but it wasn't long before we had the "all walks of life" category — an occupational therapist, housewives (besides myself), a farmer, civil servants, a bus driver....

The group provided us all with inspiration, discipline — many people would confess that they'd written their poem Tuesday afternoon "so I could have something to read tonight" — entertainment, and audience. The group also provided me with subject matter. Michael Estok, reviewing my *Wise-Ears*, writes, "story-telling and story-*listening* constitute a major part of the action." On Tuesday Night I witnessed the tremendous drive to tell stories that many people have, especially in times of trouble. The whole process of writing seems to order, to clarify, to comfort people in distress.

But I wasn't the only one whose work was affected by becoming a part of the group. Bob Gibbs' poetry is complex, profound, not easy to catch on the first reading. Desiring to entertain as well as to perplex us, he began to write stories inspired by his unusual Saint John childhood of the 1930s. After warming up with three or four stories, he began the Pompman and Hutchie stories, later published in various magazines, read on CBC, and eventually published as a collection by Oberon Press, *I've Always Felt Sorry for Decimals*. He spoke of his fiction to Cheverie: "Part of the reason that story takes the form it does is that every week I had the impulse to surprise my audience by making unexpected things happen."

Kent Thompson favoured the first-person narrator even before he began reading to the group. But the practice of reading the stories aloud made him, I suspect, more adept at capturing the voices of various New Brunswickers, especially women. He would regale us with his anecdotes of loitering in the lingerie section of Zeller's to listen to the diction and syntax of the shoppers, the language that eventually found its way into his stories and novels.

Reading aloud to the group affected Bill Bauer more radically than it did anyone else. The immediacy of the audience, his own talent, and his fascination with different voices met in perfect accord. One of his most popular personas, Everett Coogler, was born one night after I'd gone to bed and Bill had stayed up to write. He had been gloomy for a while — I can't remember why and when he woke me up and read me the first Coogler poem, I thought, "He's gone around the bend." This was a moment of revelation for me — the close connection between the comic spirit and despair. Kent said to Cheverie that Bill Bauer is "the only genius I've ever known." In the true, not debased, meaning of the word, I think he's right.

The all-time star of Tuesday Night is Dave Richards. We each remember his progress differently. Kent thinks that Dave's initial offerings were mediocre and that it was when he got married ("the day after," Kent says) that his talent became obvious. Bill says that Dave wrote interesting stuff from the beginning. I think that reading to the group did affect the style of *Coming of Winter* and *Blood Ties*, the two novels he read to us. The rolling oratorical prose of those books came partly from his devouring the Russian greats, from the Bible and Latin of his childhood as altar boy, and from reading to us out loud.

At the time of Richards, two other talents were attending — Brian Bartlett and Michael Pacey. Brian was a legend for us even before he came, because he had held book sales at his house ever since he was 10 and his discarded books betokened a child prodigy. Very early on he began to write a column for the *Daily Gleaner*, was an active member of Aida Flemming's Kindness Club, and was a bird watcher among the old folks. He joined Tuesday Night when he was in high school and continued for the four years he attended UNB. Whereas Richards wrote with no revisions at all, Brian revised endlessly, and one night he read to us the seventy-fifth version of a villanelle he was working on. He lives in Montreal now and has gone on to publish poems and stories widely.

Michael Pacey was the soft-spoken romantic son of the boisterous Desmond Pacey. All three of the triumvirate of Richards, Bartlett, and Pacey had an exaggerated notion of the worth of women; Pacey and Bartlett were particularly vulnerable. Richards found his princess early, married her and lived "happily ever after." But the women in the lives of the other two became palpable presences in McCord Hall.

Our first promising youngster was Joe Sherman, a charter member of the group. One night when he was reading a poem, I anticipated the next word, but lo and behold that was not the word he spoke. It was a surprising word—surprising but absolutely right. He was young, not especially well-read, and yet he had what seemed like an inborn capacity to astonish with his language. I understood at that moment something about the nature of poetry, the magic of it. And, alas, I realized I didn't have that and never would. Shortly after I ceased writing poetry.

The young people were always surprising us. Dale Estey began coming to McCord Hall in the late 70s. He'd taken Kent's creative writing class (as had Sherman before) and had set himself up as a writer by working two years, living frugally enough to save money for several years of writing full-time. He had written three novels by the time he began coming but had had no luck publishing. He started to read us his fourth, *A Lost Tale*. At that time, he was a rather gloomy, unsociable person with wild beard and hair and a disreputable army coat.

One spring morning he turned up on my doorstep as I was busy getting my son off to Mount Allison University. I thought, "I can't deal with Dale's despair right now," so I sent him up to the study to wait. But it was not despair I had to deal with: it was elation. *A Lost Tale* had been accepted "over the transom" by St. Martin's

Press. Some months later an article in *The New York Times* stated that, in 1980, 30,000 unsolicited manuscripts had crossed the desks of New York publishers and only two had been accepted. Dale's gloom and reclusiveness disappeared.

We had our successes but we had our failures too. We were hardly ever without someone with mental difficulties. Once, a young girl, a victim of the worst part of the 60s drugs-and-commune scene, read to us from her therapy journal. Her psychiatrist used the journal form to get his patients to pour out their troubles, and "pour" is the right word. For several years we had a sweet-dispositioned young boy who would come between stays at the mental hospital. We all felt our responsibilities acutely in these cases.

At times I felt we were doing battle with the forces of evil. A young man whom we assumed to be an American draft-dodger came to us in the early 70s. I think he was probably dodging not the draft but the law. He has become a legend to the Tuesday Night Group. One night shortly after he began attending, he read and then got up to go: "I've got to be up early tomorrow because I have an appointment for tests for syphilis." With that he grabbed the door handle and left. I don't remember how we later managed to get the door open ourselves. A nadir came another time when he read a very explicit story about incest involving a 10-year-old boy, his mother and father; the point being that the parents were liberating the boy.

One of the reasons we survived, even prospered, for so long was the generous-spirited nature of the continuing members. First, there was Kent, who was ambitious for us all. He would write articles describing Fredericton as the new Athens, the new Dublin, mentioning our names. He was always scheming to get us on radio or TV, and approached Theatre New Brunswick's Walter Learning to see if he'd be interested in plays by us. He encouraged, cajoled, got angry at us when we didn't live up to our promise. Bill Bauer said, "Kent had what I call a 'Let's do it attitude' which I responded to very much. And I've always felt that I owe Kent a great deal."

Bob Gibbs had an uncanny knack for finding what was good in a poem or a story and for saying tactfully what was wrong. We never had petty jealousies or silly in-fighting. When we had a fight, it was a rip-roaring one over matters of principle.

Another of the main reasons we survived was our sense of mission, which resulted in the founding of the New Brunswick Chapbooks. The Chapbooks published twenty-five volumes by ten McCord Hall writers and ten non-McCord writers before the press was retired. Tuesday Night also provided the genesis of the Maritime Writers' Workshop, with members providing everything from organization, to teaching, to Kool Aid. The evening readings of the summer workshop became a kind of festival, often drawing a hundred people a night.

Various members of the Tuesday Night Group were published by Ottawa's Oberon Press—Richards, Gibbs, Thompson, Elizabeth Brewster, both Bauers, Sherman—and we had four launching parties for these books, and books by other members of the Maritime writing community—Susan Kerslake, Ann Copeland, Marjory Whitelaw, Terry Crawford. On Tuesday Night we met writers from all parts of Canada and the USA, from Nigeria, Malawi, England, Wales, Belgium, Scotland, Peru, Hungary. We established links with writers in other parts of Canada—Hugh Hood, Liliane Welch, Helen Weinzweig—to name a few.

When I asked Brian Bartlett what about Tuesday Night had the most profound effect on his writing, he replied. "It provided me with concrete, close-up evidence that there were no set ways of writing. I remember how Bill and Kent used to lock horns about something that had been read. Everyone was very much his own man."

One of the consequences of our long associations was that each of us educated an audience for himself. Brian, after reading my *Wise-Ears*, wrote me a letter which was totally satisfying because he had understood the novel perfectly. Bill Bauer said "I conceived the idea, with perhaps very little to warrant for doing so, that the aim of the group was to engage in experimental writing.... So that most of what I did I regarded as a trial—to try something out that somebody said couldn't be done or to try something new." Dave Richards experiments with a different voice and prose style in each of his novels. And Bob Gibbs' *A Mouth Organ for Angels* was an experiment tried after listening to Weinzweig lecture on postmodernism.

Very few of us had a "message"; few of us expected to get rich. More of us were using the creative process to explore. This consensus drove people off, but it also allowed some to find a way to say what they had been wanting to say for a long time, to explore some experience—war, an unhappy love, a nervous breakdown, a strange childhood—that cried out for understanding.

I miss Tuesday Night Group. I think often of the members: Michael Brian Oliver, Marian Cameron, Bernie Badani, Andrew Bartlett, Selma Brody, Jeanine Grady, Sally Harysym, Sandra Allen, Nicholas Wermuth, Stephen Boston, Rick Burns, Laurence Creaghan, David Dawes, Bob Burns, Dan Lingeman, the Maxfields—John and Margaret, Dawn Pollard, Betty Ann McDorman, Mike and Jack Patterson, Jo and Martin Singleton, Victor Skretkowicz, John Timmins, David West, Rick Hatt: a partial list of those who made the McCord Hall years such an inspiriting experience.

ArtsAtlantic 26 (7.2: Summer 1986)

The Report of the New Brunswick Arts Policy Advisory Committee, Fredericton

31 January 1989

In December of 1986, then-Premier Richard Hatfield announced the formation of an advisory committee on the arts. In September of that year, 350 artists gathered in Fredericton at Forum 87 to make their views known to the committee. On January 31 of this year, the committee presented its report to Premier Frank McKenna and to the public.

They made two main recommendations, both to do with the administration of arts policy in New Brunswick. The first proposal asked for an upgraded department of the arts under its own deputy minister. The arts had languished too long in the shadow of the powerful tourism section of the Ministry of Tourism, Recreation, and Heritage.

Roland Beaulieu, minister of this portfolio, outflanked the advisory committee by announcing, several days before, and again at the presentation of the report, that his ministry was to be restructured, with four sections under assistant deputy ministers: Culture, Sports, Tourism, and Administration. Later he announced that Roger Levesque, a career civil servant, would head the culture division. This acknowledgement by the government of the accuracy of the committee's analysis bodes well.

The other major recommendation is that an arts board be established, the model to be the Manitoba Arts Council. The committee carefully set out the make-up and duties of such a board. It would be an arm's length body to advise the provincial government and to administer grants under a peer jury system.

The committee obviously had deliberated carefully about the relationship of the two new bodies it recommends. Although some artists had asked for a completely autonomous arts board selected by the arts community itself, the report states that such a board would be "plainly absurd, a recipe for disaster" which would "create a confrontational or adversarial situation." The two bodies should work together, and members of the government agency should be on the arts board.

The report made a strong case for the economic value of the arts and the necessity for increasing arts funding, reproducing a chart which showed that New Brunswick spends the lowest amount on the arts, per capita, of all the provinces. In 1988-89, the budget for the Cultural Development Branch was $1.1 million, with $800,000 of that going to cultural programmes. The increased funding should include grants to artists and writers. "Within any new agency, with new funding, a significant proportion of the grants structure — and that of other departments — should be re-directed towards longer term development," and this "principle of sustaining grants should be extended to individual artists and craftpersons."

Premier McKenna, in accepting the report, said that his government had been studying a draft copy, that an interdepartmental committee had been set up under Jim Morell of the Policy Secretariat, and that in the spring session of the legislature the government would respond to the recommendations.

In fact, the author of the report, publisher Peter Thomas, appeared to be on the same wavelength as McKenna. In their speeches, both of them stressed the accelerating importance of service and information industries, and the concern of these industries for a high quality of life when they are looking for a new home. "Industries considering location no longer weigh such factors as the source of material and lines of communication alone. The availability of cultural activities is now a major element in such decisions," says the report. McKenna echoed these words, "We usually think of art as providing people with a sense of fulfillment or completeness. But it can also have a significant effect on a nation's economic fortunes."

Hatfield's decision to create an advisory committee was the result of pressure by several Acadian artists. There is no doubt that the francophone artist organizations have been more active than those of the anglophones. For example, the final committee included only one native-born English-speaking New Brunswicker; it had started out with more, but they had all resigned. At the presentation of the report, a large proportion of the questions afterward were in French. This reflects, I think, the distrust that English-speaking New Brunswick artists have of government intervention in the arts. It is not coincidence that the ministers in charge of culture in both the Hatfield and McKenna governments have all been francophone.

The Cultural Development Branch came in for severe criticism in the report. "At best the activities of this branch can be considered a holding operation, at worst tokenism and political favouritism." Staff morale is low, and recruitment impossible. "Initiatives can only be minor. The programmes administered by the branch haven't changed for thirteen years." The Cultural Development and Crafts Branches, "wholly dominated by Tourism, a major spending agency with a high public profile and heavy past involvement in patronage practices...have degenerated into shabby ineffectuality, despite the best efforts of some members of their staffs."

As I evolve into a New Brunswicker, I myself am becoming a little skeptical of the efficacy of government funding of the arts. The majority of the funding is for organizations and for infrastructure. Volunteering for these groups takes up an immense amount of the time and creative energy of the artist, and the infrastructures take huge chunks of the funding. TNB, for example, has given us the Alden Nowlan plays, but little else of value, in spite of the fact that such talented New Brunswickers as David Adams Richards and Rick Burns have written superb plays. As one writer said, "Next year at this time not one writer will have an extra dime in his pocket because of this report."

However, the Advisory Committee, under Colin Mailer and Audrey St. Onge, spent long hours deliberating, reading 128 briefs, listening to the impassioned speeches at Forum 87, and writing a well-researched, thoughtful report. This document, with its eleven pages of bibliography, handsomely designed and printed, is a worthy one and does represent what, I surmised, was the collective will of the 350 artists and arts administrators attending Forum 87. An arts board would, without doubt, generate new ideas and excitement within the cultural community. But the machinery of government grinds oh so slowly and, especially in these times of fiscal restraint, we are still a long way from results.

ArtsAtlantic 34 (9.2: Spring/Summer 1989)

Premier's Advisory Committee on the Arts (PACA) Board Meetings

Fredericton, NB
February-April 1990

The key recommendation of the Premier's Advisory Committee on the Arts was the establishment of an arts council in New Brunswick. On February 1, 1990, the permanent New Brunswick Arts Board met for the first time. The fourteen members elected Ilkay Silk and René Cormier co-chairpersons. The board was broken up into some fifteen committees to recommend policies, and in March they presented their reports. The unanimous consensus of the committees was that the first priority should be the setting up of a jury system to give substantial grants to artists. Ilkay Silk said, "Everyone felt that we should give more money to fewer people—that was the only way the money could make *the* difference."

In the meantime, the government announced a new lottery, "Provincial Pride," the profits of which would be placed in a trust fund for the arts, expected to amount to some $400,000 a year. The lottery started January 15, and two months later the profits in the trust fund were $222,600. The province has also budgeted slightly over $1 million for the arts, including $150,000 for the administration of the Arts Board. As well, the government will match any money the board raises for the trust fund.

Bruce Dennis was doing triple duty as the liaison between the Arts Board and the Cultural Development Branch, newly renamed the Arts Branch, as well as being the administrative secretary of the intergovernmental committee on the arts, and the literary and performing arts officer. But the government has advertised for a person to fill the new position of liaison person and executive secretary of the Arts Board.[1]

---

1   In a subsequent update later in this same issue of *ArtsAtlantic*, Sylvie Nadeau was announced as the new liaison program officer.

Both Silk and Dennis expressed great satisfaction with what has been accomplished. At the April 26 meeting, an arts grant program and jury system was put in place. "We have a sense of urgency," Silk says. "We know people have been waiting for this a long time." Silk has also been impressed with the government. Both Dennis and André Lanteigne, Assistant Deputy Minister in charge of the culture division, "have been very co-operative and sensitive to the arms' length nature of the government." And Dennis has been pleased with the dedication of the board. "They all are anxious to work together. The two chairs are extremely competent."

Silk says the board members do work well together; there has been no friction between genres or language groups. Simultaneous translation has played an important part in the sense of community that has already developed in the group. Both Dennis and Silk stressed that the board is a dynamic process, not a static institution. One board member, Rodolphe Caron, warned that achieving perfection is impossible, that once the programs are put into practice, they are bound to be full of bugs. And Roland Beaulieu, Minister of Tourism, Recreation and Heritage, pleaded for "patience and understanding on the part of both government and the arts community."

Other provinces put their arts councils in place when times were flush. Both Dennis and Silk think there is a good side to starting out in terms of "fiscal restraint." The board will have to be more careful with its priorities, more sensitive in letting the citizens know what benefits are gained from the public support of artists. To that end, the board can help the artists reach a wider audience. And conversely, the board can make the artist aware that the arts don't exist in a vacuum, that they are there to benefit the people.

Although the immediate priority of the Arts Board is the individual professional artist, the board will not neglect arts organizations and the non-professional artist. "We feel that the process is more important than the product," Silk stated, that the arts organizations and the non-professionals are necessary and worthy of support.

Yet Dennis says that this board could recommend there be a separate group to look after community cultural development. Separating the two constituencies would prevent constant debates. But keeping them in one organization would provide grassroots support for the board and would help developing artists.

Many problems are still to be solved. What role will the board take in the educational system? Developing and defining its constituency is one difficult task. Who will be eligible for election to the board? Who will do the nominating? It will be three years before the board is fully in place. "Since the N.B. Arts Board is the first arts agency to have its members selected by the arts community, it will take some time to iron out the procedural wrinkles," Beaulieu said.

Some of the ironing out can be discouraging. Dale Estey, the member nominated by the Writers' Federation, found that the board was spending hours discussing minute points of no real concern. By April, the crucial things had not even been discussed, he says. "Not one sentence had been said about the all-important structure of the juries." How will they reconcile the need to be thorough and fair with the need to keep jury expenses to a minimum, so that the money available won't all go to administration? How will writing grants be allotted, for example. Will there be so much for poetry, so much for fiction? So much for French, so much for English? By March, the Arts Board had met more days than had been projected for the whole year. And there are still difficult decisions to make, such as political decisions about the funding of the big arts organizations: Theatre New Brunswick and the Beaverbrook Art Gallery.

On the other hand, the presence of the Arts Board already seems to have made a difference in the sensitivity of these organizations to the local artists. The new artistic director of TNB, Michael Shamata, has pledged "to nurture the local writers, actors, directors, designers." One cynic says that all the artistic directors have said that, but they never do. A long-standing complaint about the Beaverbrook is that it never shows New Brunswick work, although, at the end of April, a new showcase for N.B. artists was inaugurated there. Can the new Arts Board give more power to its artists through its control of purse strings?

Through a strange concatenation of events, 1990 has become a time of new beginnings in the cultural life of New Brunswick. All four of the provincial universities have new presidents. TNB has a new artistic director. Mount Allison University's Owens Art Gallery has a new director/curator. Gallery Connexion finally got Canada Council funding. The Arts Board is in place. Good will, optimism, and patience are the order of the day. We hold our breath.

ArtsAtlantic 38 (10.2: Fall 1990)

Renaissance Man

If New Brunswick were to elect a renaissance man, it would likely be Herménégilde Chiasson.

At 48 years old, he has made 10 films, written 11 books and 15 plays, and photographed and painted plenty of Acadian culture. He was recently chosen as New Brunswick's representative on The Canada Council. France bestowed on him the honourary title Chevalier des Arts et Lettres. He was the second recipient of the New Brunswick Arts Award for filmmaking and was named by Quebec to L'Ordres des Francophone d'Amerique. He has received top grants from The Canada Council. He's also on the board of the National Library and is president of the Acadian Association of Professional Artists in New Brunswick.

His unusual first name ("I'm always having to spell it," he says) is the saint's name for the day he was baptized, a common name in his birthplace, St. Simon on the North Shore.

Chiasson's education has been broad. He received his BA in fine arts from Mount Allison University. He earned an MFA in photography from SUNY at Rochester and a doctorate in aesthetics from the Sorbonne with a thesis on American photography. He studied literature and art at the University of Moncton.

He says he's lucky to have lived during a time when it was good to be an Acadian artist—the end of the 1960s and the beginning of the '70s—when artists could move easily among the various forms of art. "I had a lot of chances," he says.

The founding of the University of Moncton helped create the Acadian art movement, Chiasson says.

"Quebec is managing the French identity—which is independentism. Quebec either excludes us or tolerates us or sees us as rebels."

For many cultures, you could call what happened in Acadia in the 1960s a renaissance. For Acadia, this was not a rebirth but a birth—the original Golden Age of Acadian art—and a new vantage point from which to view the world. Before then, "there was nothing, no Acadian art."

The revolutionary "Acadian moment" passed in the late '70s, and everyone settled down. Artists no longer wanted "to get into turmoil" about ideas of what it is to be Acadian. Now art is "getting crystallized"—young artists must be more selective. The great Acadian artists moved to Quebec.

Chiasson didn't settle down. Recently he caused a stir by saying that the French media was controlled from Montreal and excluded Acadia. "I said it, and it was a bomb. To me it was a simple thing but to say it in public was the coming of age after 25 years."

He wants all artists in New Brunswick to make more of an effort communicating outside the province. "Great art asks questions but it can't supply answers," he says. "We're technicians and researchers in communication. Right now we need to have in literature someone to counteract Maillet—that we're all fiddle-playing, happy-go-lucky, eating poutine râpée." The popularity of La Sagouine must be a cross to bear.

Chiasson thinks that the deportation of 1755 as an historical event has been blown out of proportion. He believes Acadians should empathize with the English. The deportation was an error he says, "but we were a part of it. We didn't want to take an oath of allegiance because we didn't want to have to take up arms against Quebec."

"We were as much responsible as anyone else—we didn't play our cards right."

"I (once) thought that the fate of French Canadians was in exile. But I've changed. You have to have a place. To me, there are 250,000 Acadians and they all live in the Maritimes." These Acadians have no history of being deported—instead they fled into the woods and then came back when the coast was clear. "I don't believe in the ideology that Acadians are all over the world. Maybe there are other forms of Acadia, but this is the only one that had a chance of making it."

I ask what attracted him to Jack Kerouac, the subject of one of his films. "Kerouac said, 'All my knowledge comes from the French-Canadian and then I write it in English.'" Kerouac spoke French with his mother all his life, but his father insisted he speak English. Chiasson wanted to explore the question "What's American in us?" and was interested in Kerouac's view of exile—and how that and nationalism are connected.

Chiasson says they stem from the same principle, the inhumane phenomenology of exclusion. He's exploring this idea in the play he's currently writing, "Alexa's Exile." The play will be produced by Moncton's Theatre L'Escauotte.

"Acadia can keep itself alive through its writers and painters who bring food to the soul," he says.

"People fear that Quebec will split and that will be the end of everything. But I don't believe it would be the end. Quebec hasn't done much to help us along the road. Acadia is a way of life. But is this only a phenomenon of our generation? No. The fight is over. Before, we never knew we were Acadian. Now people know they're Acadian."

For Chiasson, what marked the dividing line between the two, Before Acadia and After Acadia, was the film by Pierre Pierrot, *L'Acadie, L'Acadie.* "It changed me."

Chiasson began his career at the CBC in radio and TV. There he could fuse writing and visual arts. When he became interested in filmmaking, he was forced to choose between the National Film Board and the CBC because he wasn't allowed to work for both.

He picked the NFB. Since then, he has been freelancing. "I have to live by my ideas," he says.

Chiasson is starting his own renaissance, by getting back into visual arts with a series of graphite and oil stick drawings. The three drawings on his studio wall are different in technique — reflective of his principle that he should not be stuck in one form. But they all use the images of a blonde woman, an angel and an Easter Island statue head.

His new studio complements a handsome contemporary home set in the woods near the shore of the Northumberland Strait in Robichaud. He lives in the midst of an artist colony: on one side Roméo Savoie, on the other Jacques Savoie, and in the back Gabrielle Savoie Robichaud.

In addition to his new studio, he has a space in Moncton, in the Aberdeen Cultural Centre, a bustling place for Acadian artists for nearly 10 years. Chiasson laments that these artists haven't been exhibiting lately. But, he consoles himself, they are not relying on exhibitions — they are working and just letting people come to the centre to see for themselves. Since the demise of the one commercial gallery in Moncton, most Acadian artists have found dealers in Halifax. The Aberdeen Cultural Centre is planning to open a store soon. Chiasson himself has never sent his dossier to galleries. "I'm not career-minded. I have no time for promotion."

We discover that we both had seen the Michael Snow retrospective at the Art Gallery of Ontario. I can see why this artist appeals to Chiasson — Snow's prolific experimenting with form and genre — film, writing, photography, as well as with straight visual arts.

"One thing I've found is that the visual arts is a place of experimentation. Maybe if I had wanted to have a career, I would have taken these images," he says gesturing to the drawings on the wall, "an Easter Island figure, a woman, and angels and done only that. But I didn't — that's why I admire Michael Snow." Snow has applied whatever he has learned in visual arts to other forms. Chiasson quotes Roland Barthes: "Everything has got an equivalence." A school of art like impressionism worked as well in theatre and music as in painting.

Chiasson's latest book is *Vermeer (toutes les photo du film)*. The book reads like a short schedule for a film: "He walks in the corridor. A woman walks behind him. He is staring at his glass of milk." The effect is that the reader visualizes every word, a literary form that seems quite original in its execution. Every page is a full photograph with text set into the photo. One of the themes of the book is living in an isolated place. Vermeer lived in Delft, a small town like Moncton—"Vermeer waiting for serenity in Delft." Chiasson explores the idea of living in a place that is in a definite territory, Acadia. "Art is a necessity because one must leave evidence."

The photos are taken along the road and from the air, emphasizing the reality of the physical territory. The book starts with a photo of an angel and ends with a photo of a reptile. His poetry, like his talk and his art, is a mixture of the polemic and the lyrical: "You went away opening cracks in April ice that melted fast, without noticing the spring as it hastened to come that year with a moist March wind sticking the leaves to their trees. And you went away so fast that a part of me was exiled within you: You went away by roads among water puddles, mudholes, gaping wounds in the asphalt bleeding dirty water over our white clothes."

Not long before her death, Marion McCain asked him to be the curator of the biannual McCain exhibition. He agreed to take on the challenge because he can shape the exhibition as he sees fit and will write an essay for the catalogue. This is the first time the exhibit has had a curator and has been open to all artists in the Maritimes. I've heard the criticism that the past exhibits were full of amateur work, that the outside jurors had the same view of New Brunswick as Chiasson deplores—uncultured—hence chose unsophisticated works they thought were representative. Many professional artists boycotted the last exhibit for this reason. It is to McCain's credit that she persevered until she found the right framework, that she chose this firebrand, Chiasson, to build it.

He is still playing with ideas for his curating. Great art stems from a generosity of spirit, he says, and in naïve art, you feel this generosity—these artists never got any money or fame. Chiasson says he has heard some of the naïve artists say, "I have to leave this to my grandchildren," as a firsthand witness. One title of such an exhibit might be Anecdotes and Enigmas, the anecdotes from the naïve painters and the enigmas from the contemporary.

Chiasson lived in Paris from 1974 to 1977. Later he went to London, and was amazed that he felt better than he had in France.

"The English had everything I'm used to—bacon and eggs, cornflakes." An Acadian friend agreed with him that he felt great in London, "because the people were so laid back and friendly and talked to you on the street." He also feels more at home in Toronto than in Montreal. "Toronto is like a big Moncton; Montreal is like a small Paris." When he was in Montreal, too many emotional issues surface. In Toronto, there are no such emotions. When he was growing up on the North Shore, the radio stations came from New Carlisle in Quebec; the influence of Quebec was strong. Artists like Edith Butler and Calixe Duguay move to Montreal. "I am an anachronism, moving to southeastern New Brunswick."

Chiasson believes too much energy goes into protecting borders. "The past is the past—we can't go back to the Plains of Abraham and fix things. We can't make a backwards timer."

In art and in politics he says, "we should all go on to something new."

The New Brunswick Reader, June 11, 1994.

Bill's World

This summer Bill Gaston will lead a fiction class at the Maritime Writers' Workshop. Nineteen years old, the MWW has earned a reputation for offering excellent instructors, producing eager wordsmiths and fostering camaraderie among Maritime writers.

Gaston is an experienced hand at writers' workshops — having participated in many across Canada, both as a student and instructor. This is his second time at the MWW, and he says it's different from others he has done. "They work you very hard."

Gaston reads the manuscript the participants send in beforehand, reads what they bring to class with them and reads what they write during the week. He presents an hour-long lecture. The topic is his choice. Over the years, the variety has been immense: the philosophy underlying the lyrical works of literature; a nuts-and-bolts examination of the poet's own poem and why each word was chosen; and the creative process of writing a novel illuminated by her mother's doll-making.

"It scares me when I have to do it myself but I like to go to the others."

He, the workshop participants and other instructors describe the MWW as "intimately social time." Many lasting friendships, like that of author Sheree Fitch and Helen Weinzweig, have formed.

Gaston began his sojourn in Fredericton as writer-in-residence at the University of New Brunswick from 1991 to 1993. Although he is a restless soul with a terror of settling down, his wife Dede, pregnant with their third child, did not want to roam further when his appointment at UNB was over. They bought a house and continued the role they had carved out for themselves as a vital force in the artistic community. Dede, a professional dancer, teaches at Dance Fredericton. Bill teaches part-time in UNB's English department. An "exciting prospect" for next year is teaching the graduate creative writing course in fiction at UNB. Together, he and Dede lead a Shambhala meditation group which has flowered over the three years. It now has 25 members. "It's become not an insignificant part of our lives." In the group Gaston teaches how to use meditation to overcome writer's block.

He brings up a much-discussed subject: Can writing be taught? He laughs as he paraphrases the advice of George Woodcock: The four things you must not do if you want to be a writer are marry, have children, get a job, and take creative writing courses. Gaston takes the middle road in the debate. Of course, talent and inspiration can't be taught or even nurtured, he believes, but the craft can be taught. Experienced writers have stumbled across shortcuts, discovered in other writer's solutions to problems — "Oh, that's how I could do that." The participant in creative writing courses can learn these techniques more efficiently from the instructors, without having to spend years in the discovery.

A large part of a workshop, too, is having a reading, an audience. A reader, any reader, is important to a developing writer, but a careful, knowledgeable reader such as a workshop instructor, is especially helpful. The other participants provide a representative audience, so that the writers come to know that not everyone will love the work. The writers learn, in the workshop dynamics, to choose appropriate voices to listen to — which criticism is helpful, which comes from someone not on their wavelength. A workshop is the only time writers can get that kind of immediate feedback; certainly, they can't rely on their friends because they are not critical enough.

A workshop also can teach what obvious flaws to avoid, what clichés of writing. Gaston likes to begin his class by saying that, statistically speaking, the women will write about relationships while the men will want to figure out the universe. Can they themselves overturn that cliché? When I first started teaching creative writing, I was surprised at the number of student stories that ended in suicide, an obviously dramatic but too easy ending, I came to see. Gaston demonstrates how such a cliché can be used by turning it upside down. In "The Revenge of Richard Brautigan," he creates a young street poet who is influenced by Brautigan, a writer who committed suicide. "Suicide was powerful work, no question. It made people sit up very straight. But, in the end, it was ambiguous. There was the possibility of reading a whimper in it. Poetry was many things, but it was never a whimper."

This past year Gaston has published a second collection of stories, *North of Jesus' Beans*, and a second novel, *The Cameraman*, set in Fredericton. He also has published a collection of poetry. Next year, he has another novel coming out and he is working on a third collection of stories. His play *Yard Sale* will open Theatre New Brunswick's season next fall, the result of his being a member of TNB's Brave New Words playwriting workshop for the past two years. He is working on another play, *I am Danielle Steele*, workshopped and read at this spring's Brave New Words. He appreciates the feedback he is receiving on the play because it is presenting him with some tough problems. It is structured like the peeling of an onion, as lies keep getting revealed. This process gets more and more subtle and the problem gets more and more difficult — a box he can't get out of. Will an audience care about the characters if they pick up that it's all a lie?

He has just started another novel. "I love starting a new work, with all the energy and excitement. I just love it." His enthusiasm for the writing process shows through as he talks about it. But we agree the revision process isn't much fun.

Gaston comes by his wanderlust honestly. He was born in Winnipeg, spent his formative years in Deep Cove, BC, and lived three times in Toronto, twice in Vancouver, once in Montreal, a year in France, and three years in Halifax, teaching at St. Mary's University. Because his family moved around so much when he was young, his bond with his brother is very strong, a subject he explored in the novel, *Tall Lives*, about twins who were born joined at the toe.

He uses this wide experience effectively. The stories in *North of Jesus' Beans*, for example, are set in California, Manitoba, Ottawa, BC; in a logging camp, a group home for handicapped adults, a hippie commune, and a tunnel in the snow.

In 1978 Chogyam Trungpa came to Vancouver to lecture on Tibetan Buddhism. Gaston had been searching for a religion that had a definite practice and specific guidelines for approaching reality. Trungpa convinced him, and he became a Buddhist. The tenets of Buddhism feed his writing: the value of the mundane and the spontaneous, a suspicion of the status quo.

As well, his Buddhism makes him "less interested in advertising the degraded and the violent" in his work. But the religion he practices is not "one of those brown rice affairs where everyone smiles like the pamphleteers in an airport." He believes in the Tantric tradition of "slapping people awake—clumsy as my attempts may be"—a practice that his gift for comedy (he is a very funny writer) allows him to perform very well. As one of Gaston's characters says, "If I were a Buddhist priest I would have slapped him."

One goal of the Buddhist is to relish the ordinary. As one of his characters says, "the bravery to resist twisting away from horrifying boredom, the bravery to cut the bondage of entertainment."

An instructor at a workshop can introduce his students to the work of writers who will help them in their own writing. Four writers who have influenced Gaston in the past—"The Four Johns": Fowles, LeCarre, Irving, Gardner—demonstrate to him that fiction can be popularly appealing on an entertainment level and still be good literature.

Over the years, the MWW has had many excellent instructors, drawing on many Maritime writers—Robert Gibbs, Kay Smith, Joe Sherman, Ann Copeland—and flying in others from afar, such as William Valgardson, Jane Urquhart, W.P. Kinsella, John Metcalf. The evening readings by these instructors have evolved into a kind of summer festival, drawing a large crowd from beyond the workshop. Some years, the UNB Elderhostel is running at the same time and so people from across North America come to the readings. None so far has read for 16 hours like the novelist in Gaston's story "The Work-in-Progress," although once a poet did read for 1½ hours.

Many students have gone on to publish: Sheree Fitch, Ann Brennan, Mary Jane Losier, Cathie Pelletier, Joan Fern Shaw, to name a few. Dale Estey attended the first MWW as a participant, published two novels and a book of fables, and came back as an instructor. The students come from all over Canada and the US. One student from Chicago comes back year after year.

This summer the other fiction instructor is Isabel Huggan, the short story writer whose work has been acclaimed in the US, Great Britain, France, Italy and Spain. Governor-General's Award winner Tim Wynne-Jones leads the children's writing workshop, Mia Anderson the poetry workshop, and Elspeth Cameron, biographer of Hugh MacLennan and Irving Layton, the non-fiction workshop.

The workshop is always held at the beginning of July, a lovely time at UNB's Fredericton campus. This year it runs from July 3-9.

The New Brunswick Reader, July 2, 1994.

Robert Gibbs: A Sharp Selfhood

I want to tell you about a splendid character and tell you in such a way that you will truly appreciate him, but the very characteristics that make him splendid also make him a challenging subject. Robert Gibbs, poet, fiction writer, critic, editor, English professor (retired) and raconteur is a complex and subtle man, warm-hearted yet shy, witty yet sober, erudite but unpretentious, modest though self-assured.

Robert Gibbs' poetry is characterized by a sharp and original observation of the world around him at the moment he is writing. He often composes early in the day, using the form of a verse journal. Several of his long poems delineate the light, the sound, the feel of morning in his New Brunswick. Taken together, the journals constitute an anatomy of the world at dawn:

> I wake to robins and redwings that
> stake their ground   The Nashwaak claims
> a kingsize bed over the whole interval
> The farmer's dump's afloat and his manure
> pile's wider than his farm…

The dawn becomes a sacred time:

> East of here the first riser
> out of this dark has made
> a light   a fire   a prayer
> of some kind   has looked
> his way for first signs
> and this way for last.

The poet M. Travis Lane has written: "In Gibbs' best poems…is a sense of sane, even obdurate mental balance, of measuredly, recollectedly, and rigorously articulated details…it is ourselves that are sharpened, our identities that are formed — by this unique, idiosyncratic and inimitable verse." Another contemporary has described his poetry as a combination of precision and whimsy. Gibbs has published four full books of poetry as well as several chapbooks. A particularly generous collection, *The Tongue Still Dances*, was published in 1985.

If his poetry is noted for its "rigorously articulated details," Gibbs' fiction is characterized by a return to his childhood, to the Saint John of the thirties and forties (he was born in 1930), to the geography of the imagination of a perceptive boy. Although he uses, and continues to use, the world of his childhood in his poems, it is in his fiction that the city of Saint John and area comes alive.

From 1967 until 1983, Gibbs was a member of the writing group that met in the former ice house on the Fredericton campus of the University of New Brunswick, although it was not exclusively a UNB activity and welcomed all comers. By its nature, fiction is easier to understand than poetry when it is read aloud, especially such subtle poetry as Bob Gibbs writes. Desiring a more immediate response, he started to write stories purely to entertain the group; he was quite candid about his motive.

This fiction came out of his own vast memory as well as from the collective memory of his storytelling mother and aunts. Packed in was a wealth of fully realized characters. An editor playfully complained that one story had forty characters in seven pages. After he had written a few stories, there emerged two engaging figures, Pompman and Hutchie, young orphans living with their aunt and uncle after the deaths of their missionary parents. The listeners in the Ice House were charmed.

But they weren't the only appreciative audience. The stories were published in magazines and broadcast on the CBC. The celebrated writer Alden Nowlan became a fan and decided that he himself was Pompman, the brother of the narrator, Hutchie. When six of the stories were published in *I've Always Felt Sorry for Decimals* (Oberon Press) in 1978, Gibbs dedicated it: "For Alden Nowlan — My

Best Pompman." A new collection with these characters is being published by Oberon nineteen years later.

In "You Know What Thought Did," Pompman and Hutchie begin to tell stories to each other before they go to sleep. Hutchie writes: "Pompman does funny things and says funny things sometimes. Especially at night when Uncle Earlie's heard us pray and turned out the light." One night, Pompman shakes his brother and says, "Hutchie, hey wake up, we gotta do the story." He has decided they must make up a story about Oliver and Arnold, two of their playmates. "Whenever we saw them again after that, Pompman's eyes would bug, and mine felt like they did too, because Oliver and Arnold were in our story and it felt funny to see them right there in the daytime kicking a tin can up the street or doing something else just as real." It's a feeling, if not a revelation, that many artists — visual as well as literary — surely have.

Reviewing Gibbs' novel, *A Mouth Organ for Angels* (1984), also set in Saint John, *Telegraph-Journal* publisher Ralph Costello wrote: "Readers don't have to have a vivid, free-wheeling, searching, soaring, explosive imagination to enjoy a book by Robert Gibbs. But it helps."

There was a tradition in Gibbs' family of making things. His father, a jeweller, ran his business from home, and Bob spent a lot of time in the shop, sorting through boxes of junk — beads, parts of jewelry — and watching his father melt gold and fix clocks. One of his most moving poems is about his father's death:

> I see you dad, on your high stool in
> your shop, eyeglass wrenched into play and
> fine curly gold turning up and off from
> your keen engraver as you cut 'Love for
> always and always' on the inside circus
> of a secondhand wedding ring.

His mother's family, the MacQuarries, were "respectable" people, lawyers and preachers. Family members embraced different religions

—Seventh Day Adventist, Pentecostal, Christian Scientist—and since they were all argumentative there were many related discussions. Observing these as a child, Gibbs acquired an appreciative and gentle view of the paradoxes and comedy of religion.

His mother's father's people, the Towers, were "not all that respectable." They were Irish, woodsmen, barrel-stave makers, living on small backwoods farms in New Brunswick's Albert County. They had a tradition of telling stories, of making up songs and poems. His great-grandmother would stand on her verandah and make up scurrilous rhymes about the people coming up the road. When storytelling, his mother and aunts would mimic the different voices, a skill that Gibbs inherited and has perfected.

His family continues to be important to him. He and his older brother Don, with whom he now shares a home, often visit their sister Jean, the youngest of the family, in England. There Gibbs is able to re-visit Cambridge University, where he once studied for an M.A. He has been a dedicated uncle to middle-brother Raymond's daughters and son.

Bob Gibbs must have been an amusing child. "Nobody could say anything that I wouldn't repeat," he says. When he was under five, he declared to one of his spinster relations, "Raymond says you've got a moustache." To another relative, "Mom says you talk so slow."

In grade three he started to write verse and began three novels, inspired by his reading of such childhood books as John Masefield's *The Box of Delights* and George MacDonald's *At the Back of the North Wind*. *A Mouth Organ for Angels* "is a kind of reworking" of one of his earliest efforts, *The Mystery of the Silver Staircase*. When he finished writing it (he was about 10), he took it to McMillan's Printing to ask how much it would cost to publish. The clerk treated him seriously and quoted a price of $300. But I only want one copy, the boy said. It was carefully explained to him that the cost was in the setting up. In grade eight, Gibbs read *Oliver Twist* and that inspired a story about an orphan, "Fire of Life and Child of Death." Gibbs chuckles when he thinks of the title.

Gibbs took both Greek and Latin in high school, and he was the last student in New Brunswick to take the matriculation exam in Greek. At UNB the emphasis in Classics was on the writing of Greek and Latin prose. "[Professor R.E.D.] Cattley would go into ecstasy if I got something right. I can read the New Testament [in Greek] quite comfortably. But I don't sit down and translate Homer for pleasure."

By the time he entered high school he had stopped writing, and it was only at UNB when his friend Buck Richards challenged him to write a sonnet that he began again, this time every day. He was a Beaverbrook Scholar and lived in the Beaverbrook Residence with the other Scholars. It was a stimulating atmosphere. They had come to UNB as "naïve young men and we set about discovering the new world together." Alfred Bailey's freshman history was "the most stimulating course I took in university. It was an eye-opener." In that course he learned about modern art, Freud, theories of aesthetics, Plato.

The poetry the UNB students studied and wrote in the late forties and early fifties was influenced by the British poets: Eliot, Auden, Hopkins. "But that wasn't as liberating as if it had been American poetry. It took a long time for me to see the necessity to get free of the British influence. It was not until I came back to UNB and encountered Alden Nowlan and read some American poets [William Carlos Williams, Robert Frost, Wallace Stevens…] that I adopted a plainer style. And when I began to write fiction, it had a further liberating effect on my poetry."

As an undergraduate, Bob Gibbs became active in the Bliss Carman Poetry Society and in its magazine, *The Fiddlehead*. After studying at Cambridge University and teaching in the New Brunswick public school system for nine years, he returned to UNB in 1963 to study for a Ph.D. and to teach at the university level. He then renewed his commitment to the magazine and remains an editorial presence to this day.

In 1960s Fredericton, he says, there was a "creative fervour, when Fredericton had its own poetry." Alden Nowlan, Kent Thompson, Dorothy Livesay and Peter Thomas came to town, and there was "the stimulus of the people who came to the Ice House. By the time that petered out, I could continue on my own." At the Ice House, teacher and poet combined in Gibbs to influence young poets like Brian Bartlett, who much later wrote about the group in a memoir: "Bob Gibbs showed in poem after poem what well-aimed verbal beauty and playfulness could do, and in the long run his style likely became a stronger model for mine than Nowlan's later, more plain-speaking verse."

Gibbs' writing not only comes out of an affection for his surroundings, an ironic look at the characters in those places, and a marvellous memory of an unusually stimulating childhood, but also out of a religion that is not dogmatic or judgmental, though sincerely reverent. He would be embarrassed if I recounted his true charity, using that word to encompass kindness and love. A stranger comes to his house and asks for money. Fifteen years later he is still coming and still being given dinner. An artist says that he needs money and would Bob like to buy a painting. Bob already has several, but he purchases another one. Could he turn away a stranger in need or refuse a friend?

A most convincing proof of his stature in the literary community is the way other writers seek his help. Insightful criticism has been his hallmark as a teacher, workshop participant, editor and reader of manuscripts. When the poet Joseph Sherman, another Ice House alumnus, is ready to publish, he sends the manuscript to Gibbs for his comments. Kwame Dawes, in his recent collection, *Resisting the Anomie* (Goose Lane Editions), offers "Special thanks to Robert Gibbs for his first eye." Heather Browne Prince brought her UBC creative writing thesis to Gibbs for his suggestions. "I would never have been able to finish it without his help," she says. Testimonials all, but honestly earned.

His excellence as a writer has been achieved not by living in isolation, appearances sometimes to the contrary, but by his contributing immensely to the literary life of New Brunswick. He became the director of UNB's graduate creative writing program, and his teaching has won him many protégées—Alberta poet Yvonne Trainer, for example. Upon his retirement a few years ago, UNB acknowledged his contribution by naming him Professor Emeritus.

Gibbs has been a member of Canada Council juries, edited anthologies, and written scholarly articles on the work of Canadian writers. His review criticism has been described as "civil and generous, distinguished by a determination to locate and identify the best" in what he examines. He has been a judge for the Governor General's Award and the CBC Literary Competition. He has given readings of his work all over the country (including a memorable Maritime tour with the late Earle Birney and Alden Nowlan).

Nowlan chose Gibbs as his literary executor, and in that capacity, he has edited a previously unpublished novel and poems, and consults extensively with critics studying Nowlan's work. He has edited Nowlan's *Telegraph-Journal* columns, the first volume of which, *White Madness*, was published in 1996 by Oberon, with a second in the works.

But it is the writer in Robert Gibbs who warrants this attention. One of my favourite poems is this one, about a carver of wood masks. It could be about the poet himself.

> **"To imitate nature involves the verb"**
>
> Nahamee of the Squamish
> struck out this head
> with an unwavering blade
> and this must be his own face
> flashed here
> and known as a man knows his own
> from looking out of it
> not at it

A Great Cloud of Witnessing

And when he freed himself
he cut loose the tree
disclosing every ridge of grain
known only to itself
His fingers rubbed themselves out
setting his wood's assertion
against his own features
the marks he made on it

What a sharp selfhood
he must have brought
to his cutting edge
to uncover them both here
his own and the wood's
You'd have to handle this
unsmiling head yourself
to know how man and tree
secure each other

ArtsAtlantic 59 (15.3: Fall/Winter 1997)

Local poetry has the power to broaden our community

The launch of *Salon* at the Beaverbrook Art Gallery last Friday evening was a celebratory affair marked by a heartfelt speech from the publisher of the *Telegraph-Journal* about his love for New Brunswick arts. Everyone I talked to there was excited that we were to have our own arts section. The folding of *ArtsAtlantic* some years ago had left an awful void.

In her inaugural column, the editor, Shawna Richer described me as "venerable." My heart, but not my head [I hope] swelled when I read that. Venerable means wise and extremely old. The old part is correct. I once knew a Venerable Canon, who wasn't particularly wise or old. Then there is the medieval scholar, the Venerable Bede, who was wise. Venerable or not, I'm excited to be part of this endeavour, to be able to say whatever is on my mind about arts in New Brunswick. My husband is afraid that people will throw eggs at our house. Instead of egging us, please write a stinging letter to the editor, denouncing me.

Tip O'Neill, the late, outspoken Democrat from Boston famously said, "All politics are local." I am going to steal that and say instead, "All poetry is local." Dotted all over New Brunswick are groups of poets who read their poetry to each other, arrange public readings, and hold contests.

The Wolf Tree Group meets in Sussex and Fredericton; the Chocolate River poets meet in the Moncton area. A dedicated gaggle of poets meets regularly in the Fredericton Public Library. Groups meet in McAdam and Miramichi, Saint John and Sackville. Few of these poets are invited to read at such august places as Toronto's Harbourfront or the Vancouver Writers' Festival, but many of them are invited to read across the Maritimes.

A Great Cloud of Witnessing

In a recent *Globe and Mail* article suggesting that there are many poets but few readers of poetry ("Poets aplenty, but who's reading the verse?" Nov. 2006), Brian Fawcett says that he stopped publishing his poetry in the early 1980s due to lack of an audience. Here in New Brunswick, there isn't such a deficit but sometimes there will be only seven or eight at a reading. Perhaps the audience includes a husband or a mother or an aunt, but it will also invariably include people devoted to poetry.

A blog I read regularly (www.ronsilliman.blogspot.com) discusses the poets of San Francisco as if they are well-known, although I recognize none of the names. The blogger writes of books being put out by publishers I have never heard of. The blogger says, "One of the great things about the post-avant [and the most crucial way in which it differs from the old avant] is how it understands itself as a community."

Is the reading of poetry and the attendance at poetry readings a purely local activity? I tend to go to the readings of friends and acquaintances, buy their books and read them. Often at these readings I hear poems I have heard or read several times, and when this happens, I am especially joyful. I don't attend purely out of loyalty either, but because I have come to know and love the voice and stance of the poet. I have become part of a post-avant community.

If I were a poet, perhaps I would read from far afield in order to be alert to new trends and new forms and thus enlarge this community. Recently I was asked to review a book about Elizabeth Bishop's poetry. I found I was most moved by her poetry about places I had known: Massachusetts, Maine and Nova Scotia. I was interested in her relationship to Marianne Moore, whom I met when I was young and whose work I long admired.

In my small Massachusetts village, where I grew up, in the 1920s and '30s, a revered teacher taught poetry with such passion that many of the villagers began to write it. This poetry never went beyond the village border but was widely shared within it.

Any publisher of poetry is in the financial predicament of printing expensive books to be read by a small regional audience. One of the giants of New Brunswick poetry is Robert Gibbs, but our local publishers do not put out his work. A second giant is M. Travis Lane and she also publishes elsewhere. It is troubling that to get the work of New Brunswick poets, I have to buy from Ontario publishers, a refutation of the thesis of this column.

Our friend Joseph Sherman died a year ago. Whenever he had a manuscript to submit to his publisher, he would send it to Robert Gibbs and me to vet. Because I had read Joe's poetry so carefully for so many years, knew the people and places he recorded, and had heard him read many times, I could hear his voice loud and clear. On those occasions the three of us, Joe, Bob, and I, would be engaged in camaraderie like no other; a community of three.

Salon, February 3, 2007

Mixing cultures promises to stimulate the fruit of our literary labours

I remember, with pleasure, the early occasions when the francophone arts community came together with the anglophone arts community. Rick Burns, to whom both arts communities owe a great deal, had spurred the creation of Gallery Connexion. Somehow Luc Charette heard about the new gallery and submitted work. We were excited about showing this work, Façade, his first exhibit in Fredericton, and getting to know at least one of the Acadian artists. Many of his compatriots attended the opening in 1986.

Roslyn Rosenfeld wrote in her *ArtsAtlantic* review of the exhibit: "Throughout these varied forms of expression, one has the sense of a keen intellect grappling with basic artistic issues." This articulated as well what the artists of Connexion were trying to do. Charette was on their wavelength, with his wall pieces blending painting and sculpture, contemporary art that was not only bilingual but international.

It was about that time we learned what superb policy activists the artists from the Acadian community are. They led us into battle with the provincial government; we knew that New Brunswick artists had the least amount of provincial support, but how to rectify that? A weekend conference was held at the Centre Communautaire, and the needs of the artists were discussed.

Connexion hosted a reception and an exhibit for the delegates. I had the feeling that the Acadians were surprised that we stodgy English could create such a funky place. I remember one artist telling me, awed, "I didn't know this place existed." Soon we had more exhibits of Moncton artists, Yvon Gallant for example, and they had exhibits of our artists. On the tenth anniversary of the opening of Connexion, Charette, having become the director of the University of Moncton art gallery, curated an exhibit of Connexion members and hosted a celebration.

In 2000 the Moncton community began the Northrop Frye literary festival, including writers in both languages. Later they added writers in other languages. I could see again how much Moncton supported its artists. I gave a reading at that first festival, one of 42 writers. I had never read before to such a large gathering, up on the Aberdeen Centre stage, the audience in darkness, with lights playing on me. I felt like a rock star. Reading at Harbourfront in Toronto was not as exciting. There were reading venues all over Moncton—restaurants, galleries.

When I began to write profiles of artists and craftspeople for the *New Brunswick Reader*, I visited the Aberdeen Centre in Moncton several times. What a lively place. Fredericton's fledgling Charlotte Street Arts Centre is modeled after it. The artists and writers made films, had their own theatre company producing their own plays, had two publishing houses. Their sense of community was palpable. Some of the Moncton artists moved to Montreal, but many stayed home, and I have the impression that the artists of Moncton think of themselves collectively as Acadian New Brunswickers, not as an offshoot of Quebec. They have a long history and culture to draw upon, but they really want to make something new and contemporary, not "folklorique."

Herménégilde Chiasson was a motivator in this arts community, and when he was named Lieutenant Governor, a brilliant choice, he became a motivator for the arts in the whole province.

Art and craft is international, obviously not requiring translation. It takes a little longer for literature to mingle. It has happened in my lifetime here that we became the only province that is officially bilingual. As a transplanted unilingual American, I find that exceedingly stimulating. Many of our students are in immersion classes. This is clearly expensive and as we are always being told, we are a poor province.

Perhaps we aren't doing immersion as well as we might, but where else in North America is it being done better and as a matter of public policy? So far, the growing number of bilingual young people hasn't affected our literature in English, although it is only a matter of time. A three-year old girl growing up in a bilingual household was recounting her dream to her parents. A woman has fallen on the railroad tracks and was hollering "help me, help me." She recounted the dream in French, but the "help me" was in English. What will scenarios like this mean for the literature of New Brunswick?

On another subject, a poet took me to task for writing that Maritime publishers don't publish Maritime poets. Goose Lane Editions has hired a local poetry editor, Ross Leckie, and they have recently published several New Brunswick poets. My correspondent also reminds me that Gaspereau Press in Nova Scotia has published local poets. I also note that Broken Jaw Press has published some New Brunswick poets and that other smaller publishers, Allison Calvern's poppy press for example, have lately been putting out chapbooks.

Salon, March 3, 2007

Provincial writers' federation falls short

Over the past several years, many writers have initiated discussions with me about the weakness of the Writers' Federation of New Brunswick. We usually end up debating how to revivify it, although some people suggest that it would be better to let it die a natural death.

The federation has never been as strong as writers' groups in other provinces—Newfoundland or Nova Scotia, for example, and I can think of several reasons why. New Brunswick did not catch the crest of the wave of federal arts funding in the 1970s, and our independent arts board was formed only a few years ago, twenty years after other provinces had one. The federation has never had the government or private donor financial support enjoyed by sister organizations. In 1987 I visited the Winnipeg building that houses the provincial arts organizations, and I was envious because there were studios for artists and musicians and offices for writers—even electric typewriters; it was a place of excitement.

At the inception of the Writers' Federation of New Brunswick in 1982, we on the founding committee had to decide whether to welcome all serious writers, to limit it to professional writers, or to have a two-tiered system like the federation in Nova Scotia, with one tier for all writers and a more prestigious upper tier for published writers. We made the decision to open it to all writers. Consequently, it has never been considered an honour to belong. Well-known writers have supported the organization over the years—Fred Cogswell, Michael Nowlan, Allan Donaldson, M. Travis Lane and M.T. Dohaney among others—but I see few of our most highly-regarded writers at the meetings.

Another burden is that New Brunswick does not have one major city. The federation has held its annual meetings in six different places. When the Nova Scotia federation meets, all the members know they'll be coming to the big city, Halifax. They are enticed to come because the office is there, the stimulation is there. They are even enticed to come because the shopping and restaurants are there.

Another reason for the lack of strength in New Brunswick is a tendency for our prose writers not to belong to professional organizations. The Writers' Union of Canada, for example, has few members from this province. It has never had a New Brunswicker as the Atlantic regional representative, although University of New Brunswick professor Kent Thompson was one of its founders. This reluctance doesn't seem to apply to the province's poets and freelance journalists, who join The League of Canadian Poets and the Professional Writers of Canada in large numbers and who have really formed the backbone of the Writers' Federation in recent years.

The federation is invisible. It's tucked away in a third-floor office on Queen Street in Fredericton. The space was chosen for its affordable price, but is seldom populated now. If someone were to make the arduous trek up there, they would not often find anyone to greet them. A drive to move the office to the new Charlotte Street Arts Centre was stymied a few months ago. A catch-22 is that as the membership has dwindled over the years, a lack of dues money means even more invisibility.

The organization does not do enough lobbying for its writers. Why has the Arts Board not granted the Alden Nowlan Award for Excellence for three straight years? Couldn't the University of New Brunswick be persuaded to appoint a New Brunswicker as writer-in-residence? It hasn't had one since 1990. The federation created the Alden Nowlan Festival, but the event didn't attract much interest or business sponsorships and last fall was not even held.

When I ask poet Shari Andrews if the organization has helped her, she says, "Definitely. It helped me branch out and, with the contacts I made, form a support system with other poets like Heather Browne." The federation sponsored her for paid readings during National Poetry week. She entered its competitions, won prizes, and thus had her work evaluated. The competition was one of the organization's strengths, and so I was distressed when the decision was made to open it to all Canadians, and last year the two top prizes went to non-New Brunswickers.

Prose writer Rhona Sawlor says that she met other writers at various federation activities. Through these contacts, she found a job successfully shepherding the Maritime Writers' Workshop for several years.

Organizations have their cycles, rising, falling and rising again. Despite all the disadvantages I have chronicled, the Writers' Federation of New Brunswick had many productive years. At a book launch last fall, a writer who had been active in the group came up to me and with pain in his voice said, "Nancy, what's happening to the Writers' Federation?" I know he is hoping that the federation will rise again.

Salon, March 10, 2007

In the arts, one person can make a difference

On April 19 the Beaverbrook Art Gallery will open the third Writing on the Wall exhibit, the brainchild of poet Joseph Sherman. He described it this way in a brochure: "Writing on the Wall invites established New Brunswick poets to respond to a work of art of their choosing, selected from the Beaverbrook Art Gallery Collection." He explained it as the "ekphrastic concept of mobilizing poets who are interested in interdisciplinary projects." Ekphrastic poetry interprets an artwork of a different medium.

Joe curated a similar project in Prince Edward Island, where he lived, and then initiated one in Fredericton, where he had once lived and where his mother still does. He selected the poets and went with them to the gallery where they chose a painting, either on display or in the bowels of the storage vault. The poet then wrote a poem inspired by the painting. In Fredericton, six poets have participated. Because I was his friend and wrote for his magazine, his widow suggested to the Beaverbrook Art Gallery that I take over curating the project. For this third exhibit, M. Travis Lane chose a painting by Molly Lamb Bobak and will unveil her poem Thursday evening.

In the arts community one person like Joe can make such a big difference. As editor of *ArtsAtlantic* he single-handedly kept the magazine alive, soliciting writers, editing and selling ads, all while keeping in touch with the artists of the whole area. For the 20 years he edited the magazine, he brought the artists of the Atlantic provinces out of their hiding places and put them before the public. The extent of his work was demonstrated when someone else took the magazine over and it very soon folded. Joe organized readings, helped start a series of poetry chapbooks and did all this while still publishing wonderful poetry. He was honoured with the Order of Canada, and when he died in January last year, many different media outlets across Canada paid tribute to him.

I was thinking again about the impact one man makes when the Beaverbrook Art Gallery and Gallery Connexion exhibited the work of Rick Burns this winter. He was the driving force behind the creation of Connexion, which inspired and stimulated many of our young artists. He taught at the College of Craft and Design, where again he influenced many. He was endlessly experimenting, trying out new forms and materials. His enthusiasm, his laugh, and his love for all the arts, were catching. Not only did he paint and make constructions and installations, he wrote stories and plays. I never felt as alive as I did in his presence.

Kent Thompson was another person who made a difference, and happily he is still alive although he has left the building. He revamped *The Fiddlehead*, taught creative writing, initiated a writers' group that lasted 16 years. He travelled around the country as a tireless promoter of our writers and waxed euphoric in various national magazines about Fredericton as the new Dublin. Pretty soon, other writers were echoing his words. He was one of the founders of The Writers' Union of Canada. He established a relationship with Oberon Press which published many New Brunswick writers. His and Michaele's home was the site of many wonderful arts events.

Tom Condon is another man who made a difference in arts and culture. He oversaw the expansion of the University of New Brunswick, spearheaded the restoration of the Imperial Theatre and was an early supporter of the Writers' Federation of New Brunswick. He was a mainstay of many other art projects, Symphony New Brunswick for one.

In Fredericton, Charlotte Glencross has single-handedly led the creation of the Charlotte Street Arts Centre. One of the attributes of these people who make a difference is that they are able to get others on board. They raise money. They enlist help. They generate enthusiasm. Charlotte even managed to get the Canadian Army involved in the restoration. The centre has already in its short life been a catalyst for the arts — in visual arts, dance, filmmaking, poetry readings. Before she took on this project, she had been a most helpful and innovative civil servant in the New Brunswick Arts Branch and a teacher of weaving at the College of Craft and Design.

Our Lieutenant Governor, His Honour Herménégilde Chiasson, is also a man who has made a difference. A true Renaissance man, he works in filmmaking, poetry, visual arts, and theatre. He is a leader and an inspiration in all of these. When he was named Lieutenant Governor, the whole arts community, English and French, cheered, and their enthusiasm has been justified.

The names of these and many other vital human beings may be forgotten in the far future, but they will have left their indelible marks on our community, the only immortality we really know anything about.

Salon, April 14, 2007

Written accounts do more to support the arts

I am definitely a media aficionado. We get three daily and two weekly newspapers plus several monthly magazines; I read the NY Times online; I listen to the radio, both the CBC and the new Rogers station. Recently we bought a television set and DVD player, installed it in the living room instead of relegating it to the basement, and so watch more TV and films. I have a blog and regularly read twenty other blogs. You get the idea — I embrace all media.

In the past, when a new form of communication appeared, people predicted it would spell the end of the others. Radio would hasten the demise of newspapers, as would TV, as would the World Wide Web. Everything wonderful was going to be done with computers and the Internet; print would disappear. However, when I look into the near future and ask myself which of these will be doing more to support the arts, I have to answer, print.

The CBC-TV has a short arts segment on its six o'clock local news; the local hosts of CBC radio often speak with writers with new books or artists with new exhibits. But these come and then immediately disappear. The Internet is great for looking up facts — is Freeman Patterson's garden on Bellisle Bay? for example. The blogs that I read often include the bloggers' reviews of books or lectures about new music, but unless I print them out, they disappear. We need print because it can be saved.

I am biased because print has always been the love of my life. Nothing helps writers like old-fashioned book publishing, but book reviews and accounts of launchings in the newspapers surely help, not only with sales, but with letting us know what is going on in the literary world. Reviews of exhibits, accounts of openings, and photographic images help the visual arts and crafts. These accounts endure. You can go hunting for your clippings if you need them.

A Great Cloud of Witnessing

About 15 years ago, I was on a Canada Council jury where the other jurors were complaining about their local newspapers' coverage of the arts. I was proud to be able to extol *The Daily Gleaner*'s coverage, and I could tell they were surprised. Could any good thing come out of Nazareth? For a period of time, the *Gleaner* had one of the best music critics in Canada, Anthony Pugh. He was succeeded by another excellent reviewer, Vivienne Anderson. Jo Anne Claus was a first-rate critic of theatre. She was succeeded by another good reviewer, Anne Ingram. Christina Sabat was indefatigable in her coverage of the visual arts and crafts, with reviews, accounts of openings, profiles. She was succeeded by the excellent writer Ray Cronin.

These people moved on; some left Fredericton, some died. They were not replaced, so that now the Gleaner has very little arts coverage. I don't know what precipitated this change in policy. I know that reviews can be tricky because a bad one angers the person being reviewed, as well as his family, friends and publisher or arts venue, not good for selling papers or ads. *The Atlantic Provinces Book Review* discovered this and changed its policy from having lengthy, knowledgeable reviews to mere notices, altering its name in the process.

Just when things looked bleak for arts coverage in the province, the New Brunswick Reader came along. At first it featured crafts but soon it covered all the arts. I have mentioned *ArtsAtlantic* in previous columns. Someone said to me that no one who wanted to write about the arts in the Atlantic provinces would be able to do so without consulting that magazine. Alas, *ArtsAtlantic* folded, the Reader quietly left us, but along came *Salon*. Many people have expressed to me their pleasure in this section and I, too, am delighted with it. When I was asked to contribute, I was so enthusiastic that I said yes in spite of the fact that I'm too old for such a strenuous activity as writing 800 words a week on the arts in general. Some day I hope it will be said that no one who is going to write about the history of the arts in New Brunswick will be able to do so without consulting *Salon*.

Goose Lane Editions and the Beaverbrook Art Gallery have just published two books, both beautifully written and illustrated, about New Brunswick artists Bruno Bobak and Miller Brittain. We have two recent biographies of Alden Nowlan, both well-done, complementing each other. We need other books about our artists and writers. One about the Pownings or about Nel Oudemans or about Ray Fraser would add to our arts history because we do need a written record of what our artists and writers have accomplished.

Salon, May 19, 2007

The fine and often thankless art of book reviews

A book report is the first analytical essay that anyone ever writes, starting perhaps in fifth grade. We seem to know innately how to compose this first book review, and teachers for generations have deemed the writing of it an essential ingredient in a curriculum. A review, even if it is only read aloud in the classroom, is also important for a potential reader.

The books I buy I invariably have discovered through book reviews. Unfortunately, unless you review for one of the big-name periodicals, book reviewing is a poorly paid activity, a fact you might also learn in Grade 5.

When I review a book, I read it several times, I research the author, and I sometimes read other books by the writer. I want to be fair to the book so I write and rewrite. I am not alone in putting in this amount of work. For the review, I might get $35. Why would any sensible person take on such a task?

Last summer I agreed to review two books. I had looked at the first one, a novel, and read a little to make sure I could be fair to it. Why spend all that effort on an unworthy book? Fortunately, I continued to like it. I had some expertise on what the writer was doing because she left hints of the books that had influenced her. I recognized these and appreciated them. I received $35 for this review, but it took me perhaps only 20 hours to write it.

But alas, I hadn't seen the other book before I agreed to review it and was alarmed to find that it was a dishonest book. What was worse, I really didn't have enough expertise to back up my points and so in addition to having to read the book twice, becoming more annoyed the second time through, I had to do a lot of background reading. Then I agonized: would my bad review cause the writer to commit suicide or at the very least send her into a deep depression?

Was I making a mistake because I wasn't sufficiently expert? This review took perhaps 40 hours to write and for it I received nothing but the gratitude of the editor.

Does a writer get anything from a review of his book besides the free advertising? Some writers don't read reviews, good or bad, but I do. Most importantly I get a sense of an audience. Reading aloud to a group also gives me that sense. When I get a bad review, my husband reminds me that people could enjoy a book or not according to their mood. A reviewer might have a sick child and a deadline she is not going to meet.

My memory of reading the first review I ever received is nearly as fond as my memory of first setting eyes on my husband. It was by T.J. Rigelhof in the late, lamented *Atlantic Provinces Book Review*. He later gave my third novel a rave review in the *Globe and Mail*. Bless you Mr. Rigelhof.

On the other hand, a later novel of mine received a slam, also in the *Globe and Mail*. This story ends happily. A few years after the review appeared, I attended a gathering in Toronto of writers who had new books coming out. Also attending was the woman who had written the damning review. I came to realize that she was trying to avoid me, and I amused myself by chasing her around the hall. A writer doesn't often get a chance to wreak such revenge on a reviewer. Rigelhof was on my wavelength. The woman I chased around the hall was not.

A University of Maine professor, Vernon Lindquist, wrote positive reviews of several of my novels, but when *Samara the Wholehearted* came out, he expressed his displeasure with it because the summer camp I described didn't have ramps for disabled people. One of his family members was disabled. My novel wasn't realistic, he wrote, because these days all such organizations have easy access. A reviewer, like any reader, brings his own experience to the grand mission of reading. Years later Lindquist wrote me that *Samara* was his favourite of my novels.

A Great Cloud of Witnessing

A poet I know said she would die happy if just one of her books got reviewed in the *New York Times Book Review*. Be careful what you wish for. A few weeks ago, a novel by Karen Connelly, a former writer-in-residence at the University of New Brunswick, received a rave review there. The review begins, "Amoebic dysentery, maggots, sadistic guards, a reeking latrine pail—these are the constants in Karen Connelly's tale of political prisoners in Burma, a novel that, at least initially, makes you wonder who will read on." With friends like that, who needs enemies?

Salon, June 23, 2007

Many heads are better than one

For 16 years, I was a member of a writers' group started by Kent Thompson and informally named "The Ice House Gang" because we met in UNB's refurbished ice house. I had read about many communities of artists, the one collected around Abbey Theatre and W.B. Yeats in Dublin, for example, but until I became part of one, I hadn't known just how inspiring such a group could be. My own modest literary career was the result of belonging to the Ice House Gang. Many books of poetry and fiction were spawned there, as well as the NB Chapbooks, the Maritime Writers' Workshop, the Writers' Federation of New Brunswick and a revitalized *Fiddlehead*. We eventually ran out of steam, sadly, and folded, but other communities sprang up out of the ashes.

Artists have clustered around Gallery Connexion for many years now. Over that time many different people have had studios in the building that houses the gallery. A leader in this community was the late Rick Burns, as I have written before. He attracted writers, visual artists, craftspeople, musicians and Craft College students, all of whom found a home there. One memorable evening the gallery sponsored a multi-arts gala. Lutia Lauzon brought her collection of exotic musical instruments—various whistles, thumb pianos, clackers—and as dusk fell, she played her harp and invited us non-musicians to join in as the spirit moved, assuring that we would make music. I was skeptical, but the miracle was that we did make an eerie harmony—the writers, the craftspeople, the artists, the real musicians. It was such a moving experience that I used it in one of my novels.

In the late 19th century, for a short while Fredericton was stirring with what poet Charles G.D. Roberts called "a strange aesthetic ferment." Roberts, Bliss Carman, Francis Sherman, and others, would meet in the handsome Anglican rectory of Roberts' father. In a marvelous essay, Dalhousie University professor Malcolm Ross analyzed the conditions for this ferment: a climate of culture and intellectual excitement generated by Bishop Medley and demonstrated in the church architecture Medley promoted. John Leroux has written about this in *Salon*. Stimulation came from England in the form of exciting new music, visual arts, and literature, as well as the architecture. In his seminal essay, "Creative Moments in the Maritime Provinces," scholar and poet Alfred Bailey writes about this group, about the excitement generated by the publication of Roberts' poem "Orion" and its effect on Carman. These creative moments don't last long, as Bailey implies in his title, but they do create a stimulus that reverberates.

Kay Smith, Miller Brittain, P.K. Page, Erica and Kjeld Deichmann, Jack Humphrey and Ted Campbell formed a gathering in and around Saint John that has always seemed to me to be the kind of bohemian community about which an historical novel could be written. For a while in the 1980s a similar group thrived in the Hampton and Shampers Bluff area, with the writers Elspeth and Ray Bradbury, Freeman Patterson, and other artists and craftspeople.

Why are such clusters so enjoyable and produce so much work, I have long wondered. Once my son was on a Little League squad led by a professional coach, and I got a glimpse of how a team is created. The players were a ragged bunch, but Mr. Born managed to make them into a team that performed far better than anyone expected. The members of our Ice House Gang did seem to feed off one another. Robert Gibbs said he wanted the immediate response that we fiction writers received, his poetry requiring more time to appreciate, so he began writing short stories. He proved to be a natural comic storyteller with an astonishing memory for details and incidents.

Our community in the ice house included only a few visual artists although we did associate with many others. Bruno Bobak designed the NB Chapbooks, Marjory Donaldson silkscreened them, and Bruno made portraits of some of the group. An early member, Joe Sherman, became the editor of *ArtsAtlantic*. Perhaps the architecture and ambiance of the ice house did contribute to the work engendered there.

The evangelist reports that Jesus said, "Where two or three are gathered in my name, there am I in the midst of them." I don't think you have to believe in a supernatural power to experience the joy of having something greater arrive in your midst as you gather with a few people in a quasi-spiritual challenge. It seems, however, to be a feature of these communities that they do run out of steam; the strange aesthetic ferment goes as flat as does the initial ecstasy of young love. Soon the first flush settles down to the more mundane, but equally important, lifetime of devotion.

Salon, September 15, 2007

A man who embraced us all

Tomorrow at 2 p.m. in Wesley United Church in St. Andrews, friends and admirers will gather to pay tribute to Peter Thomas who died in July after a two-year fight with cancer. I have written before about those who, through their intelligence, creative vision and energy, have made a difference to the arts in New Brunswick. Peter is a prime example of this.

Michael Taylor, writing in *The Fiddlehead*, remarked on the way Thomas kept his deep roots in Wales while putting down deep roots in New Brunswick.

"Peter was as much an inpatriate as an ex. How thoroughly and admirably he immersed himself in the culture of Atlantic Canada. How unstintingly he gave of himself to the cultivation of the arts in the region," Taylor stated.

Thomas did indeed embrace the province. He loved its history and wrote two books about it, both remarkable not only for their careful scholarship, but for their immense readability. *Strangers from a Secret Land: The Voyages of the Brig "Albion" and the Founding of the First Welsh Settlements in Canada* was published by the University of Toronto Press, was nominated for the Governor-General's Award, and won the Canadian Historical Association Regional History Award and the Welsh Arts Council Non-fiction Prize.

In his second book, *Lost Land of Moses: The Age of Discovery on New Brunswick's Salmon Rivers*, Thomas wrote a history of the province in the 19th century through its salmon fishing. I don't know how he managed to write such a fascinating, readable history just by using various fishing narratives, but he did.

In his preface, he wrote, "Sport has never been isolated from social history or the economic or political facts of life, and these sporting narratives of New Brunswick also offered a running commentary on great contemporary events and themes."

Thomas loved to fish in our rivers. A fishing friend said wistfully, "He was a magnificent angler. He made such beautiful casts." While traipsing through the woods and fields, he became interested in its abandoned apple orchards, finding out the names of the various old species. I remember that he and his wife Helen almost single-handedly saved the block between Smythe and Northumberland streets in Fredericton from slum landlords by sensitively renovating three of its old houses and creating beautiful gardens for them. Thomas petitioned the city to make the narrow street one-way, and while researching its history, discovered it was once called Goose Lane because one of its inhabitants raised geese.

He was an inspiring, if somewhat irascible, teacher of English at the University of New Brunswick. In 1981, he became the editor of *The Fiddlehead*. In his first editorial, he laid down this principle: "… a more positive assertion of our Atlantic origin will be made — not by an arbitrary definition or proportion of content but by ensuring that each *Fiddlehead* goes out with a distinct flavour of place, of the culture of Atlantic Canada."

To this end, Thomas solicited work from the region's writers and instituted an essay series, "Out of Place." Douglas Lochead, David Adams Richards, Alden Nowlan, Réshard Gool, Milton Acorn and Elizabeth Jones each contributed essays. He made a useful, insightful distinction: "Locale, not the local: it's the imagination of our place we seek to reflect, not its mirror image."

In 1980, he took over Fiddlehead Poetry Books from Fred Cogswell. A year later, he expanded the company by creating a new imprint, Goose Lane Editions, with the intention of publishing the fiction and history of the province.

Thomas helped organize and co-chaired the symposium where, one memorable weekend, French and English artists gathered to kick start what became the New Brunswick Arts Board. Prior to this, we were the only province without an arts coalition. Peter was no ivory tower professor; he dealt shrewdly with the government in getting the board off the ground.

His oeuvre includes three books of poetry, two books of literary criticism, as well as the editing of a collection of Fred Cogswell's poetry and a festschrift in honour of Douglas Lochhead. His novel, *The Welsher*, is comic in the somewhat melancholy way I think of as particularly Welsh, beginning as it does with a funeral, the comedy residing in the witty, acerbic tone of the narrator. The main character describes the burial ground, "I was unprepared for this tender autumnal bower, the purr of wood-pigeons, the newly-emerged sun disproportionately generous."

I have always loved these lines from his early collection, *A Cure for All Diseases*:

> Thrushes singing on the Rhondda thorn
> and the thin mouse edging along the wall,
> its head revolving like a toy,
> Iorrie and Benge, a hundred sober men,
> and the wet grave floating straws.
> Twenty-four years of dying;
> then you died.
>
> The time is difficult for me today
> and seeps away; I look back
> over my shoulder for the shadow.

Salon, September 29, 2007

The uncertain future of books

Twenty years ago, I began to write a novel set 20 years in the future. I wanted to know what became of Samara, the baby born at the end of my previous novel. One of the futuristic items I imagined was a portable computer, "the size of a paperback book," which could be plugged into magazines the world over. On it you could get articles, even translated foreign language items. I still have an image of the computer in my mind, and when I saw an ad for the new Kindle on the Amazon website, I was brought back two decades because the device looks just like one I had imagined.

Steven Levy in a recent *Newsweek* writes about this device, and Amazon advertises it with a video. Kindle is indeed like the one I imagined, a portable computer, the size of a paperback, on which you can download not only magazines but books and newspapers. On it a bestseller costs $10, half the cost of the hardcover. Many people have said that such devices will never replace books, but others theorize that although baby boomers, who rule the world now, might not go for them, young people who all love their omnipresent technological gadgets will embrace them.

Can anyone envision the future evolution of books? A lot of people are trying to. I have purchased a few e-books, downloaded them, but then printed them out because I found that reading a whole novel on the computer was not pleasant. I couldn't fall into the book, lose myself. When I read, at a certain point I am no longer seeing individual words, no longer am holding a volume. This is especially true of novels but also is true of certain works of non-fiction. Interruptions are awful — I will fall out of the story. The people who have developed Kindle are well aware of this falling-into-a-book phenomenon and have designed the device with special e-ink, the special serif font, Caecilia, and other features that not only mimic books but enhance them. I'm not yet willing to gamble $400 on a Kindle or its competitor, the Sony Reader, to see if reading on it does indeed have the same effect as reading a hardcover. I will wait.

Will the book disappear, and if so, when? How would its disappearance affect us in New Brunswick? An immense part of our economy is dependent on trees being turned into paper although I gather that New Brunswick paper is used for newspapers rather than for books. Will browsing in our bookstores be wiped out? Many of my purchases come from impulse buying. I now read three newspapers online (those that I can't get locally), but it isn't satisfactory because scanning isn't possible. There is little advertising, and I suppose that it is advertising revenue that keeps newspapers going. Strangely enough, I also find that advertisements are useful.

Will whatever evolves be good for future New Brunswick writers? Perhaps they will be able to have readers in far-flung parts of the English-speaking world. Regular readers of my blog live in Utah, several cities in England, Upstate New York, for example. I don't know how they found me. Would my publisher's capacity to put my novels on a Kindle get me more readers in other countries? One sure thing is that nothing would ever go out of print, a writer's dream.

Would being able to get books so easily and cheaply make it more feasible to publish those that aren't big money makers, poetry for example? Will local publishers have to digitalize their new lists? The manuscripts are already in computer form, but they would have to be structured to the Kindle's specifications. They will be cheaper, but a writer might sell more of them and thus make up for the royalty loss a cheaper one would entail.

Visionaries who are excited about these devices postulate that readers will be able to make suggestions to writers, who then will be able to change the content of their books. An author of a non-fiction volume can update it or make corrections according to reviews. Readers of a novel might complain so loudly about its ending that the novelist would change it. I know that I would like to change many things in my published works. The *Newsweek* article quotes a phrase often spoken by these visionaries: Readers will read in public. Writers will write in public. Readers of a book on the Kindle, not just reviewers, will be making remarks to other readers, as they now do on blogs. Writers will be posting their work on Kindle for others to criticize. Already several writers are blogging their works in progress, asking for suggestions. Serial novels might come back into fashion. I wonder: did I encounter the future 20 years ago?

Salon, December 15, 2007

Artists need cash to create

Here's a chilling phrase: "the businessization of the arts world."

It appeared in a front-page article in the *Telegraph-Journal* with the headline "Newest goal: Business-like approach to the arts."

The New Brunswick Foundation of the Arts invited François Colbert, a professor of arts management, to tell us how to make cultural organizations profitable. Foundation chairwoman Anne Bertrand, who coined the phrase, said the arts and culture community needs to look at itself and examine how to appeal to the public without compromising its creativity.

"Create art and culture people want to see, that they will pay to go see," she said.

Colbert said various government sectors in Canada put $7 billion into the arts. "So there's no lack of funding." He must have been talking about the production of the work artists have already created.

Becoming profitable is a worthy goal. Ballet companies and symphonies must cater to the public to survive. They know they won't be as profitable as the World Pond Hockey Tournament is, but the Frye Literary Festival does well, and after 26 years, Goose Lane Editions is still in business.

No one, however, makes a profit during the making of a painting or literary work. Creating takes time; several years for a novel or a concerto, during which the artist is not making money. He hopes to profit eventually, but he is not getting a weekly wage. He might try to make something people want to see but whether people do or not is a lottery. Painters want to sell their work. Writers want to make enough money to live on, but appealing to the public is not easy.

Once, when my husband and I needed money, we decided to write a Harlequin together. The very first writer of a Harlequin came to study at the Maritime Writers' Workshop. As a lark, she and her roommate began to write a romance together. I thought, Aha, maybe Bill and I can solve our cash flow problem! We are both writers; how hard could it be?

We got the guidelines from the publisher, created characters and a situation; the time-honoured plot was obvious. I read Bill's chapter. "You can't have comedy in a Harlequin." He read mine. "You can't have religion." Maybe if we'd been destitute, we could have finished it. But I can tell you, it was a lot harder than it looked.

I think it's important to keep this distinction in mind: artists create, arts businesses produce those creations. Certain poets hit the publishing jackpot without compromising themselves. Robert Frost, Billy Collins and Dylan Thomas come to mind. But most poets don't. No writer could make a living writing short stories unless he was published in *The New Yorker*. I have known hundreds of writers but have never personally known one who was published there.

The public can see what the art gallery or the publisher is doing. If the symphony orchestra produces lousy music, we know it. But what do we know about the writer toiling away in his hovel? What the devil is he writing, we ask, some post-post, modern junk that no one wants to read? I was talking to a visual artist about writer's block, telling him he was lucky because if he had a block, he could just take a brush and make some marks on the canvas. I demonstrated. It wouldn't help a writer out of a block just to write gobbledygook. He protested vigorously, "If I just went like this (he imitated me), that would be just like your scribbling. It wouldn't help me at all."

How does an artist justify to a jury that he will use the $15,000 or $3,500 wisely? He sends in samples—a music demo, slides of paintings—a resumé, letters from people who swear that the beggar will indeed paint and won't spend the money on a jaunt to Aruba.

In the end, the juries have to go on faith; it's a matter of percentages. Out of 10 awards, maybe four writers will finish the novel and only one will be published. Lousy odds for our hard-earned tax money.

I have never applied for a creation grant. I make that disclaimer so that you know I am not arguing for myself but for the many artists who scratch for a living. As far as I can glean from their websites, in 2007 The New Brunswick Arts Board awarded $171,000 for creation grants and in 2006 the Canada Council of the Arts awarded project creation grants of $100,000 to New Brunswick artists. That's an awfully small piece of the $7 billion pie.

Salon, February 16, 2008

You can't browse at online bookstores

I read that independent bookstores are folding in every city. Fredericton's Westminster, however, survives, even seems to thrive. What is its secret? The legendary Frog Hollow Books in Halifax endures with a new owner. Also enduring in Charlottetown as well as in Halifax are the two Bookmark stores. For children's books, Woozles in Halifax is a favourite of parents. In Rothesay another children's store with a fine reputation, Benjamin Books, survives. Westminster itself has a large children's section; these books seem to be moneymakers, subsidizing those written for senior citizens.

The big stores, Chapters in Canada, Borders in the U.S., give local stores stiff competition, but I suspect that internet services, Amazon for one, are their main rivals. The web is astounding for the obscure books you can find. Looking up Viktor Shklovsky to make sure I was spelling his name correctly, I discovered a book of his—that I coveted but that had long been out of print—was now available from Dalkey Archives. As well, in 2007 Dalkey published his book about the novel that had at long last been translated.

The trouble with online bookstores, however, is that you have to know what you might want. Nothing can take the place of browsing in a bookstore. Many years ago, my husband came back from a UNB bookstore sale with a gift, W. E. Hockings' *The Meaning of God in Human Experience*. It gave me a new way of thinking about immortality; not bad for a remaindered book. Some months ago, while browsing in Westminster, on impulse I bought a book which got me thinking about contemporary music and led to my musings in State of the Art.

Serendipity and its more mystical sister, synchronicity, often appear in my life in the form of books that wend my way. Over several years I had accumulated 11 of the 12 volumes of *A Dance to the Music of Time*, and just before I was going to read them,

I went into a poorly-stocked used bookstore, and behold, the missing volume. For fifty cents. Fredericton has a good used bookstore, The Owl's Nest, and Moncton also has a good one, The Attic Owl.

The independent bookstore is essential for new or struggling writers. An article by Julie Bick in the *New York Times* described the immense clout that Seattle now has in promoting books because Amazon, Costco and Starbucks are headquartered there. Why Starbucks? I thought as I began to read the article. Those of you in Saint John perhaps already know why; every few months Starbucks chooses one book to feature in its stores and that book will sell 100,000 copies. How pleasant to read a book while you are sipping your fancy coffee. Fredericton's Chapters has a scaled down Starbucks right in its store, complete with tables and chairs. Westminster has a comfortable chair but no coffee. In Bangor, the big box store Borders not only has coffee, it serves lunch. The tables are always occupied by people chatting, reading, using their laptops on WiFi. But even Borders is in financial trouble.

The mammoth discount company Costco can ensure the livelihood of any writer if it chooses her books for its stores. It is unlikely, however, that Costco, way off in Seattle, will hear of a New Brunswick-based writer, but these writers do have a hope with local stores. On its website Westminster lists its bestsellers, many by local authors. At least once a month a writer will launch his book in the cozy store.

When I was growing up, tradesmen came to our door: the milkman, the A&P man. Vic the Bookseller came to the door of my father's workplace. Vic made the rounds of the Boston newspapers, carrying a satchel of new and used books. He made it his business to learn what would tempt his customers. I have inherited many of these temptations, including the complete works of George Eliot. An article in the *Boston Globe* was illustrated by a cartoon of my father buying a book from Vic, the ultimate in a local bookstore.

So many good things have disappeared that I find it difficult not to think back to a golden age even though I know rationally that such a thing never existed. In a few days the oldest bookstore in Canada, The Book Room, a store that opened in Halifax in 1839, will close for good. In his press release, the owner gave the reasons: "The coming of big-box-bookstores with their large inventory at discount prices; the expansion of books into grocery and drugstores; the ease of ordering books at discount prices over the internet and the dual pricing of books with higher selling prices in Canada than in the United States…" Soldier on, oh Westminster, carry on, oh Benjamin Books!

Salon, March 29, 2008

Books in the hands of the writers

At the Small Press Fair held in Gallery Connexion in Fredericton, I was surprised to find many chapbooks, zines, stories told in comic book form, and eccentrically illustrated pamphlets. I shouldn't have been surprised because the computer makes these easy to produce. They brought me back to 1967 when a group of us created the New Brunswick Chapbooks, a series that included some of the best poets in the province.

At first a volunteer typed the poetry; later we paid someone. Back then I was a lousy typist; now I can easily be perfect. One day M. Travis Lane phoned me in alarm because the typist had rearranged her poems as if they were prose. We had the books printed in offset by the Provincial Artisans. Now an inkjet printer would spew the pages out in jig time.

Bruno Bobak designed them, and Marjory Donaldson silkscreened their bands of colour. Various artists donated their work for the covers. I was proud of how handsome they were, but after a while the poets agitated for books that were even more handsome because professionally printed. This necessitated applying to The Canada Council, filling out forms, worrying about money. Even with my friend Dale Estey helping me, the process became such a pain that I gave up the project in 1982. Now after all these years we are back to cheap books.

One of the tables at the fair held chapbooks put out by the press BookThug[2]. Like the NB Chapbooks, they are published in limited editions, stapled, sometimes containing only 15 pages. They are cheap — $10; we sold ours for 60 cents. The press is about to launch a fiction series; we tried that too. I should warn them. BookThug sells its wares online at Apollinaire's Bookshoppe, whose motto is "selling the books that no one wants to buy."

---

2   BookThug renamed itself Book*hug in 2018

Some of the books at the fair were self-published. I used to be snobbish about this practice, but I have changed my mind. The Maine Alliance of Writers and Publishers now gives prizes for the best self-published books. My husband, an expert on Maine books, says that often the self-published books are better than those published commercially.

Software publishing programs enable you to make a book the right size with handsome fonts and even with the ability to scan in illustrations. If you are diligent, you can market your books yourself. New Brunswick writer Peter D. Clark has placed his books in gas stations and tourist stops. He has his own website. The internet probably would have helped the Chapbooks. I see that some of them now fetch $15 to $35 on websites.

The word chapbook originates from their being sold by chapmen, peddlers who sold their wares from door to door or in the village square. In my last column, I wrote about Vic the Bookseller who came door to door. Billy Valgardson told me that he sold many copies of his books at the annual fair in his hometown of Gimli, Manitoba. Wayne Curtis sells his books in various small stores along the Miramichi River.

Lately the media has been reporting scary financial news. Over the last few years, I have been impressed that some ordinary folks now live like only the wealthiest could when I was growing up. People have bathrooms that are like the spas of exclusive health clubs, but at the moment people in the USA are losing these homes with their Jacuzzis. What does this portend for books? Will poets have to go back to being published in a cheaper form? The worst aspect of being 73 is that I know I will never hear the end of some stories. It is like beginning to read a novel even though you know that its last 30 pages are missing.

Economist Christopher Ruhm says there is good news in a recession: people smoke and drink less, get sick less, and consequently don't die as young. Maybe they will have to stay home and read more. They would have to read books from a library or reread the books they already own, but when boom times come again, they might retain the reading habit and be able to buy books. You can purchase three books for the price of one pedicure. Those who were publishing in chapbooks might be well-known enough to be published in hardback.

The samizdat (from the Russian words for self-publish) literature of the Soviet Union was hand-written or typed with carbon copies and distributed hand to hand. Because this practice was so dangerous, the reader experienced a special frisson while reading the manuscript. I have read a lot of typed manuscripts, and although it is not a risky practice, it is exciting to be the first (and maybe the last) to read a new work.

Salon, April 5, 2008

Into the inner lives of poets

For the last few weeks, I have been communing with the work of three poets. Former Frederictonian Brian Bartlett has a new book out, *The Watchmaker's Table*. On successive Sunday mornings, health troubles kept us from church and so instead I sat in my cozy corner, read Brian's poetry, and thought about what is important in life. The first morning the sun was streaming in, and little knolls of snowdrifts in the backyard were patterned with unusual shadows and unidentified paw prints.

Brian creates a life lived that is precious and sacred. His family, ancestors, students, colleagues, and the natural world are all lovingly, vividly portrayed. A bird on top of his chimney starts "babbling" while the poet is sitting on the couch reading Heraclitus. "Any day you're welcome to whatever warmth I can offer, / especially if down the chimney you chortle, Mindfulness, / mindfulness! in your fluent, fractured way." In "Breathing and Reading," the son, accustomed to being read to at bedtime, wants to read the book himself, but wants the father with him. The two lie on the son's bed, companionably reading their separate books until the son falls asleep. "They divide the hour / like a loaf of bread offered by a stranger / when hunger, cold, and storm / slow their steps far from home."

Michael Pacey came to visit his old friends. I asked him to bring new poems to read. One poem made me laugh out loud, "Reading Proust." A long poem about using a pencil versus a pen demonstrates a completely original sensibility: "The feel of pencil: walking, in deep sand / into the wind, against the grain / and very thirsty; / scratching eczema with a knitting-needle. / Chalk on slate. / The smell: school (vomit, shavings, mucilage)." Another totally original poem explores the connection between the senses and the brain, using the legend of Saint Denis, who after his beheading, picks up his head and walks home. The final stanza: "The last one hundred steps, sheep-bells / and smells from the fields / hold me for a moment, holding my breath, / holding my blind head outstretched like a lantern."

I have followed the work of these two poets for 35 years, beginning when they were in high school. I have heard them read their poems countless times, have read them almost prayerfully, and the upshot of this is that I feel that I have crept into their inner lives. This is a privilege I do not take lightly.

I have only just met the third poet, Michael deBeyer. As the curator of the Writing on the Wall project at the Beaverbrook Art Gallery, I chose Michael as the writer to commune with a painter. I didn't know him or his work, but Lynn Davies recommended him and lent me his book. I realize that if I come to know a man through his poetry before I ever see him, I meet him with a different mindset.

Michael chose a Bobak oil, "Atlantic Coast," painted in 1959 when Bruno was about Michael's age. The purpose of Writing on the Wall is to highlight a particular work in the collection, and this surely happened because few people have seen the painting recently. Now it is splendidly displayed by itself along with the poem Michael wrote to give his reaction to it. In his essay about his choice, he explained, "Being, then, is as critical as place to this painting." He expresses this again in the poem, "It is not time, but occasion / and duration in one. The tide / breaks too. The day turns to mirror / the light its grey mornings were."

In his book, *Change in a Razor-backed Season*, deBeyer invented a way of investigating an idea in two ways. He writes a paragraph on a subject and then a poem which he calls Echolalia. A poem titled "Echolalia: The Hallway" follows prose titled "The Hallway." In prose is this sentence: "Consciousness is like a beautiful high-walled garden keeping us from the miracle of ourselves." In "Echolalia: The Hallway" he repeats in poetry: "The noise of articulation is beautiful, a consciousness thinking, I am the words."

Poetry originated, it is theorized, because in a strictly oral culture the rhythms made it easier to memorize long passages and thus keep history alive. Why, in evolutionary terms, should it continue to thrive? It is less useful to me than the directions to my new washing machine. It thrives because it does what we all desire and need, to be allowed inside someone else's mind and imagination, if only imperfectly.

A poet has no need for story or artificialities. He opens himself up to us. There is no temptation to do otherwise: he knows he will probably never make a lot of money, will never become a rock star. Purity is not guaranteed, but it at least can be anticipated. The poet's subject is his own nuanced view of his inner life.

Salon, April 26, 2008

A world that arises from a sentence

While I was on vacation, I began to write another novel. I was inspired by reading Colm Toibin's novel, *The Master*, a portrait of the novelist Henry James. Tobin describes James' method: "The slow, sly systems used to write a novel, the building of character and plot through action and description and suggestion…" This is the method of everyone who writes a novel, although unfortunately the "sly" part is sometimes ignored. I myself like the slow part, starting with a sentence or a character or a scene, and from that building a whole world. I have begun nine since my last one was published in 1994 and have finished four, have revised, combined, changed from third person to first person, and changed locations. Why have I become such a flibberdigibbet about writing novels, I worry.

After I had written on the new novel for several mornings, I set down this sentence: "They had the only house with a name in the city." I don't know why this came out; perhaps it was that my brain was busy thinking of names for the characters. I was also observing the names of the cottages in our vicinity, all of them using a variation of Sea, Shore, View, Ocean. For the house in the novel, I discarded Hall and Place as being too pretentious for the one I was picturing. At last, I remembered Wordsworth's Dove Cottage and for quite a few pages I used "Cottage." I gave it the name Larkspur Cottage, but for reasons I can't remember, I rejected that flower and finally came up with Heliotrope Cottage, an awkward sounding name, but it was the name the previous owners had bestowed on it so it couldn't be blamed on the central character. Every year the original owners planted a garden with heliotrope, and the central character continued that tradition. Because I had never seen a heliotrope, when we returned home, I bought one. Its vivid lilac flowers are blooming now.

I called the main character Miriam. "Call me Ishmael," is the famous first sentence of a fabulous novel. The name Miriam charms me, even though I have no relatives or close friends with it. A few years ago, I wrote a novella about another Miriam. Miriam's Heliotrope Cottage owes a little something to Shirley Craft's house that contained the daycare where our granddaughter was wonderfully happy. The heliotrope garden owes something to the garden of our friends Helen and Peter Thomas in the same neighbourhood because, of course, Shirley's backyard was full of sandboxes and swings.

I have heard writers talk about the agony of working on a novel. That perplexes me because, for me, there is nothing as pleasurable as being completely immersed in my fictional world. Any form of concentration is pleasurable, whether it is being absorbed in a good book or watching a particularly good ballgame or playing Shanghai Rummy. Your cares disappear for a blessed hour or two.

Perhaps I cheat a little by not writing about the most horrible things in life. One book I took on vacation was Laurie King's *Keeping Watch*. I enjoyed her other books, so when I saw this one in Owl's Nest, I bought it. The prologue was set in a tree where a Vietnam veteran had set up paraphernalia for spying on a child molester. The mystery, I gathered, was about catching pedophiles. I could not read past the prologue. King's forte is using specific, graphic details. I marvel how she could write such a novel because she would have had to imagine horrible acts.

One reviewer wrote, "Some stories scour the soul. This one is full of things that hurt: scary, horrible, humiliating things."

Perhaps I don't agonize because I don't have to put bread on the table with the proceeds of a novel.

I have taught many creative writing courses and been in many writers' groups, and in nearly all of them there will be at least one good writer who eventually produces a good novel. I can think of at least 20 of these unpublished good novels. Often the writers will produce only that one novel. Perhaps they get discouraged because it doesn't get published. Or they go on to other pursuits, making pottery or jogging. Or life intervenes. But I wonder why the sheer pleasure of the endeavour doesn't keep them going.

In a review of the reconstituted James Agee novel, *A Death in the Family*, Will Blythe writes: "In the end, all that a writer has to pass on is not myth and anecdote, but scene and character, evoked in memorable prose...readers may feel they are seeing into the very heart of existence—the utter strangeness of being alive in a particular family at a particular time and place." That's a goal worth shooting at.

Salon, July 19, 2008

Alden Nowlan, the great energizer

I've been remembering Alden Nowlan and thinking about the impact he made on the New Brunswick arts community. Stephen Scott has been commissioned to paint a posthumous portrait of Nowlan and wants to get to know him. He came to talk to Bill and me about Alden, and we spent a lovely couple of hours out on the back porch reminiscing. Scott wants to capture the essence of the man, not just a photographic representation. If any artist can do that, he is the one.

When Greg Cook's biography of Nowlan, *One Heart, One Way*, came out in 2005, Bill read it first, commented on how good it was and loaned it to several people. I didn't read it then, meaning to pick it up later. After talking to Stephen, I got it out. It's good, a very personal biography. It should have been given awards. Cook gives us a vivid picture of Alden's childhood. He conjures up the winter the teenager spent in his cold bedroom, hardly leaving it, a black coat covering his window, sleeping during the day, reading by the light of a kerosene lantern at night, eating very little. Cook skillfully integrates Nowlan's poetry with his history.

I think my affection for Alden grew because he reminded me so much of my father, who had also grown up poor without a mother, a big man who also was underfed. Like Alden, my father was self-taught, reading voraciously. They both drank too much and who could blame them, knowing their childhoods. Alden venerated the love he found in his wife Claudine and son Johnnie, as my father did for the love he found in his wife, Grace and his two children. (Grace, incidentally, was also the name of Alden's mother.) My father said to me, "I have loved extravagantly." From Cook's biography, I understand how extravagantly Alden loved.

Bill and I visited him often, but we were not a part of his inner circle. We had children who were being babysat, and I wake up at 6 a.m. no matter what time I go to bed, so we were never there late at night when all the hijinks were hatched, The Flat Earth Society, for example. We called him Alden, but those of the inner circle called him Al. I did notice, however, that Alden himself called others by their full name, Gregory, not Greg. I think, however, that he liked Bill and me. He asked me to look at a manuscript of his stories (how presumptuous of me to have agreed!) and invited us with Gerry and Leta Clayden to the first dinner party he gave by himself once when Claudine was away. Robert, not Bob, Gibbs also called him Alden and wasn't a part of that inner circle either, but Alden chose him to be his literary executor, one of many examples of his wisdom.

Because Alden was wise, no doubt about it. I think he was the only real genius I've ever known. He had, again like my father, a stunning memory. Because he was self-taught, he hadn't been brainwashed as those of us who went to university were, and so what he said was often utterly original. The University of New Brunswick, the provincial government, the Canada Council, and the Guggenheim Foundation never got more for their money than they did with their grants to Alden.

Stephen Scott talked to us about his own need to reevaluate himself, to find a new supply of energy. He is hoping that communing with Alden will provide that. Wouldn't it be great if 25 years after his death, Alden could still supply creative energy to a young artist? He did that for all of us, and in particular to his young acolytes, Brian Bartlett, Ray Fraser, Al Pittman, Jim Stewart, among many others. There are writers who can supply their own energy, but you only have to read literary history to see that a group of writers energize each other. Often there is one in the group who invigorates the most. Alden was an admirer of Samuel Johnson; the Nowlan cat was named Hodge after Johnson's cat. I imagined Samuel while Alden was sitting in his big chair, cigarette in hand, surrounded by books, talking, leading the conversation. Supplying energy. No wonder he ran out of it. It's also easy to imagine Cook as Alden's Boswell.

I learned that Alden's people came from New Ross. Many years ago, Michael Bradley wrote the fanciful *Holy Grail Across the Atlantic*, piggybacking on the infamous *Holy Blood, Holy Grail* (forerunner of *The Da Vinci Code*), theorizing that Jesus Christ's descendants had come to Nova Scotia, settling in New Ross. If I imagine Alden as Samuel Johnson, I can also imagine him as the descendant of Christ.

Salon, August 2, 2008

The manuscripts in my attic

For my birthday I received *The War of Art* by the novelist Steven Pressfield and *The Creative Habit* by the choreographer Twyla Tharp, both full of advice for creative people. I gave advice in writers' workshops for more than 30 years; I often wonder if I did more harm than good.

I came on the scene before these workshops were popular so I never attended one as a student. A young friend who had gone to many workshops, a workshop junkie she called herself, asked me to teach one with her. I have since taught many, from weekend courses for people who hadn't written anything to a graduate seminar in fiction. I started when I hadn't published even one story. That sounds presumptuous in the extreme, and it was, but I think I did my best teaching early on because I was so enthusiastic and optimistic.

At that time, I read to see how certain admired writers get their effects. I read how-to books; I collected interviews with writers. I devoured with great enthusiasm Sherrill Grace's study of Malcolm Lowry; instead of cutting things out as most how-to books suggested, Lowry added telling details, making his sentences thick and meaty.

My student Madeline Hare invited me to her house to show me the writing space she had made for herself under the stairs. On a shelf above her table were books I had mentioned in class; she had bought them all. The writing space and the books made me hopeful that I had contributed pleasure to her life. I was immensely touched.

Wayne Johnston was in my husband's graduate creative writing class. Johnston's MA thesis became part of his highly acclaimed *The Story of Bobby O'Malley*. "What could I teach this guy? He just needs time to write," Bill said. A workshop in any art or craft has this as its biggest selling point: you get time plus incentive to create. You perhaps do get a shorthand course in some technical aspects, but these are things you could probably learn by yourself. You get a knowledgeable critic in the teacher, but I learned from poet Robert Gibbs that praise is the best criticism because it is important to learn what you do best. For many years I was in a writers' group with Gibbs. His ability to point out the good parts of any poem was remarkable.

How many times have I read or heard a successful writer give this advice to novices: Just write. So simple. Pressfield says, "There's a secret that real writers know that wannabe writers don't, and the secret is this: It's not the writing part that's hard. What's hard is sitting down to write. What keeps us from sitting down is Resistance." The book is about overcoming Resistance. With a capital R.

But I believe a more fundamental reason "wannabe writers" don't write is that at the end of all that self-discipline, you don't really have anything tangible. A manuscript is not the same thing as a sweater or a quilt and not the same thing as a book. Reading a manuscript is hard work, nothing like the pleasure in reading a book. I now refuse to read manuscripts because I no longer have the immense energy that it requires.

The discipline needed to overcome your Resistance to writing is not like the discipline needed to go for a walk in order to improve your health. Walking is pure self-interest, and writing can't be just for yourself; you have to anticipate the pleasure of a possible reader. The pleasure I get from the e-mails I receive from readers of this column is colossal. When I say one e-mail makes my day, I really mean it. A while ago a friend I hadn't seen for 40 years wrote to say she had re-read all my novels. Wow!

What does keep us all creating is difficult to put into words that don't sound foolish or spooky. Ralph Waldo Emerson wrote, "We but half express ourselves, and are ashamed of that divine idea which each of us represents." I have to believe that my 10 unpublished novels somehow express the divine idea that is Nancy Luke Bauer, just as valuable as the socks I once knit that unraveled on the first washing.

A Great Cloud of Witnessing

Biologist Rupert Sheldrake's theory of morphic resonance is: "Each individual both draws upon and contributes to the collective memory of the species. This means that new patterns of behaviour can spread more rapidly than would otherwise be possible. For example, if rats of a particular breed learn a new trick in Harvard, then rats of that breed should be able to learn the same trick faster all over the world…" The manuscripts in our attics, Sheldrake says, do contribute to the collective memory of our species.

Salon, October 4, 2008

Extracting emotions from rocks

Don McKay recently gave a spell-binding lecture at UNB, titled "Ediacaran and Anthropocene: Poetry as a Reader of Deep Time." The former UNB professor and distinguished poet (he has won two Governor General's Awards) served up an adroit mixture of the erudite, the entertaining and the thought-provoking.

He explained that geologists have declared a new period in the Proterozoic era, the first new one so declared in 120 years: the Ediacaran Period. The name comes from the Ediacara Hills of Australia where a previously unknown class of fossils was discovered. McKay, relocated to Newfoundland, learned that these Ediacaran fossils are also present in the Mistaken Point barrens of the Avalon Peninsula. He described the flora in that place, where, on his knees, he saw the fossils.

Harry Hess, the geologist who formulated the plate tectonic theory, coined the phrase "geo-poetics" to convey his feeling of astonishment at his own theory. That phrase and that astonishment has become a bridge for McKay to cross over the gulf between science and poetry.

When McKay was on his knees in the barrens, he could stop and have, for a few seconds, a moment of astonishment. In fact, "wonder" and "astonish" were words repeated often in the lecture. The contemplation of these fossils and of the time periods in geologic ages yielded for McKay "the wonderful possibilities of being."

His own recent work has included poems about rocks: basalt, limestone, gneiss. I confess my lack of insight: when I read some of them in *The Fiddlehead*, I was unmoved. I bought his book *Strike/Slip* and, armed with the information of the lecture, I have been studying the rock poems with appreciation.

A Great Cloud of Witnessing

I realize that because of my couch potato tendencies, my being caught up in the world of books and art, I don't often have moments of astonishment in nature. My street was built on a tamarack bog, and I know there are fossils in the wilderness that is our backyard because my son found one. I could go out there, and, on my knees, look for one. Still, I am more likely to have moments of astonishment contemplating humankind.

But how great to be McKay on his knees in a remote barren in a remote province, observing something wondrous and then writing a poem. Why is it that human beings can't sustain this wonder for more than a second? Perhaps, he mused, because, in evolutionary terms, if a man were on his knees being astonished by a fossil, a tiger could sneak up on him.

From the Ediacaran Period of 542 million years ago, McKay jumped forward to the Anthropocene Epoch, postulated by geologists but not yet officially recognized. This epoch began at the turn of the 18th century with the industrial revolution and so is named after human beings. To paraphrase Pogo: "We have met the fossils and they are us." Thinking of ourselves as the central species in an epoch allows us to imagine ourselves in deep time, backward to the era when we emerged as a species, forward to the industrial revolution, and into the future when all that will remain of our species are our fossils. This imagining gives us the gift of "defamiliarization," being able to catch a glimpse of ourselves without the film of the familiar.

Most of us appreciate poems involving wildflowers and birds, McKay's previous subjects. But it is a tour de force to extract emotion from rocks. As I was re-reading these poems, I was surprised that I hadn't responded to them originally. My grandfather was a paving stone cutter. Most of the men in my village worked in the granite quarry; some came from Sweden and Italy to do so. The cellar of our home was made of granite blocks. McKay, the environmentalist supreme, perhaps wouldn't like the holes left in the landscape by the quarrying, but he would appreciate the cellar blocks. I have five rocks in my bureau, one from the moor of Wuthering Heights that a friend brought me.

When my children go through this drawer, they will puzzle over the rocks. By then I will be in deep time, being astonished, I hope.

McKay picks up a quartz crystal from his desk and ponders it: "The crystal floats like a lotus on my palm, bending the light from a dying star to dance upon my coffee cup this fine bright Cenozoic morning." Isn't that an incredible image?

Unlike the wildflowers and birds used as metaphors of transience, rocks speak to us of longevity. In "Petrified" McKay melds transient humans with the enduring rocks: "You are the crystal that picks up / its many deaths. / You are the momentary mind of rock."

As Simon Schama has written, "One of our most powerful yearnings: the craving to find in nature a consolation for our mortality."

Salon, December 6, 2008

A personal rapport with an artist one hasn't met

For the last few months, I've been involved in an energizing art experience — working with the poet Nela Rio. We are preparing the Writing on the Wall exhibition to be opened in April at the Beaverbrook Art Gallery. In past years for this project poets visited the gallery and selected a work which they hoped would inspire a poem. The work and the poem were then exhibited.

In October, at a workshop on writing about art, Nela read a poem, in Spanish, about the iconic Beaverbrook Art Gallery painting *Santiago El Grande.* Before she read her poem, she explained how much the painting meant to her. I thought: the perfect person for Writing on the Wall. In previous years, the chosen poet had selected a work of art at random, with no deep relationship with the artist. This year would be quite different.

Nela and I have spent two mornings and two afternoons discussing her affinity for Salvador Dali. I quote myself in an email to Beaverbrook Art Gallery curator Terry Graff. "I have just come back from a most fascinating afternoon with Nela. I just wish you could have been there. I know you are going to be excited about what she knows and feels about Dali."

Nela is originally from Argentina, from a Spanish-speaking family of Italian descent. She retired a few years ago from teaching Latin American literature at St. Thomas University. Her poetry has been translated into several languages, has been published widely and has been the subject of an academic symposium. Nela is also a visual artist, short story writer, and international activist for women's rights.

She has had a personal rapport with the artist for a long time. Working with her has not only been an art history lesson, even more it has been a lesson in how to bond with an artist although you have never met him. This bonding is demonstrated in many ways. For example, without knowing Nela's feeling for Dali, a scholar compared her work to his. She discovered that her favourite poet, Federico Lorca, was also Dali's favourite—her son is named after Lorca. Another scholar compared her poetry to Lorca's.

Santiago El Grande is filled with light and triumph. The dominant feature is the horse, dramatically rearing up, ridden by Santiago—Saint James—the patron saint of Spain. Nela learned that Dali had been inspired by Jose Gambino's sculpture in the Catedral de Santiago de Compostela. On a trip to Spain, she searched for the sculpture, wandering the huge church, disappointed when she couldn't find it. Finally, she sat on a bench to rest, and there, hidden behind a wrought iron grill, she saw the work.

The violence of it shocked her. Santiago was indeed riding a horse in the same rampant attitude as that of the horse in our Dali, but he was slaying Moors; their bloody and headless bodies were strewn around the horse's hooves. This work depicted Santiago Matamoros—Saint James the Moor Slayer. Nela speculated on how Dali could have reconciled the two visions, and how she herself could. In the second poem of her triptych on Dali she wrestles with that problem.

When Nela moved to Fredericton, *Santiago El Grande* seemed to welcome her to this outpost. She visited it often and knows every part of it well. I'd never paid much attention to the mysterious woman in the lower corner until Nela singled her out: "And at the foot of this resplendent awe of the knight inflamed / The silent image of the woman in white captures us, / Her head turned, her face partially veiled, / A singular, questioning gaze toward us" (translated by Elizabeth Miller). Gala, the woman in white, is the wife of Dali, an image he used in other paintings.

Santiago El Grande is a product of Dali's mysticism period, Nela says. I hadn't noticed the tiny people at the bottom of the painting. She says that they are "witnessing." She pointed out Dali's characteristic sky, also in other Dalis in the Beaverbrook Art Gallery collection. The scallop-shaped structure in the background was inspired by architectural features of a cathedral in Toulouse.

A Great Cloud of Witnessing

She brought me a reproduction of a Dali she particularly reveres, *Muchacha en la ventana*, depicting a woman looking out a window. A few years ago, she wrote a poem imagining herself as that woman.

We are renovating our bathroom, and my daughter-in-law suggested we paint the walls brown. This seemed unorthodox, but when I saw the brownish-grey walls in the Dali painting, I thought, aha, that indeed is the colour.

A further coincidence — my aunt sent me towels for the bathroom and the curtains for the ventana are the same teal colour. The colour scheme for the bathroom will be courtesy of Salvador Dali via Nela Rio. From the sublime to the mundane.

Salon, February 14, 2009

A brain conducive to creativity

For International Women's Day I spoke to the Unitarian Fellowship on the topic of "women getting older, and what that means to their creativity." The invitation to speak was prompted by a column I had written on late bloomers.

My talk was divided in three parts: the first on some new research into the brains of older people that suggests to me that older women are well-positioned to exercise their creative powers. The second part was about the way the trajectory of an older woman's life also aids these powers. The third part was derived from my column on late bloomers.

In the 1970s it was politically incorrect to say that women and men are different: "our biology is not our destiny." Perhaps it was necessary to make this absurd point in order for the equality of men and women to become a reality. But now that it has happened, researchers are encouraged to study the differences between the sexes.

I mentioned here before that one of the most illuminating books I have read in years is Louann Brizendine's *The Female Brain*. From the time a female is born, chemicals are coursing through her to prepare her to have babies. These chemicals have to affect her creative powers. Merely holding her baby releases the hormone oxytocin. This hormone is even released when an adoptive mother holds her adopted baby. Oxytocin is incredibly powerful, but it begins to disappear when women grow old, allowing them to retreat into themselves. Other disappearing hormones also weaken women's drive to look after everyone.

The research of Professor Francisco Ayala and others has shown that men and women think differently when viewing art. Men use only the right half of their brains, their right parietal lobe, when they are appreciating art, whereas women use both right and left sides of their brains. The connection between the two hemispheres of the brain is better developed in females. Professor Ayala suggests that women contextualize the information and think more about the details of what they are seeing, assessing the position of objects according to broad categories, such as above or below or left or right. Women tend to be more aware than men of objects around them, including those that seem irrelevant to the current task. Perhaps the brains developed differently because women were gatherers, needing to see small things like berries and roots, whereas men were hunters, needing to map large areas.

The process of the contextualization of details is of great interest to me. Older people have the awkward problem of forgetting names. Recent research at MIT has uncovered a surprising fact: old people's memories function better in some ways than young people's memories do. The researchers report that "children rival adults in forming basic memories, but adults do better at remembering the rich, contextual details of that information." Adults have a more developed prefrontal cortex, an area of the brain long associated with higher-order thinking, planning and reasoning. The prefrontal cortex is responsible for creating memories that are richer in details.

Other research shows that the reason for old people's having trouble remembering a name is not that their brain is declining, but that their brain is "taking in more data and trying to sift through a clutter of information, often to its long-term benefit." Older people take in more information from a situation, and then combine it with their greater store of knowledge and experience. This clutter prevents your coming up with the name of the smiling woman you meet in Sobeys.

Writing fiction and creating visual art both involve putting details in context. So here we have studies showing that women are better at putting details in context, and other studies showing that older people are better at it.

I suggest that not only the biology of an older woman but the trajectory of her life is conducive to creativity. In my time, even if a woman worked outside the home, she did the housework. As a consequence, a woman never retires. At first this struck me as unfair, but now I see that it is a boon not to have to retire. As well, from the time my children went to school, I have written for several hours a day. I have never had to retire from that practice either. Retiring is not part of the trajectory of my life.

George Eliot published *Middlemarch* when she was 53 and *Daniel Deronda* when she was 57, both works of astonishing complexity. Neither book could have been written by a young woman. Harriet Doerr published her first novel, *Stones for Ibarra*, when she was 73. Reviewers praised the book for her use of evocative detail.

Near the end of her life an old woman is searching for answers, not for fame or power or money.

Salon, March 21, 2009

Portraits that capture the essence of a persona

A spontaneous collective "oooh" went up from the large crowd when the portrait of Alden Nowlan was unveiled at UNB's Harriet Irving Library. I've never heard anything like it, the gut reaction to a splendid work of art. If you would like to, you could visit the library foyer and have a cup of Starbucks coffee while you sit and contemplate it. The painting is full of life, almost as if Alden were smiling down at us, albeit a little ironically. Stephen Scott was an inspired choice for the commission made possible by the endowment of the late professor Alvin Shaw.

Scott had never met Alden, but he read his work and the two biographies. He talked to Alden's wife Claudine and to Alden's friends, including my husband Bill and me. He viewed photographs. But this still doesn't explain how he could get the essence of Alden's persona into the painting, that "sense of felt life," to use Henry James' phrase. Magic? When I talked to Stephen afterward, I could tell that he had become friends with Alden in the way you can with a dead writer. The essence of the man is in his poetry and his autobiographical novels so Scott could commune with him. In much of Alden's work, as in that of other excellent writers, there is the same "sense of felt life." It's entirely fitting that Alden's portrait exhibits this.

Leopold Kowolik and Inge Pataki of Gallery 78, the gallery that represents Scott, were at the ceremony. After the unveiling I asked Leopold, whose opinion I value highly, what he thought of the portrait as a painting because he hadn't known Alden. "Magnificent" was the word he used. "It's magnificent. The way he has put it together is magnificent." Later he said that the frame of the painting "had been shifted," as if the artist and the subject were in the same room together. This gives the portrait "a real presence," he said. I didn't know exactly what he meant, but as I look more at the portrait, I am beginning to see.

Claudine was sitting in front of me, and when the ceremony was over, I asked how she liked it. "Very much," she said in her characteristically understated way. But when I was talking to her later, she said, "When they unveiled it, my heart went and I couldn't breathe for a second."

Alden's literary executor and close friend Bob Gibbs asked me how I liked it. "Yes," he said. "Yes. It is so good. It has such life to it." Later he said that one of the reasons he likes it so much is that it hadn't idealized Alden. Alden is sitting in a posture typical of the man. "And the palette has a lovely harmony of muted colours."

The portrait hangs alongside one of Bliss Carman. The library has portraits of two other poets, Alfred Bailey and G.D. Roberts, but these need restoration before they can be hung.

Bruno Bobak painted a posthumous portrait of Katherine McLaggan that once hung in the lobby of McLaggan Hall. I have looked for it, but it is gone. I wonder where it is now. It's also brimming with a sense of felt life. I never knew Dr. McLaggan, but the portrait expresses strength and determination.

Bobak also painted a joint portrait of members of the UNB English Department, *Kent's Punch*. It includes Nowlan, Gibbs, Bauer and four others. Bill is painted in profile. When I first saw it, I thought, Bill's lower lip doesn't stick out like that. And then I turned and looked at him, and lo and behold it did. Later I noticed that his aunt's lip did too, a family trait I suppose.

John Updike wrote about a portrait, "the mouth is the key to likeness." In Scott's portrait, Alden's mouth has an ironic, maybe even sardonic smile. Alden did not suffer fools gladly. Some poor devils went home from Windsor Castle stinging from Alden's keen observations. But you have only to read the poems to know how empathetic he was with suffering humanity. That was the smile that Scott has captured—what fools these mortals be, but also how endearing these mortals be. The eyes and the forehead in the painting have a hint of sadness, or is it pain? As Bill observed, individual people were always the subjects of Alden's poems, unusual for a poet.

The success of a portrait as a work of art is not just in the likeness captured. I have gone over to the library again to study it, took a photo to put on my computer desktop. But the photo doesn't reproduce the amusing brush strokes of the shoe. Or the way the brush strokes on the wrinkles of the jacket arms give life to the whole body.

Salon, April 4, 2009

Support for a land of scribblers

In the newsletter of the Writers' Federation of New Brunswick, Marilyn Lerch challenged writers in our province to create a stronger community. She hopes to spur action on this creation at the AGM taking place in Saint John May 8 to 10. President Lerch writes: "…we must find ways that will lead to a fairer distribution of knowledge, expertise, resources, commitment and good will among our members. We must bend our efforts to building a community of writers."

Lerch wants to "erase those insidious lines separating the professional from the emerging." She exactly articulates our hope for the federation when a group of us founded it. In some provincial federations you could only be a full member if you had been published. We thought it better that anyone who writes be eligible to join.

Lerch suggests that the WFNB establish "branches" around the province. Unofficially that has already been done with little bands meeting to discuss their work and to hold literary events. A Miramichi group, Words on Water, under the leadership of Judy Bowman, sponsors readings; it recently invited Wayne Curtis to read at Saltwater Sounds.

The WFNB has always been province-wide, the leadership sometimes based in the Fredericton area or the Saint John area or the Edmundston area, and now in the Moncton area.

In Kent County, Grace Morris and Roy Gould of Ford's Mill wanted to help save poet Al Purdy's Ontario house. Four WFNB members, Ed Lemond, Kim Gautreau, Lee Thompson and Marilyn Lerch, read at the fundraising event: a dinner, additional readings by six local writers and an open set. Seventy people showed up at Greenwood Lodge; the readings went on until midnight.

A Great Cloud of Witnessing

In Fredericton alone I know of six sets of writers who meet to read their work to each other; there must be others. I have belonged to many such groups over a period of 40 years, and so I know how valuable they are for some, but not all, writers. In these I gained a sense of audience. I remember poet Robert Gibbs acquiring his prose voice before my very ears while he mesmerized us with his wonderful stories. A group can help writers become disciplined or cure isolation misery. With a caveat or two, I have been vastly entertained by these gatherings.

In her president's message, Lerch urged university professors to join the WFNB. In the beginning many professors were supportive: Allan Donaldson at UNB Fredericton, Michael Thorpe at Mount Allison, William Prouty at UNBSJ, to name only three of many. In New Brunswick, university professors hold power and influence. When I first came here, I was amazed to learn how much—I had only to say my husband was a professor and a merchant would cash the cheque of this stranger. That power is perhaps not as strong as it once was, but it still counts heavily.

Our support from the provincial government has always been limited. The historical reason for this is that we didn't catch the great tide of the late '60s and early '70s when it was *de rigueur* for governments to support the arts. We were the last province to form a writers' federation. If we could get every writer in New Brunswick to join (at $40 a year), we would have a powerful political voice, for we are a land of scribblers, no doubt about that. In my opinion, what the organization needs is enough money to pay the part-time executive director for just a few more hours.

It can't be run totally on volunteer effort although, of course, it mainly is. Hundreds of hockey coaches, managers, board members, schedulers, snack providers and lacers of skates run the provincial hockey leagues. But, if I interpret their website correctly, Hockey New Brunswick has five paid staff people who make sure things stay organized. The Saskatchewan Writers' Guild also has five paid staff members. The Writers' Federation of Nova Scotia has three paid staff. The WFNB pays one person for 12 hours a week (although they have always worked more for free).

A lovely WFNB community project has come to fruition. Members offered to teach people to read, and they wrote about their experiences. The result is a book, *Paths to Literacy*, soon to be published by Goose Lane Editions. Another project is just getting started, a three-year plan of outreach to rural members.

Two years ago, I was worried that the WFNB was on life support and would soon be just a memory. Now I sense that life is coming back into the organization, led by the enthusiasm of Lerch. The equally enthusiastic Gwen Martin is now its fundraising consultant. Lee Thompson, the new executive director, brings the gusto of youth. To celebrate this new life, the name of the AGM has been changed to WordSpring.

Salon, April 18, 2009

Renewed life for two arts groups

Two of my favourite arts organizations, both once hovering on the edge of the abyss, stepped back instead and are now roaring along new roads. Whew! These two are favourites not only because I was present at their births but because I believe that both contribute hugely to the arts community.

The original home of Gallery Connexion was the basement of the Justice Building in Fredericton. When the basement flooded and was then condemned in 2008, the gallery's part-time director, Meredith Snider, and its president, Carol Collicutt, paddled furiously to keep Connexion afloat. Its board of directors also worked hard, meeting nearly every week. Tim Yerxa at the Playhouse gave the gallery an office.

And then an angel flew in, Brian Johnson of Kingswood Park — the award-winning golf course and family entertainment centre. Johnson offered the basement of the Chestnut Complex to Connexion at an affordable rent and worked with them to renovate the space. It will open sometime in November, but Snider gave me a preview tour. The public can also get a preview when the Salmon Run Auction is held there Oct. 24.

Because the gallery is in the basement, it still has the funky ambiance I have loved from the beginning. I like too the serendipity that Connexion, with its artists and craftspeople, is in the building that once sheltered the Chestnut Canoe factory. *Salon* contributor John Leroux offered to provide the floor plan. Bosatra and Comando of Yuge Designs are creating the interior setting.

The main space, The Rick Burns Gallery, is 1,100 square feet and retains its original stone wall. A smaller space is named 1922 Gallery because this date of the building's construction is chiselled into a wall. New to Connexion will be a café run by Kingswood. It will have a small stage for performance art, music, poetry readings, you name it.

To be viable financially, Connexion has to have artist studios; the rent of these seven spaces will help pay the gallery rent. But even more important, to be viable creatively the gallery has to have artists on-site to provide mutual inspiration. The publishing house Goose Lane Editions has its offices in the building next door, and Snider hopes this will contribute to the artistic buzz.

The second organization roaring off on a new road is the Writers' Federation of New Brunswick. Thanks to president Marilyn Lerch, the board of directors and part-time director Lee Thompson, new life has been injected into it. I marvel at the time, energy and creative imagination this has obviously taken.

If you are depressed by reading gloomy news and gloomy fiction, get *Breaking the Word Barrier: Stories of Adults Learning to Read*, compiled and edited by Marilyn Lerch and Angela Ranson and published by Goose Lane Editions in conjunction with WFNB and Laubach Literacy. Seventeen members of WFNB were paired with men and women who had learned to read only when they were adults. The writers tell the moving accounts of these students. One learner says, "It was like sitting at a card table and always being dealt bad hands. It was very frustrating." All 17 had been dealt bad hands in life, but with the help of tutors, they persevered and triumphed. These are stories of true grit.

The book includes an excellent essay by Herménégilde Chiasson on the magic of reading. "Reading is a form of affection. It is an intimate moment of sharing information, a way of bonding around a story, a way of participating in the marvels of the imagination." In early October WFNB held a successful fall fair in Florenceville. I have received glowing accounts of it from several friends. "Ann Brennan and her daughter Rayanne did a terrific job of making it a great day, complete with a bean supper and three kinds of pie for dessert." Ann was on the founding committee of the federation.

And, "It seems to me that there is a feeling of energy and momentum in the writing community at this point in time. There were quite a

A Great Cloud of Witnessing

few new faces for the workshop, and even more came in the evening for the kitchen party." One friend said, "it takes a lot to make my wife comfortable, but she was." To connect with writers all over the province, the fall and spring annual meetings have recently been held in various venues.

Writers serve the arts community but not in as visible ways as actors, dancers and painters do. They contribute to local newspapers, give readings in schools, teach, compile the history of individual communities, and most important, keep alive the option that any New Brunswicker can be a writer.

I wish an angel would fly in for WFNB because it desperately needs a full-time director and an office space.

Connexion and WFNB: also stories of true grit.

Salon, October 17, 2009

Power in one's talent being recognized

On successive days I attended two celebrations honouring excellence in the arts. The first was a gathering in Will and Debbie Van Den Hoonaard's lovely home overlooking the Saint John River Valley, the second such party they have given for Jo-Anne Elder. The hosts were gracious, the goodies interesting — a bowl of pomegranate seeds for instance.

Jo-Anne, for the third time, has been nominated for a Governor General's Award in English translation. She is a whirlwind: translating, teaching, volunteering, writing fiction, editing a magazine, organizing festivals and travelling to conferences. Sounds like a full life, doesn't it? And all this is in addition to being a devoted mother to seven children.

Her third nomination for the GG suggests to me that she is one of the best translators of Acadian poetry in the country. I've worked with her on several projects requiring translation. She does the job impeccably, sensitively and on time, even ahead of time, one of those people you can rely on completely.

She received this nomination for her translation of *Seul on est*, the winner of last year's GG for French poetry. Her nomination reads, "In *One*, Jo-Anne Elder's bold, yet delicate translation provides English-language readers with thrilling access to the poetic world of Serge Patrice Thibodeau — in which the majesty and intimacy of the natural world are mirrored in a human experience that sees itself, both agonizingly and ecstatically, at one with nature."

The second celebration of excellence in the arts was at the Lieutenant-Governor's mansion, with its view of the river from the other side. The affair was elegant, also with interesting goodies — cream puffs stuffed with pumpkin and sweet potato among others. I heard, for the first time, the new Lieutenant-Governor speak; Graydon Nicholas is a most charming, self-deprecating man.

A Great Cloud of Witnessing

The occasion was the presentation of the annual Lieutenant-Governor's Awards for High Achievement in the Arts. These have been renamed from the Excellence Awards; for example, the Miller Brittain Award for Excellence in the Visual Arts is now the Lieutenant Governor's Award for High Achievement in the Visual Arts. I assume that the change was made to correspond to the Governor General's Awards.

Because three of the four recipients were Acadian, the proceedings were mostly in French, and I once again sat there like a dummy, wishing I were bilingual, hearing people laugh and not knowing what they were laughing about, catching such words as *donc, ce soir, parce que, aujourd'hui, je pense* and thinking to myself, why can't I catch the important words?

Ray Fraser received the Lieutenant-Governor's Award for High Achievement in English Literary Arts. He was nominated by a writers' group in Miramichi led by Cynthia Losier. Alden Nowlan is quoted in the award booklet, "(Fraser) is one of the most gifted writers I know, and among his gifts are two that are all too rare: a zest for life and a sense of humour." Ray is on a roll because five of his books are included in the recent release from Nimbus Press, *Atlantic Canada's 100 Greatest Books*.

Marcel-Romain Thériault received the award for theatre. At last summer's play festival, I saw his terrific play, *On and Off the Shelf*, translated by Jo-Anne Elder. Rino Morin Rossignol received the French literary arts award. He is the consummate jack-of-all-trades: poet, essayist, journalist, playwright, translator, novelist.

Roméo Savoie received the visual arts award, the second time he has received it. I hadn't realized that you could receive the award twice. He is obviously well-beloved in the Acadian community.

I was pleasantly surprised to learn that the award stipend has risen to $20,000. When I received it 10 years ago, it was $5,000. Twenty-thousand would be a significant percentage of the income of most full-time artists and would allow them to work many months worry-free. From now on, only three awards will be given annually: for visual arts, performing arts and literary arts, the latter alternating between English and French.

The occasion brought old acquaintances to mind: Toby Graser, Kathy Hooper, M. Travis Lane, Stephen May, Nancy Schofield, Greg Cook, Luc Charette, among others. Luc told me he has been appointed the executive director of ArtsNB. For 22 years he was the director of the Galerie d'art Louise-et-Reuben-Cohen at the Université de Moncton. He decided it was time to try something new.

Karen Ruet's dramatic photographs of Fraser, Savoie and Thériault grace the handsome awards booklet, designed by Julie Scriver.

The artists I know make art because not doing so is discombobulating — the brain rebels. All the same, to have a jury of their peers say about their work "this is good" is like eating a gourmet meal, not as life-sustaining as a boiled egg every morning, but a powerful stimulus nonetheless.

Salon, November 21, 2009

Reflecting on endings and beginnings

Karen Ruet had a lovely column in the *Daily Gleaner* about Ralph Kirkbride, who died Dec. 14. Ralph was the quintessential art aficionado, well-known and well-loved by the arts community in Fredericton. He not only supported this arts community by volunteering on many different committees, he truly loved our visual arts and crafts and was a knowledgeable collector. An exhibition of the artwork Kirkbride assembled would be a fitting tribute to him.

I encountered photographer James Wilson at the opening of an exhibition. We had worked together on a bicentennial project back in 1984. He said he reads my column because they are "edgy." I was telling a friend this, that I thought the columns were probably not edgy enough, and the friend said he too thinks they are edgy. I now have a new appreciation of the word.

I've known poets Michael Pacey and Brian Bartlett for 40 years, since they were teenagers and have been a witness to all stages of their creative life. Every once in a while, Michael visits us to read some new poems. Those of the last few years are wonderful: original, witty, full of insight. His lines and images stick in my head when not much else does. He recently came to read us a new series about ordinary household objects. From "Medicine Cabinet":

> Consulted in domestic emergencies,
> like a fuse-box. The Bible.
> Glowing.
> Behind a mirror, hidden
> like a wall-safe; babysitters, party guests
> break in, root among the rolls of gauze,
> ointments, pills
> in search of gossip.

Michael wondered if the dreams I wrote about a month ago were predicting that my world was being downsized to the essentials: "…these (large) houses have dwindled to shabby quarters in rooming houses, with little furniture, only overhead lights, and three-quarter metal beds with thin mattresses."

This reminded him of W.B. Yeats' lines: "Now that my ladder's gone, / I must lie down where all the ladders start / In the foul rag and bone shop of the heart."

My husband's stroke has caused us to contemplate moving from our large bedroom to a smaller one on the first floor.

I just received Brian Bartlett's new book *Being Charlie*. Brian has been a great fan of Charlie Chaplin for many years. Recently he watched all 80 of the Chaplin movies and wrote a series of 106 haiku about them; this chapbook is a selection of 52 of these. They are charming: "On the face of a child / dead three days — a smile / made by the undertaker."

About these poems Brian writes in an afterword, "Although I'd been writing poetry since my teens, I was lukewarm about haiku until I was in my 40s. Thanks in part to Robert Hass' *The Essential Haiku: Versions of Basho, Buson, and Issa*, my eyes and ears finally opened to both the subtlety and the immediate impact of the greatest haiku, to their variety of mood and tone, their wit and emotion."

I described Carolyn Atkinson's summer celebration of Juliana Ewing's birthday. Here is an Atkinson winter haiku: "In the stark window / above the snow-covered porch / red geraniums."

I wrote about the new marketing strategy for classical music — beautiful women on their own websites. During Christmas week PBS broadcast *La Bohème*, starring the No. 1 diva in the world, Anna Netrebko. I went on her website; no surprise, she is a beauty in fabulous gowns.

A Great Cloud of Witnessing

The Impressionist exhibition at the Beaverbrook Art Gallery closes Jan. 4. I want to see it again before it leaves town because I'm afraid I have the wrong image in my head of the Monet.

Beginnings: so much to look forward to in 2010. I hope to read Rex Weyler's *The Jesus Sayings*, lent to me by Stephen May; Anne Michaels' *Fugitive Pieces*, bought in a used bookstore; Mary Catherine Bateson's *Composing a Life*, ditto; Sebastian Barry's *The Secret Scriptures*, a novel lent to me by Robert Gibbs; John Shelby Spong's *Eternal Life: A New Vision*, a hardcover I bought at Westminster Books; and Catherine Gildiner's *Too Close to the Falls*, a memoir lent by Anna Mae Snider.

A child asked me to subscribe to magazines in aid of his school; *Canadian Art* and *Quill and Quire* are both new to me.

Maybe I will finally read *Bleak House* or even the seven novels I haven't read in Hugh Hood's 12-volume New Age series.

The new Gallery Connexion will open.

I might begin a project I have in mind, photos of the self-effacing wildflowers I find in our neighbourhood, a project inspired by the panoramic photos of Scott McFarland. Or perhaps I will complete the two unfinished novels or my memoir. Maybe even write a haiku.

Resolution: Savour the changes taking place in my life.

Salon, January 2, 2010

Framework of hope is built on past successes

Doug Saunders had an encouraging article in the *Globe and Mail* on Dec. 26. The gist of it was that many aspects of the world are better now than they were 10 years ago. So much doom and gloom populate the news that I treasure glimpses of hope; they are precious because they are rare. Much of what Saunders wrote came as a surprise. For example, "The intensely personal, morally demanding Pentecostal faith is by far the fastest-growing religion in the world, now with 640 million followers and double-digit growth rates every year."

Saunders points out the pros of the Pentecostal faith — against drug addiction and prostitution — as well as the cons — against homosexuality and birth control. The migration to cities, improved education, the stemming of AIDS, the ballooning of such technological wonders as computers, Internet, cell-phones, all have changed the world dramatically and mostly for the better.

The article got me thinking about the arts in Fredericton, that so many aspects are better than when I first arrived in 1965.

I think of cooking as an art; when we arrived in Fredericton there were only three restaurants and those undistinguished. Now we have 10 excellent restaurants and at least 10 more that are good. The same is true of Moncton and Saint John. When we arrived, expecting that because we were near the ocean we could buy fresh fish, we were amazed that we couldn't get any. One year a fish shop opened, but by the time I heard about it, it was closed. Now we can get fresh fish whenever we want.

The Craft School huddled in a few poor-looking buildings on Woodstock Road. It gradually grew, took over a heritage building on Queen Street, became a college — The New Brunswick College of Craft and Design — and established a relationship with the University of New Brunswick so that it can now offer a degree.

The crafts world burgeoned, partly due to the school, partly due to immigrants enriching it. Now we are second to none in the quality and variety of our crafts.

The art centre at UNB Fredericton had been established for several years when we arrived, but with the appointment of Bruno Bobak as artist-in-residence, the teaching of his wife Molly Lamb Bobak and the hiring of Marjory Donaldson it became the hub of the visual arts. The Beaverbrook Art Gallery stretched itself, offering exhibitions by provincial artists, becoming a real force in the community. Tom Smart was greatly involved in this connection. Gallery 78 was established, helping artists to make a living. Commercial galleries were also established in Moncton and Saint John — Peter Buckland and Trinity, for example.

The literary world blossomed before my very eyes. The small Fiddlehead Poetry Books became Goose Lane Editions, and now it can boast that it is Canada's oldest independent publisher, a force to be reckoned with in the publishing world. I have three shelves of books by people I know, and they only constitute a small percentage of those published by New Brunswickers. When you add the books written by people who passed through the province, such as Bill Gaston and Wayne Johnston, the number swells.

We can attend an amazing number of concerts. Symphony New Brunswick and the New Brunswick Youth Orchestra appear to be thriving, as well as many different quartets, duos, trios and soloists.

Astoundingly, the government chose one of our most distinguished artists, Herménégilde Chiasson, to be our Lieutenant-Governor. His term must surely have affected all the New Brunswick arts because he is a filmmaker, poet, playwright, painter, winner of national prizes. In addition to being an articulate francophone, he speaks fluent and eloquent English.

We did begin to have an appreciation of our architecture and began to save our heritage buildings. John Leroux's monumental history surely helped fuel this appreciation.

In the mid 1970s the province, under Richard Hatfield, established the Arts Branch and began to fund the cultural scene. In the '80s the New Brunswick Arts Board was formed.

There have been some disappointments. The person who took over *ArtsAtlantic* from Joe Sherman couldn't make a go of it, leaving us without an arts magazine. *The Atlantic Provinces Book Review* disappeared, leaving New Brunswick writers without serious reviews. The Writers' Federation of New Brunswick still is ludicrously, even insultingly, underfinanced — no one's fault but a fact nonetheless. Many of the buildings erected in the last 40 years were ugly, or to be kinder, unremarkable. The Brunswick String Quartet disappeared.

I received a Christmas card with the quotation by computer guru Alan Kay: "The best way to predict the future is to invent it." I gather it is a famous quote, but I don't remember having heard it. I have been pondering it. The blossoming of the arts in New Brunswick didn't just erupt like Athena from the head of Zeus; the flowers were planted by enthusiastic aficionados.

Salon, January 9, 2010

Finding a pattern with soothing words

I discovered long ago that I need to write in order to remain sane. This activity doesn't produce the narcotic effect that reading an engrossing novel does. Instead, writing down words in a sequence provides me with a soothing organization that replaces in my brain what William James called "one great blooming, buzzing confusion." I also discovered when I listen to the radio that words, even the most interesting words, put me to sleep, whereas music keeps me awake.

Rudyard Kipling famously uttered, "Words are, of course, the most powerful drug used by mankind. Not only do words infect, egotize, narcotize and paralyze, but they enter into and colour the minutest cells of the brain…." His novels do have the ability to tranquilize, to let us dive deep into another world and so forget our troubles for the moment.

My husband Bill's younger brother Tommy suffered a birth trauma that left him unable to speak. Bill remembers the pain he and his parents felt waiting for Tommy to say his first word; that he never did was the great tragedy of their lives. When a young relative took a while to talk, Bill worried. When he heard that she had said some words, tears came to his eyes. Miraculously, Tommy, now 72 years old, is being taught sign language, and this newfound ability to use words makes him less frustrated and less aggressive.

The American novelist Reynolds Price writes, "The root of story sprang from need—need for companionship and consolation by a creature as vulnerable, four million years ago and now, as any protozoan in a warm brown swamp. The need is not for the total consolation of narcotic fantasy…but for credible news that our lives proceed in order toward a pattern." I have quoted this in two previous columns.

Near the end of my college years in 1956, in a desperate state I went to the resident psychiatrist. She gave me Miltown, a tranquilizer launched in 1955. Under its influence I wrote an exam which my professor described as gobbledygook. He was clearly alarmed and wouldn't even let me see what I had written because he thought it would distress me. To realize that there was a possibility that I would not be able to write "credible news" scared me so much that I became a teetotaller, no longer taking even an Aspirin.

My friend Bob Gibbs is struggling with the complexities of a new computer. He writes, "I'm still learning and want to try pasting by sending you a poem I wrote in the summer of 2008. Donald [Bob's brother] was having a CAT scan at the DECH, and I was waiting in the lobby, reading John Bayley's memoir *Iris* about Iris Murdoch and watching the people coming and going by the revolving door. The CAT scan was the one by which Don's cancer was detected. All the time I was sitting there I was composing the poem and had it pretty well finished by the time Don was through. It's called "These Our Entrances: These Our Exits." So here goes, if I've set it up right."

>Counterclockwise this door
>turns   It takes in more
>than it lets out…
>
>…Without looking up
>
>I watch the endless round of halt
>and hale   caught together between
>clear blades that snatch at others
>too as they pass down the hall
>to *urgence* or *diagnostic imaging*
>where right now my brother Don
>lies prone   his inside out
>to see if there's a blood-leak anywhere…

Iris and her Friends is Bayley's memoir of his wife, the novelist Iris Murdoch, as her Alzheimer's progressed. I am not surprised that Bob was both reading and composing a poem while he awaited confirmation of what he dreaded. He wasn't reading an Agatha Christie mystery either, no "narcotic fantasy."

Many other writers have used the power of their own language, not to "narcotize" themselves, but to discover a significant design. St. Thomas University philosophy professor Leo Ferrari and his wife, the writer Lorna Drew, used language to chronicle Ferrari's struggle in *Different Minds: Living with Alzheimer Disease*. M.T. Dohaney kept a journal, subsequently published as *When Things Get Back to Normal*, of the first year after her husband died.

Bonnie Massey told me that on January 29 I could see the Wolf Moon, the biggest and brightest of the year, so-called by Algonquin tribes because hungry wolves howled at it. That night was bitterly cold with a howling wind. I've never seen a wolf in the wild, only in a zoo, tamed and forlorn, but the word still resonates. At 6 a.m., I looked out the window and saw the phenomenon, huge and formidable. Massey's words didn't "narcotize" me, but, staring at the moon, and knowing its name, I did experience a frisson of pleasure.

Salon, February 6, 2010

In memory of Helen Weinzweig

When the death of Helen Weinzweig was announced on Feb. 11, I began to reminisce about her association with this province: the Maritime Writers' Workshop, the writer-in-residence program at the University of New Brunswick, the lives Helen touched here.

It must have been professor Kent Thompson who suggested we ask Helen to teach at the workshop in 1981. She came back in 1986 and in 1988-89 was the writer-in-residence at UNB.

For a private tribute to her, I reread her book of stories, *A View from the Roof*. It was published in 1989 by Goose Lane Editions and shortlisted for the Governor-General's Award. I had forgotten that the book has an erudite preface by its editor, my friend John Timmins, with a cover illustration by another friend, Stephen May. It was designed by another friend, Julie Scriver. So many connections.

Her first novel, *Passing Ceremony*, was published in 1973 when Helen was 57. Her second novel, *Basic Black with Pearls*, was also shortlisted for the Governor-General's Award, in 1980. The two novels are short — *Passing Ceremony* is 120 pages and more than half of those are only a paragraph or two long. Helen started writing in 1960 when she was 45. Her literary career spanned only a few years, a book a decade, and contained few words. Yet, her work had a great impact on the Canadian literary community.

Her writing is experimental in the European style. Not surprising, because she spent her first nine years in Poland. Alain Robbe-Grillet, Italo Calvino, Jorge Luis Borges were among her favourite writers. She was married to the composer John Weinzweig, so it is not surprising, too, that *Passing Ceremony* used a musical structure.

In an interview with her in 1981 for *The Fiddlehead*[3], I asked her why she wrote. She answered, "I bore easily. The only thing that

---

3   *The Fiddlehead* No. 132, Spring 1982, pp. 12-17

didn't bore me and never will is language." She discovered that if she stayed inside her head for three days, she would plant an ongoing image that would stay with her for the next four days even with interruptions and responsibilities.

One of the students Helen influenced was a young Sheree Fitch. Sheree writes me, "At a time in my life when I was most fragile, she had me to her home, she fed me, she nurtured me, she took me to plays, museums and galleries, swimming at the University Women's club. She showed me a world that felt a world away from mine. She gave me her time and wisdom and shared her love of literature. She told me I was a 'true' writer when I felt like I would just never 'fit' anywhere. She loved my nonsense! I loved her and cherished her friendship—but I also felt loved by her."

George Fry writes me, "…she was a huge influence on me. I was her student at the writers' week and I got to know her quite well and used to meet up with her in Toronto." Dale Estey, who taught at the MWW with Helen, writes, "I had dinner with her and her husband in Toronto. I have never felt so intellectually intimidated." Robert Gibbs told me that his novel *A Mouth Organ for Angels* was influenced by Helen's novels.

I wonder how many people were influenced by the Maritime Writers' Workshop. Once Joan Fern Shaw and I went out to supper. She told me the story of her sad life, that she was dying of cancer, how much the workshop had meant to her. She came to the workshop maybe four times. She published two well-received books of short stories and won several prizes. Her first book, *Raspberry Vinegar*, owed much to Helen, she said. Four of the seven students in Helen's 1981 workshop went on to publish. Sheree and Joan—but who were the other two?

We started the workshop because we had many local writers who could serve as instructors. To add glamour, every year we invited a "star" from away: William Valgardson from British Columbia, Joan Clark from Newfoundland, John Metcalf and David Helwig.

Ann Copeland came all the way from Sackville. Some came twice. All these writers were wonderfully generous with their time, both during and after the workshops. Cathie Pelletier came from Fort Kent, Maine. She was much influenced by Metcalf and corresponded with him for a long time. She has gone on to publish to much acclaim.

Reminiscing about Helen also got me thinking about the petering out of the workshop in the last few years. But we did have a good run.

Salon, March 20, 2010

Recollections of artists, life lessons

When my friend, the poet Joe Sherman, became the editor of *ArtsAtlantic* in 1979, he had difficulty finding someone to write about New Brunswick artists. He asked me if I would give it a try. Eventually I wrote 22 articles for the magazine.

Because of these, George Fry asked me to write an introduction to his book *The Landscape of Craft*. Neil Reynolds, an aficionado of crafts, read the introduction and asked me to write about them for his editorial creation, *The New Brunswick Reader*. Every week, until my father got sick necessitating trips to Massachusetts, I wrote profiles of craftspeople and visual artists, even supplying the images for the covers: heady stuff.

A while ago I was looking at the list of artists I have written about in these publications and 13 others as well. This set me wondering what they are doing now. Many of them I can keep track of, but some have disappeared from my view. I couldn't remember two of the craftspeople. I remember the studio loft in downtown Saint John of one of them, remember the person, but can't remember what she made. Was it something to do with fabric? I Googled the other one, know his craft, but can't remember him or his workshop. We had a flood in our basement, and although it didn't affect my archives, I decided my files would be safer at the Harriet Irving Library. This was a sensible decision, but I regretted it on this occasion.

I do remember the other 80 or so artists I've written about. I remember their homes or studios, their passion for and their patience with their work.

David Silverberg was the first artist Joe asked me to profile, a wonderful introduction to art journalism. Because the article was to be my first and because I had no qualifications for the job, I spent an immense amount of time on the project, reading about engraving, going to the UNB Arts Centre to see his work and then twice visiting him in his studio at Mount Allison University. He is larger than life—ebullient, ardent, charismatic. Later I revisited him for the *Reader*. When my daughter Grace studied at Mount Allison, she modelled for him. We bought one of the engravings he made from his sketches of her.

David McKay and I shared the third floor of the Baptist Sunday school building, once the York Street School. My office was 40 by 40 feet with 15-feet-high ceilings. I convinced myself that it was the very classroom where Charles G. D. Roberts had taught. David had the former auditorium for his studio—huge, bright, with flowering maples always in bloom. I kept a journal about our interchanges in the hallway and used it as an article for *ArtsAtlantic*, an interesting form, I thought. Eventually the church turfed us out, but we each found a home at Gallery 78 where we were colleagues for another 17 years. I don't think there can be many people in the world who know and love David McKay's work as well as I do.

I used to get around the Atlantic provinces, and one of the most memorable of my visits was to Prince Edward Island to interview Daphne Irving. Joe asked me to write about her because he thought we would be kindred spirits. We were. She had translated several of her religious experiences into paint, and then she conceived the idea that she could use paint to come to a mystical understanding of God.

I was introduced to the Moncton art scene: Guy Duguay, Luc Charette, Danielle Ouellet, Herménégilde Chiasson and the exciting Aberdeen Cultural Centre. Guy died young, about 40. I wish I had known him better because he was such an intriguing person.

The poet Robert Gibbs was a mentor to Joe. When Joe was going to publish a book, he would send the manuscript to Bob and to me. He seldom took my advice, but he always took Bob's. When he asked me to write a profile of Bob, I foolishly said yes. I agonized over the project. Deadlines came and went. Finally, in desperation, I sent in a piece. I received a most judicious note from Joe, saying, in essence, that my piece stunk. His wife Ann thought so too, he said. I was grateful because I knew what it took for him to send me the note. I had known in my heart that it was lousy, and I would have been sorry to have had it published. I scrapped it, went back at the assignment, and the article turned out pretty good. Phew! A stern editor is a great comfort. Memories are a great comfort too.

Salon, April 17, 2010

Making it strange in Odell Park

Some people train so they can climb Mount Everest. I'm going to train so that next July I can go to the theatre and make it all the way through the play.

I was having a fine time at Len Falkenstein's production of *Macbeth* in Fredericton's Odell Park, but at the intermission decided I wasn't in good enough shape to make it through the second half even though my friends Julie Scriver and John Morgan were looking after me. I was afraid that Falkenstein might have to deal with a dead body he wasn't expecting.

The experience was wonderfully weird. If, as the Russian critic and novelist Viktor Shklovsky writes, one of the functions of art is "making it strange," making the familiar unfamiliar, Falkenstein, aided by Shakespeare, succeeded.

When the crowd of us walked by a field, we were startled by a strange sound—a witch rising out of the long grass doing something unearthly with her voice. Another witch in a tree right above our heads surprised us with her racket. Then a third came through the woods. Magical.

Because we had to walk to 17 different places in the park, there was an extra dose of the camaraderie that makes theatre-going unique among the arts. One man had his wide-eyed boy in a pack on his back. A woman explained to her child that she didn't have to be frightened by the witches because it wasn't real—"it's like a movie."

Falkenstein has the knack for choosing the right setting for the various scenes. The first murder scene was played deep in the park under tall pines. Eerie music came from behind us. For the drunken porter scene, the incessant knocking at the door echoed across the woods. The park itself became a major player with its trickling brooks, sturdy bridges and old rock walls. At dusk, real crows cawed. "Light thickens, and the crow / Makes wing to th'rooky wood."

I saw the familiar park, as well as the familiar play, in new ways.

Unfamiliar worship settings also make rituals strange: a midnight mass in candlelight or an Easter sunrise service on the banks of the Saint John River with snow falling gently.

Matthew Heiti, as Banquo, was brilliant, playing the part with an insouciance that created a different character from the one I had known. Macbeth, too, made us believe in his hesitations and transformation. Warren Macaulay played that demanding part admirably. Theatre can't fool us into believing it is real in the way that movies or a page-turner novel can, where it is easy to trick us into what poet Samuel Taylor Coleridge called "the willing suspension of disbelief."

In the 21st century, we're seeking a different kind of artistic experience. Movies can't replace the theatre. A long time ago my husband and I saw a summer production of Hamlet with the ghost rising out of a trapdoor in the round stage, saying "ooh, oooh," wearing a white bed sheet like a kid at Halloween. It was embarrassingly amateurish, but we agreed that we've never been able to think of the ghost in the same way again.

Nearly 20 years ago, we were asked to host a monologue performed by the actor Claire Coulter. We were to invite our friends into our living room, serve them wine and cheese. One friend, sitting comfortably on our couch, told me afterwards that he was terrified he was going to fall asleep, as you often do when someone is reading you a story at bedtime. Coulter gave a memorable performance of *The Fever* by her friend Wallace Shawn, who noted in the back of the book, "This piece was originally written with the idea in mind that it could be performed in homes and apartments, for groups of ten or twelve."

Falkenstein, giving us directions when we were all gathered together at first, suggested we notice how often Shakespeare used the word "nature," and indeed it did jump out at me on several occasions.

Even though my unwilling flesh made me leave at intermission, I do have an inkling of how the play turned out. For one thing, Shakespeare gives pretty broad hints near the beginning when the witches prophesy. It was the working out of the plot he was after, I think, not trying to keep me on the edge of my camp stool to find out how it all goes down. If you're reading the play, you don't have to turn to the end, worried that Macbeth won't get his just desserts.

I have written before that Len Falkenstein is a treasure. From July 22nd to August 1st his NotaBle Acts summer theatre will showcase more than 12 original plays, indoors or outdoors in four different venues; full-scale, workshopped, or just read aloud.

Salon, July 10, 2010

Reflections on journeying the road less travelled

A concatenation of events has had me sauntering down memory lane. My daughter Grace told Ross Leckie that I wanted to find a good home for our collection of issues of *The Fiddlehead*. Ross, editor of the magazine, said he would like to have them because the office had few or no copies of many of the issues.

I spent an afternoon going through them, taking out those that had work by my husband. Bill had a few stories and poems published there before he himself became an editor.

The number of writers who published in *The Fiddlehead* and later became well-known is impressive.

I was surprised to find a story by Henry Roth who published one blockbuster novel in 1934—*Call It Sleep*—and then remained silent for 60 years. John Metcalf's masterful story, "Robert, Standing," was first published in the magazine. I'd forgotten the drawings by Joseph Kashetsky and Fred Ross. M. Travis Lane wrote an amazing number of reviews, no doubt the most thoughtful the poet being reviewed ever received. I got to wondering whatever happened to various people; for example, Michael Brian Oliver and Elizabeth Rodriguez, two poets I'd published in the NB Chapbooks.

St. Thomas University professor Tony Tremblay had invited me to write a piece on the McCord Hall writers' group for his Wikipedia-style website of New Brunswick literature. A few days ago, I got out an article I had published in *ArtsAtlantic* in 1986 on the group. More fond memories: the night that poet Bob Gibbs read us his first story—he told us he was envious of the fiction writers because they were more entertaining than the poets. In my article I quote Michael Estok reviewing my novel *Wise-Ears*, "story-telling and story-listening constitute the major part of the action."

As I wrote there, I did witness "the tremendous drive to tell stories, especially in times of trouble. The whole process of writing seems to order, to clarify, to comfort people in distress."

"McCord Hall," a.k.a. "Tuesday Night," later christened "The Ice House Gang" by Alden Nowlan, spawned the New Brunswick Chapbooks, the Maritime Writers' Workshop and The Writers' Federation of New Brunswick as well as a host of published novels, short stories and poetry. It also spawned many lifetime friendships. Bill once said that each of us educated an audience for ourselves. Bill, Bob Gibbs and I were there for the whole run of 15 years. Maybe I'm being arrogant, but I'm sure no one reads Bob's work with more insight and delight than I do.

Those were exciting years for me. My children were young, fascinating (they continue to be fascinating), New Brunswick was a new home, intriguing. Kent Thompson arrived in 1967, two years after we did. He began the McCord Hall group in 1968; converted *The Fiddlehead* from a small, stapled poetry magazine into a more substantial one that also accepted short stories; started a little theatre in the basement of UNB's Carleton Hall; swept us into the vortex of his own incredible storm.

In the midst of all this sauntering, my daughter and I went to a play by Rick Merrill about Alden Nowlan that was being workshopped at the NotaBle Acts Theatre Festival. The play was constructed of Alden's own words: poetry, fiction, interviews, letters. Because of his innate modesty his own words didn't convey his extraordinary charisma. On our way home from visits with Alden and Claudine, Bill would often remark that we had been in the presence of a genius. We knew him for 15 years, from the time he arrived at UNB in 1968 until his death in 1983. As writer-in-residence, he inspired many jeux d'esprit—the Flat Earth Society, the plays he wrote with Walter Learning—as well as the productivity of the cadre of writers, politicians, musicians who gathered around him.

A Great Cloud of Witnessing

The fall issue of *The Fiddlehead* is going to have Brian Bartlett's essay on Bill, so I've been going through his CV and bibliography for information, and through his unpublished poetry to pick a selection for the magazine. I had forgotten how many wonderful unpublished poems there are. I'm finding them here and there in our disorganized household.

In 1965 we had a big decision to make when Bill finished studying for his PhD in North Carolina. Massachusetts? Maine? Or New Brunswick?

Where is that? people asked. "Is it over the water?" asked our pediatrician. It was my decision to make, Bill said. I knew he wanted to come to New Brunswick, but my mother wanted us to come home to Massachusetts. As Robert Frost wrote: "I shall be telling this with a sigh / Somewhere ages and ages hence: / Two roads diverged in a wood, and I, / I took the one less traveled by, / And that has made all the difference."

Telling it with a sigh, yes.

Salon, July 31, 2010

Memories of Molly

Although Molly Lamb Bobak and I have never been close buddies, our paths have crossed so often and I have seen her paintings, even studied them, for such a long time that I feel near to her.

One memorable day in 1999 we stood together in the Legislative Assembly to receive our New Brunswick Excellence Awards. She asked me how I was going to spend my award money. I said on my son. She laughed and said she was spending hers on her daughter.

She had a studio on the top floor of Gallery 78 across from mine. When we met at openings, we would talk about our teaching. Once she asked if any of my creative writing students had talent, and I exclaimed that many of them did, more native talent than I had. Her students too had talent. We wondered why these students didn't produce more—a waste, we thought. They don't keep at it, we decided.

My husband learned that the Bobaks were papering their dining room ceiling with the gold inserts of Matinée cigarettes packages, so he saved his for them. When their project was finished, Bill continued to save the nifty inserts for a project of his own.

I came to appreciate her art in a deeper way when I was commissioned by *ArtsAtlantic* to write about Molly. In addition to interviews, I spent a lot of time in front of various paintings I found around town. Now, I could be in Timbuktu and if I saw a Molly painting, I would recognize it immediately.

I re-read my profile of her, thinking to quote parts of it, but I wanted to quote all of it. For example, she said she was frightened about the state of the world, that people are confused: "That's what sorrow is, confusion." I didn't fully appreciate that aperçu at the time, 1989. But when I re-read it, I thought, sorrow is confusion: so exactly right, but such an original idea.

She told me that she was worried about art. She thought art had distanced itself from people and from the world. But all was not lost. There were good young painters around. The best of them was Stephen May. "There is not a false or a phony brushstroke. You should be doing an article about him!" Which I did. She quoted poets W.H. Auden and William Carlos Williams. She recited Williams' line, "An artist has to make it in his own village, the place of his own soul." This *Salon* spread and the Beaverbrook gala suggest that she has.

I usually hate to re-read my writing because it always seems so inadequate, but I have to admit that I liked my Molly article. I think I captured, if not her essence, at least a pretty good facsimile of it. The article caused me to get out her book, *The Wildflowers of Canada*. It's a pity that the publisher put that title on it because it really is a wonderfully joyful memoir, full of insight into the education of an artist in addition to its beautiful watercolours. If you haven't read it, go find a copy. Alden Nowlan wrote about it, "[Molly Lamb Bobak] is a natural writer, with a refreshingly unselfconscious, winsomely conversational prose style, which resembles her watercolours in that it looks easy and yet hardly anybody can do it." The last part — looks easy but is rare — describes Alden's own prose style, so he would be the one to recognize the quality.

Of her first September in Fredericton, she writes, "The early fall weather was mellow and clear. The maples were turning scarlet; the butternut trees were violet, smudging into opaque yellow; towheaded meadows and fields surrounded Fredericton, and the blue Saint John River flowed through the town. John Corey showed us how to look at life here and later he showed us how to love the winter too." What follows is a delightful description of Corey's lessons.

Molly's interiors are my favourite of her paintings. I think of Bonnard and Vuillard when I see them. They weren't her influences, however; Shadbolt, de Staël, Cezanne were. I wrote about these interiors, "… indoors shade into outdoors, where a person is contiguous with the room and seen only as one source of light among others rather than the dominating focus."

My first crack at curating the annual Beaverbrook Art Gallery exhibit, Writing On the Wall, was with Molly's *Blue Interior*, interpreted by poet M. Travis Lane. Travis chose that painting from all the ones in the gallery's collection. The last lines of Lane's poem are: "And I grow frail. I will be dust, dew, nimbus. / Say of me: She did not sink to darknesses. / She clambered into light." Yes, clambered into light.

Salon, September 25, 2010

Falling for a federation

What could be better than this: a beautiful fall morning, sitting in a restaurant a few feet from the mighty Miramichi River with a view of the magnificent bridge, eating eggs Benedict, chatting with three writing buddies?

Dawn Watson, Kathie Goggin and I had travelled together to the silver anniversary celebration of the Writers' Federation of New Brunswick and there met up with our mutual friend Sheree Fitch.

The event honoured the founders of the WFNB. I was one; Mary Jane Losier, Ann Brennan, Allan Cooper, Mary Brebner, Valerie Evans, Michael O. Nowlan and Tom Condon were others. Those of us founders who could attend gave presentations of our memories of the beginning.

Waiting for the proceedings to start, a vignette flashed into my mind. At the inaugural meeting in the fall of 1982, it became evident that we would need an interim president. On a scrap of paper I scribbled down a question to my seatmate, Michael O. Nowlan, "Would you consent to be nominated?" He grinned, his face lit up, and he scribbled down, "Yes!" I saved the piece of paper—it seemed like an historic document—and when the Harriet Irving Library consented to house my archives, I sent it there.

Way leads on to way. From 1968 to 1983 Kent Thompson hosted a group of writers in UNB's McCord Hall. The Maritime Writers' Workshop arose from that group. Early participants in the MWW started the WFNB. New Brunswick was the only province without a writers' federation.

So many pleasurable moments: I was hugged by old friends Wayne Curtis, David Adams Richards, Doug Underhill and Allan Cooper.

Are New Brunswick men big huggers, or is it just that I am especially huggable? I talked with founders Brennan, from Johnville, and Losier, from Bathurst, who drove from their homes to Fredericton many times for meetings about the formation of the federation. Ann's daughter Rayanne is now WFNB president.

I renewed brief acquaintance with executive director Lee Thompson, poet Ian LeTourneau and UNB writer-in-residence John Barton. I saw again poet Marilyn Lerch, WFNB's dynamic past president, and poet Diane Reid. I met Carla Gunn, author of the highly praised *Amphibian*, who read from her novel-in-progress. I heard news of old friends. Mary Brebner, the Campbellton founding rep, is now a Calgary lawyer. I met Evelyn Butcher who remembered my husband's reading of *Unsnarling String*.

The owner of Lightning Demand Press, the publishing offshoot of the Book Inn, gave a presentation. Later in the day, I went to the bookstore to see their amazing Espresso Book Machine. I'd heard of these but had never seen one. The LDP machine is one of only five in Canada, the only one in the Maritimes. The operator put in a PDF of a book manuscript, the machine whirled—I could see its action because the outside is glass—and in four minutes out came a sturdy-looking book, perfectly bound with a handsome cover.

A few years ago I wrote a family history. Forty-five family members wanted copies, so I laboriously cranked them out on an old printer. It would have been great if I could have produced an actual book.

Saturday afternoon, five members gave readings to launch their new books. Allan Donaldson launched *The Case Against Owen Williams* and Cameron Gunn (Carla's cousin), *Ben and Me*, both reviewed here in *Salon*. Deborah Carr gave a strong reading of *Sanctuary: The Story of Naturalist Mary Majka*, making me eager to read the biography. Sheree Fitch read from her intriguing "dark" adult novel, *Pluto's Ghost*. Wayne Curtis delighted us with his memoir, *Long Ago Far Away*.

A Great Cloud of Witnessing

In the midst of pleasure there was sadness. Janet Hammock told me that my friend Liliane Welch died September 22. I met Liliane at a writers' workshop I gave at Mount Allison University in 1975. She would often send me manuscripts of poems and later went on to publish widely and prolifically. Immersed in my own problems I had lost touch the last few years. I hadn't received a copy of her annual book of poetry and, now that I come to think of it, hadn't received a Christmas letter.

Liliane was dynamic not only as a poet but as a professor of French at Mount Allison. I remember our first walk out on a Sackville marsh, discussing her love of poetry and her dream of writing it. I, a couch potato from birth, was always impressed with her summer sojourns climbing European mountains with her husband Cyril. She wrote a lovely poem about the birth of my first grandchild.

A weekend filled with memories.

Salon, October 23, 2010

Casting a vote for the arts

Most people don't put much stock into what politicians promise. We know they say what we want to hear, not because they are dishonest but because we won't elect them if they don't. In a perfect world they would do as promised.

I'm not a member of any party, but I do know that there are lovers of the arts in all of them. This opinion was reinforced at the election forum sponsored by the Fredericton Arts Alliance. All the candidates were advocates for the arts, well-spoken, intelligent and civil. They even seemed to like each other.

Adam Scott Ness, an independent, is keeping alive the democratic ideal that anyone can run for office. He seemed to be having a great time. The Green Party candidate, Louise Comeau, was all for the arts, but when asked about reinstating the funds for international travel for artists she said it would be better for them to stay home and not contribute to airplane emissions.

Jesse Travis of the NDP was well-versed in the issues. The NDP has never been in charge in New Brunswick or federally, so I don't know how its tenure would affect the arts. I was, however, alarmed when a columnist I admire, Jeffrey Simpson, wrote, "The most irresponsible promise of the election campaign thus far belongs to Jack Layton"—a promise to Quebecers to re-open the constitution can of worms. Ouch.

Keith Ashfield had many impressive statistics at hand to show how much the Progressive Conservative government had done for artists. My Canadian Facebook friends are nearly all artists, and most of them seem to be against Stephen Harper. I don't know why. In New Brunswick the Progressive Conservative Party has been good to the arts. Funding for the arts started under Richard Hatfield. He gave his support to Alden Nowlan as the UNB writer-in-residence. Ashfield has been active in getting funds for the Beaverbrook Art Gallery and other arts organizations. He has been a good politician for his artist constituents, attending exhibit openings and concerts.

The Liberal candidate, Randy McKeen, surprised me with his grasp of the arts issues and especially with his charm. He said he would model himself after Andy Scott, who had formed an advisory committee on the arts. When Scott formed the committee, he told us the arts were an important part of the Fredericton riding, and he felt he didn't know enough about them. That was awfully savvy of him. And savvy of McKeen to follow in his footsteps.

One topic for debate was how can the government encourage private investment in the arts. McKeen endeared himself to me by saying that private philanthropy is not available to emerging and cutting-edge artists. Private donors give to established, admired organizations.

This forum, and the one in the fall for the provincial election, focused heavily on visual art. Fredericton writers don't seem to be interested in politics. I saw only two other writers in the audience. Writers are quite engaged in other parts of the country. Margaret Atwood wrote an op-ed piece in the *Globe and Mail*, a parable linking a vacuum cleaner salesman to Stephen Harper. Parables are notoriously difficult to write.

There was time for only two questions from the floor, and spry young men beat me to it. My question would have been about a new copyright law. The Writers' Union, Access Copyright and musicians' unions are lobbying for a law to replace the outgrown one that doesn't deal well with new technology. A law tabled by the Conservatives died when the election was called. Writers were mightily against the new law. It did seem like a kick in the teeth—proposing several broad exceptions to copyright, including "fair dealing for education."

The Writers' Union sent a questionnaire to the parties. So far, only the Green Party and the Liberal Party have answered. The two parties promised to bring in a bill that would be fair to writers, publishers, visual artists and musicians.

The possibility that self-employed artists could be included in such benefits as EI, maternity and sick leave was discussed. To implement such a plan, Andy Scott had introduced a private member's bill that died when an election was called. All the candidates were for such a bill.

New Brunswick gets a small piece of the federal arts funding pie. The province has 2.5 per cent of the population but receives only 1.5 per cent of arts funding and only .7 per cent of Canada Council for the Arts funding. Ashfield said arts funding is done by juries. MPs can't meddle; everyone will agree. I've written about this before. Maybe it's time to write about it again.

Salon, April 30, 2011

Inky poetry

When a thoroughly original poet comes along, I want to celebrate his work.

I have written about Michael Pacey so often you probably think he pays me as his publicist, but I assure you he doesn't—although he did give me a copy of his first full-length collection of poetry, *First Step*.

For quite a few years now, Michael has visited us every once in a while to read his new poems. Bill was his professor and I was his first publisher. We were always entertained and asked for copies. Very occasionally I would offer a suggestion, but the person who was the most helpful is our mutual friend Brian Bartlett to whom the book is dedicated. Brian is a master of wise editing for many poets.

The work in *First Step* has just the right amount of whimsy, humour and seriousness. "Compacted of wit and sagacity" as Robert Gibbs writes.

M. Travis Lane, introducing Nela Rio and Robert Hawkes at a recent Odd Sunday at Molly's, made a distinction between poetry of ink and poetry of blood. She prefers the poetry of blood, as she labelled that of Rio and Hawkes. It's an interesting, useful distinction. I'm still pondering it. Later she clarified "the poetry of blood" as poetry from the heart.

One of my favourite poets is Richard Wilbur—I even gave the preference to the main character of one of my novels. I soon realized this fondness began to define her. Because she was from New Brunswick and Wilbur is from New England, I tried to change the poet she was devoted to. By that time, I couldn't—he was too much a part of her. I had to figure out a way—somewhat awkwardly—that a high school sophomore in Woodstock would have heard of Wilbur.

I suppose Wilbur would be considered a poet of ink. I admire his rhyming. He can rhyme his poetry without making it doggerel: Descent/went or dynasties/ honesties. Are rhymes "inky"?

They are difficult to bring off. I think of this when I listen to songs written by local musicians — singer-songwriters — playing on their guitars such tuneless music that I could never replicate it. They sing lyrics that are spurred forward by their rhymes: "gittin'/happen," "name/came," "there/somewhere." "Breeze/seas" is a popular Maritime rhyme although the songs are usually sung with a fake Dixie accent. The whole process baffles me. I suppose these songs are akin to the hundreds of bland poems or the many derivative conceptual art projects.

I've tried my hand at writing bland poems. Some of them rhyme: "glisten/listen" or "bone/stone." Using the past tense is helpful: "died/ replied/cried."

I like poems of the blood, too, but they are also difficult to create. Male poets invariably write about the birth of their first child, usually not among their better poems. Joseph Sherman's mother and wife both complained to me that he hadn't written poems about them. My husband never wrote a poem about me. I did complain just once. Although I had cooked him many meals (I just figured out about 35,000), he never wrote about one of them. But he did write a poem about a meal he had cooked for himself — a canned Smedley's Steak and Kidney pie. Bill was definitely an inky poet.

Michael Pacey might also be considered an inky poet. His subjects are an eraser, a pencil, a vacuum cleaner, a hockey stick, vomit. "I vomited all over Europe."

His rhymes are so subtle, so inconspicuous I can't even be sure they are placed deliberately. Could it be he has such a keen gift for verbal music he just naturally drops them in? I suppose "feathery/ heathery" is deliberate. "Burrs/fur/word." "Hand/span."

A Great Cloud of Witnessing

The title poem, "First Step," is a tour de force about St. Denis, who after his execution, picked up his head and walked home. How well Pacey can use alliteration: "Swing it like a parcel / picked up at the post office, an empty pail of paint."

And metaphors. I will never be able to handle a berry box without thinking of these lines: "Weighing roughly the same as a moth" and "paper-thin like walls in Japan." Or open a medicine cabinet: "Consulted in domestic emergencies, / like a fuse box. The Bible." "[B]abysitters, party guests / break in, root among the rolls of gauze, / ointments, pills, / in search of gossip." When he first read me that line, I laughed out loud.

Here is a generous collection of 53 poems, every single one noteworthy. Robert Gibbs, in a back-cover blurb, noted the two poems on a compost heap: "Exemplary to all would-be gardeners, this collection could serve as a handbook on how to grow a poem." Bill Gaston writes, "These poems' wry, lean and precise eye give fresh life to the word extraordinary."

Salon, May 14, 2011

Not for ourselves alone, but for all

I've just travelled the first stage of my pilgrimage to the art sites of New Brunswick. I visited Sussex, a tiny, perfect village with a charming downtown, a trout creek running through it and gorgeous vistas of hill farms with silos and green fields. If I lived there, I would want to build a fence around it to keep out all the bad guys.

What made Sussex a good place to begin my pilgrimage is its arts community. The Sussex Literary Initiatives and Cultural Events — SLICE — is unusual because it's not an organization and doesn't have a leader. It is, I gathered, like a flock of birds, instinctively coming together to generate enthusiasm for the arts.

A while ago this flock of writers, artists, craftspeople, photographers, teachers and lovers of the arts held a spectacular launch of Beth Powning's novel, *The Sea Captain's Wife*.

I came for the AGM of the Writers' Federation of New Brunswick, hosted by SLICE. It was so successful that on our way home one of my fellow pilgrims worried no other town would be able to compete. The whole region was involved — the Masons, the Lions, the schools, everyone from fourth graders to my contemporaries.

At the Sussex Artists' Co-op on the first night, two high school students with beautiful voices, Kelly Knox and Tom Ans, serenaded us. Townspeople brought homemade finger food and poured wine.

The next day, the Masons served us a full-course dinner with pork as delicious as I have ever eaten. That night, the Lion's Club bingo hall was transformed into a garden, "Writes of Spring," with trellises, trees, flowers from the Corn Hill Nursery, quilts and paintings.

A table was laden with so many desserts they could have fed Princess Louise's Hussars. I wish I had the talent to wax poetic over the scene.

A Great Cloud of Witnessing

Although the people of SLICE insist they have no chairperson, on this occasion they did have movers and shakers: Patricia Stout, Jane Gillies, Kelly Cooper and Beth Powning among others.

Some of the town's teachers were enthusiastically involved. From its beginning the WFNB has had a close relationship with teachers. They invited us writers into their classes, read our books, began to write and then became members.

As in Chaucer's account of a pilgrimage, *The Canterbury Tales*, many stories were told. Judy Caissie told me the story of her heroic granddaughter and the genetic disease causing her blindness. My travelling companions, Diane Reid and Kathie Goggin, told me stories, which, while not quite as racy as those of the Wife of Bath, were entertaining. They of course had to listen to mine.

Many writers read their fiction: Alexander MacLeod read a powerful section of his, "The Loop." Chad Pelley read a harrowing account of an accident.

The winners of the WFNB competition read: Johanna Bertin on her trip to Morocco; Jane Gillies' story with an O. Henry ending. Barry Grenon took home the David Adams Richards prize and Jennifer Houle the Alfred G. Bailey prize.

As usual there were workshops. I've been to so many they make me feel old. Well, I am, of course. How many times in my life have I been told not to use adverbs as Pelley told us? I feel so bad for adverbs and adjectives I even wrote a column defending them.

In the workshop "Monetize Me!" Allan Lynch said a freelance journalist should be charging $75 an hour plus expenses. At that rate I should charge $3,000 for this week's column — a bit unrealistic.

MacLeod said his story was about the relationship between need and capacity, a stimulating idea. He always writes about something compelling to him at the moment.

He never thinks, "What will I write about now?" because his father once said to him that was like "wandering around the mall."

People ask me how I think of subjects for this column.

They do come to me, but now if I ever find myself "wandering around the mall," I know it will be time to retire.

Such oddments entice me to come to these events. Even more, I get a sense of the whole province and its writing. I meet people with like interests. I greet people I haven't seen for a while: Lee Whitney, Keith Eldridge, Ann Brennan. I love listening to the stories, both fictional and real.

The WFNB has had two energetic presidents recently—Marilyn Lerch and now Rayanne Brennan. The result is a doubling of its membership.

Last year, Rayanne and the executive director, Lee Thompson, travelled around the province encouraging people to participate. The WFNB website now has profiles of 100 writers.

The motto of Sussex is "not for ourselves alone, but for all." It would do for the WFNB as well.

Salon, May 21, 2011

Your last and final 400 words

I've always thought it was a legal requirement for a family of a deceased to put their relative's obituary in the newspaper. I'd imagined the cost would be a hardship for some people. Writing one might be difficult for grieving offspring not used to wrestling with words. But while I was having a discussion about the subject with some friends, I was told it's not an obligation.

Some people plan their funeral; some even write their own obituary. My husband and I hadn't discussed the process, and after he died—a year ago tomorrow—I sat in his hospital room not knowing what to do next. My daughter and youngest son took over; the funeral home knew what to do. My oldest son offered to write the obituary.

Afterwards, I realized how well he had captured Bill's essence. My cousin said she was surprised the universities Bill attended or the books he'd published hadn't been included. But, in fact, those things weren't very important to him, and the obituary did emphasize what he stood for, an accurate synopsis of his life: "May we all care for each other as much as he cared for us."

For most people, this newspaper record is the only printed biography they will ever have, the first and final summing up of their life, the only historical document of their existence between their birth, marriage and death certificates.

What got me interested in genealogy was the discovery of a yellowing obituary of my great-great-grandfather. I read he had been shanghaied by pirates, and I wanted to know more. The obituary of my great-grandfather stated he was walking the railroad tracks to get spring water and didn't hear the train whistle. Aha, I thought, his gene gave my family its hereditary deafness.

The template for writing obituaries is this: circumstances of birth, education, job, the names of those left behind. Mehitabel was born, she married, had children who married and gave her grandchildren, and then she died. But I notice many people want more than that. They want to express what made a person special: she loved those children and cooked them delicious dinners.

The men might have had a sense of humour, would tell family stories, be passionate about their hobbies — bowling, woodworking. A grandfather showed a grandson how to fish or hunt or whittle.

Usually a relative writes the obituary, sometimes assisted by a funeral home employee. I like it when I read that the mother's hobbies were knitting, bingo and gardening because what makes an obituary interesting, as in all writing, are the details. In the last 10 years in Maine and Massachusetts it was often stated the deceased — both males and females — was a fan of the Red Sox. When you read obituaries, as I do even for people I don't know, you realize what is important in a life.

Sometimes there is an intriguing clue to a mystery or a story not told: in the list of the surviving children, a daughter you never knew about.

I've mentioned before I don't like the war metaphor for disease: "Mehitabel waged a valiant battle against cancer."

What weapon could she have used against this enemy? What the metaphor means is she didn't complain too much, went along with any indignity of scar, bald head or colostomy bag.

It's too bad these newspaper records don't allow for anecdotes — a fuller description of being shanghaied by pirates. In 300 or 400 words, a life must be summed up. A few people, like Wallace McCain recently, will have many more words said about them, but for most of us, 400 words will have to do.

The obituary is the view the writer has of the deceased. Alice Munro said, although she wrote fiction using her mother, she didn't write about her children because she didn't want to offend them — they were going to choose her nursing home. One of mine will write my obituary.

Mary Ella Milham led two lives. For each of these she had a separate obituary. She was a professor of classics at UNB Fredericton, and for that life the Fredericton obituary emphasized the courses she taught, the scholarly work she published. Her other life was as a native of Waukesha County, Wisconsin, living on a heritage farm. The county newspaper emphasized she was descended from five original settlers and wrote pamphlets for the historical society. That obituary stated that she began at UNB Fredericton in 1968 instead of 1954. She was proud of being at the university in the early days, so the mistake would have bothered her.

I don't intend to write my own obituary, but I am toying with the idea of doing it as a writing exercise.

Salon, June 11, 2011

The theatre of real life

I've had a fine summer of theatre with more to come.

King Lear in Odell Park was a vigorous experience both physically and emotionally. John Ball, "in the role of a lifetime," to quote director Len Falkenstein, was terrific as Lear. Ball understood the play and he helped the audience understand it. The actors had to not only learn huge parts, act, overcome the acoustics of outdoors, but also traverse rough park terrain.

A memorable image in the iconic storm scene was of Lear thrashing through ferns while thunder played in the distance. Elizabeth Goodyear wonderfully transformed Shakespeare's Earl of Gloucester into the Countess of Gloucester, making that familiar role unfamiliar, always a good thing in the arts.

The NotaBle Acts Summer Theatre Festival celebrated its 10th anniversary as a vehicle for plays written by New Brunswickers. I got to see three, missing twelve.

This year, the full-length play and complete production was *Alden* — the story of Alden Nowlan, using his own words from his poems and his autobiographical novel *The Wanton Troopers*. When I heard Robbie O'Neill was playing Alden I was skeptical, but he was utterly convincing. I guess a professional actor can do that. Several of my friends used the same word about the play — mesmerizing. The father was played sympathetically by Hugh Thompson. The warm family bond of Alden, Claudine and Johnny was as I remember it. When Rick Merrill ventures into his own words, the play is not as successful. Maybe I'm being petty, but I want to set the record straight.

Three UNB professors were portrayed as pretentious twits with ludicrous accents. I never knew professors like that at either UNB or STU. Alden's good friend and literary executor Robert Gibbs is as unpretentious a human being as there ever was even though he is brilliant, a fine poet, a knowledgeable scholar. Leo Ferrari was droll and full of hijinks with a charming Australian accent. Alden's benefactor Fred Cogswell had a speech impediment with a Carleton County accent and could not have been further from the silly professors. Both universities, and the UNB English Department in particular, protected Alden, kept him as writer-in-residence for 16 years. They knew what a treasure was in their midst.

As played, Alden's lack of rapport with the students did him an injustice because he was surrounded by talented students, and he stimulated much fine writing.

The two one-acts, *Hide and Go Sell* by Chris Nyarady and *Walking to Idaho* by David Wojcik, were great fun, played with zest by young actors.

One of the differences between watching something on TV and going to live theatre is how much the surroundings change your perceptions. Real life gets mixed up with art. Parents experience this when they watch their child play Tiny Tim in Dickens' *A Christmas Carol*, whispering in a voice they know is choked with fright, "God bless us, every one."

Sitting on my three-legged campstool watching John Ball thrash around in the ferns, I understood something in the play I had never seen before. It parallels my husband's and my father's deterioration from brilliant men to stroke-ridden creatures. Shakespeare, the cast, and the surroundings made me see the tragedy of that in a new way.

I appreciated the skill of acting when thin dynamic Robbie O'Neill transformed himself into a man I knew well, cancer-ridden Alden Nowlan.

At the end of the two one-acts, a question-and-answer period was moderated by dramaturge-in-residence, Don Hannah. Chris

Nyarady said he has been writing *Hide and Go Sell* for five years, constantly tweaking it. His delight in having it chosen to be in a festival in Vancouver was palpable. He, the actors and his pal Jordan Dashner, the director of the play, talked back and forth with such enthusiasm. I remembered how I'd participated in just such a cheerful group when I was their age—the hope, the energy, the sense that this would go on forever. When Dashner was creating a memorable evil Edmund in Lear, I remembered him playing with my granddaughter in daycare.

I have more theater to come. I missed out on *The Bricklin: An Automotive Fantasy* last year by Paul Ledoux and Allen Cole—the tickets were quickly sold out. A close associate of Richard Hatfield told me that the actor who played the former premier last summer was so like him that it made her weep. George Fry waxed lyrical about the musical. I'll see for myself.

I'll also see another production of *King Lear* at the Theater at Monmouth in Maine. All these years not seeing the play performed and then twice in one summer. At my age, I'm ready for it.

At TAM, I'll also see my daughter Grace in Noel Coward's *Blithe Spirit*, playing the medium Madame Arcati. I haven't seen her in a full-blown part for several years.

Salon, August 6, 2011

Rabbit in your headlights

Today is the fifth anniversary of *Salon*, launched Jan. 26, 2007 at a gala party at the Beaverbrook Art Gallery. Its first edition was published the next day. How happy I am that it still carries on. Every week, I learn about a New Brunswick visual artist, writer, musician, craftsperson I hadn't known about. Various worthy creators I do know have been celebrated, even my close friends. I'm pleased with the response I get to "State of the Art," suggesting *Salon* has a wide readership.

I don't know why other art publications don't last. I was on a Canada Council for the Arts jury 20 years ago where the other members were complaining about the lack of arts coverage in their cities' newspapers. I was proud to be able to brag about the splendid writers *The Daily Gleaner* had — reviewers Christina Sabat for visual arts, Anthony Pugh for music, Jo Anne Claus for theatre, among others.

Alas, that golden age ended. The paper still has a fine arts column by Karen Ruet. Every newspaper in the world has a sports section and several dedicated sportswriters — no danger of their disappearing.

As I wrote last week, I've been looking for analogies. Those about writing grab me especially. American journalist Roger Rosenblatt cited an analogy by E.L. Doctorow I had read before. It hit home the first time I read it and even more so this second time around. "E.L. Doctorow likens his writing process to driving at night, when you can see only as far as the headlights illuminate."

This is the way I write novels, and for a long while I thought I was doing it the wrong way, but couldn't get my imagination to work the way more successful novelists wrote. How comforting Doctorow's analogy is. Rosenblatt goes on to examine it. "This method will take you only so far, since at some point in the act of writing, the ending will crook its siren finger and beckon you to leap into the light.

Yet it is the darkness where the thrills occur, and the lurid pictures, and the base thoughts, and strange words to describe them, and you giddily are lost among unseen and unheard of things."

I've heard writers say they had the whole novel in their head and just wrote it down. Or they had a plot they filled out. Or they pinned elaborate diagrams to their study walls. Or "I wanted to show how a woman can overcome her terrible childhood." Once, when we were strapped for money, I tried to write a Harlequin romance, where the plot, length and even the number of chapters are set out. I couldn't do it.

Sheree Fitch quoted Alistair MacLeod's analogy that a story should be as long as a string. This works better with a short story than with a novel. A short story can be any length until it gets too big and is then a novella. But a novel, to be classified as a novel, has to be at least 40,000 words. Still, it can be any length after that. As long as a string. Or, using the headlight analogy, as long as I don't hit that moose.

The Fredericton Public Library and Goose Lane Editions hosted "Winter Tales," a series designed to give a glimpse of how a writer constructs a book. The new managing editor of Goose Lane, James Duplacey, was master of ceremonies at one of the events, asking questions of the writers, carrying on a discussion with them about their books. I liked the format.

At one event, non-fiction writer Bob Mersereau talked about his two highly successful books on Canadian music—how they evolved, with anecdotes about the various artists he interviewed. Every once in a while, I think to myself that I must ask Bob about this or that, mostly in my attempt to understand the concept of the singer-songwriter. He came to sit with me after the readings, and the questions I wanted to ask him had gone right out of my head.

Poets Ian LeTourneau and Sharon McCartney rounded out the evening, alternating their discussions with readings of their poems.

Both of them commented on the wonderfully friendly writers' community we have in Fredericton.

In her discussion of the sonnet, Sharon used another writing analogy. When asked if writing a sonnet was difficult, she said it could be easier than writing a poem without a set form because without that form you are writing "without a net." No necessity for rhyme or number of lines impels you forward. You are driving as far as the headlight illuminates. Even more than writing a sonnet, composing song lyrics gives you a safety net—the need for rhymes and rhythm. They drive you forward even when the rhyme is a cliché and the rhythm is pedestrian.

Salon, January 28, 2012

When someone great is gone

I didn't start off to write of people who contributed immensely to our province, but, serendipitously, it has turned out that way.

I well remember the excitement surrounding the production of the plays by Walter Learning and Alden Nowlan in the 1970s: first *Frankenstein: The Man Who Became God*, then *The Incredible Murder of Cardinal Tosca* and finally *The Dollar Woman* in 1977, each one more impressive than the last. Theirs was a great collaboration.

The first play was entertaining because it was such a surprise — a real play, a good work, written by two people we knew. I remember the second had an engaging plot. A memorable image is the remarkable set with a train coming out of a subway cave. But *The Dollar Woman* moved me the most because it was about this place, dramatic yet nuanced, an original story.

The decade from 1967 until 1977 was exciting in general for me, a newcomer. There was the feeling that New Brunswick was participating in a national renaissance and was holding its own. If anyone expresses doubts to you about what public money can do for the arts, get them to read the history of those times. Has any other community ever got so much of worth as this province did by supporting Alden Nowlan as writer-in-residence?

In his 10 years here, Learning nearly single-handedly created Theatre New Brunswick. Alden and Claudine Nowlan hosted hundreds of students, visiting poets, local writers. He provided a model for how to be a writer. To be a writer, you write. You don't have pretensions to be a writer.

I was apprehensive about seeing *The Dollar Woman* again. Would it stand up to my memory? I wasn't sure why they were staging it at the St. Thomas University Black Box Theatre rather than at The Playhouse. The acoustics there are sometimes not kind to my elderly ears.

But it was even better than I remember it. It has a subtlety that most popular plays don't. Even the villain turns out to be sympathetic. No one has been able to solve the problem of what to do with paupers. How can society look after people who are unable to look after themselves — the simple-minded, the insane, the senile or the physically weak? One of Jesus' "hard sayings" is "The poor you will always have with you, but you will not always have me." What does that mean? It's called a hard saying because we don't know what it exactly means. Nowlan and Learning manage to capture just that ambiguity. Even though the play has a philosophical basis, it's dramatic, not just a series of speeches.

The story goes, Nowlan was researching the history of Campobello Island when he came across this unusual way for a town to take care of its poor. They auctioned off the paupers one by one; the lowest bidder won. The town paid that amount of money to the winner to take care of the person — feed, clothe and house them. The person who won could try to get as much work out of the pauper as he could.

The alternative was to build an almshouse. Lewis White, the lead in the play, "the overseer of the poor," understood that putting someone in an almshouse wasn't an ideal answer. The town I grew up in had an almshouse, called the poor farm. My mother's sad cousin lived there.

Not only was *The Dollar Woman* about New Brunswick by two New Brunswickers, but this time it had "an all-star New Brunswick cast." On my way out, someone commented to me that they were surprised that Learning was such a good actor with such presence. "Presence," whether onstage or off, is just what Learning has oodles of. Presence and energy, and a wonderful voice.

Marshall Button was terrific as one of the poor — comic and tragic alternately. Nora Sheehan, one of the people looking after the poor, managed to embody the problem. In fact, everyone in the cast was good, most of them professionals. How could New Brunswick have mounted a play with so many professionals?

Director Ilkay Silk made the most of the intimate setting of the Black Box Theatre. For some reason I can't pin down, I heard every word without straining. The professionals projecting? Whatever "projecting" means.

On another note, I was sad to read that Molly Fry died on March 1. Has the province ever benefitted more from the work of any couple than it has from George and Molly Fry? George built the New Brunswick College of Craft and Design into the outstanding institution that it is, and Molly designed and put in place our provincial kindergarten. Not to mention all the encouragement and inspiration they both have given to artists, writers, craftspeople and teachers.

Salon, March 10, 2012

The Eclectic Reading Club

On a recent evening, as I was sitting in an audience of about 25, I got musing about one of my favourite subjects, the difference between authentic tradition and fake tradition. By "fake tradition," I mean such activities as dressing up in costumes of one's ancestors—lederhosen; wearing a costume of your hero; a Stetson hat and cowboy boots; adopting an exotic ritual, like witchcraft. These can be fun, akin to playing make-believe, but they don't nourish the soul as deeply as authentic traditions do.

I'd been invited to visit the oldest reading club in Canada, in continuous existence since 1870 when it was established by Rev. James Hill, the rector of Trinity Church in Saint John, "to help him and his friends while away the long winter evenings." The current members treasure the traditions started those 142 years ago. They dress formally in tuxedos and evening gowns. Sherry is served when you arrive. The members are not following these traditions sardonically, although they obviously sense how charming they are.

The Eclectic Reading Club is not a "book" club. In a book club, the members choose a book and all of them read it in order to discuss it. A few years ago, Oprah started the renaissance of the book club. The "reading" club is about books, but with a different focus, and in this case an unusual format, derived in the 19th century and followed year by year—an authentic tradition passed down over time.

I was made to feel welcome and had no sense that I was an intruder or that the members thought themselves to be elite, just fortunate to belong to this special organization. They were eager to tell me about the club. I knew some of them and even if I hadn't met them, other names were familiar to me.

The 50 members take turns presenting a program with a theme. The previous month, Rolene Betts, an American by birth, presented on contemporary New Brunswick literature. She had asked me, an American by birth, for advice. The program I attended was presented by Beth Powning, also an American by birth. A few others in the club are immigrants, one from England and several others from the U.S. How hungry we are for authentic traditions.

The subject of Beth's presentation was "The Road," divided into three parts, as is the ERC tradition. Wine and spirits were served at the end of the first part, and again at the end of the second part. At the end of the third part, crustless triangles of sandwiches, "small cakes" (a New Brunswick term I love), and cocoa — cocoa, several insisted to me, not hot chocolate — with whipped cream were served.

The three parts of Beth's presentation were "Leaving Home," "Lure, Thrill, Freedom," and "Perils, Rewards, Home." It was Powning's evocative treatise on going on the road, with passages from some of my favourite books. She read a passage from her own memoir, *Home: Chronicle of a North Country Life*. She and her husband left her Connecticut home at the end of April where it was spring-like and drove all day into the night to Markhamville, 870 kilometres away, where it was still deep winter. Edwin Way Teale wrote that spring comes north at the rate of 15 miles a day. Beth's parents waved bravely as they set off on this adventure.

A woman originally from England, Ann Hadfield, read a passage from a memoir by the Englishman Laurie Lee about leaving home. Lee's mother also waved bravely as he set out. My mother and father would always wave bravely as I left home. One time my husband and I left, my parents bravely waving. We had to do an errand before we got on the highway. My mother had my father drive her to Route 495 so she could intercept us and wave again. She died unexpectedly a few months later, so my last vision of her is her standing at the edge of the highway waving.

Dean Turner, a man with a good, strong reading voice, read a passage from that quintessential road novel, *On the Road*. Jack Kerouac had originally set out from Lowell.

A Great Cloud of Witnessing

Each section of the presentation ended with a piece from my much beloved *Back Roads to Far Towns*, a journal in haiku by the 17th-century Japanese poet Basho making a pilgrimage.

Rolene Betts and her husband John Betts, MLA for Moncton-Crescent, drove me down to Grand Bay-Westfield to the charming home of William and Carol Sutton, hosts for the evening. While the program proceeded, we could hear cars, a motorcycle and then a train in the background.

To paraphrase 19th-century poet Elizabeth Barrett Browning, "How do I love thee, New Brunswick? Let me count the ways. I love thee for thy cherishing of tradition and for allowing me to participate."

Salon, March 31, 2012

Workshop wake up

On a lovely July morning, I sat in my favourite room at UNB Fredericton, looking out the window to the Saint John River and the hills beyond. For 37 years, this usually hot July week has been the time of the Maritime Writers' Workshop, first held in this room of the Memorial Alumni building.

When the instructor asked us to introduce ourselves this year, I unexpectedly had trouble holding back tears. Great memories were flooding in. Once, through that window, we heard a plaintive "Mom-eeee" from student Sheree Fitch's little boy, impatient for her to come out; a usually sober, mild-mannered instructor once drunkenly climbed the mast of student Nelson Adams' Grand Lake schooner; and then there was the glamourous woman who came back every summer with a man who was obviously not her husband.

Mary Lund, a self-styled junkie of writing workshops, conceived the scheme of holding one in Fredericton. I had never been to a workshop, but she convinced me that it would be a worthwhile venture. So many good writers lived in New Brunswick, we could staff it just with locals. To lure customers, we invited one "star" from away.

I was attending this year for nostalgia's sake, but, as a bonus, I learned a lot. Wendy Kitts had packed her blockbuster "My Life in Pajamas: How to start a career as a freelance writer" with helpful tips—so many things I didn't know about freelancing in spite of the fact I had been doing it for 30 years.

My friend Sassimint Grace took the course given by Valerie Sherrard, "Writing for Children and Young People." Sassi wrote me, "The course material included everything from technical aspects of writing to hints for researching and preparing for publishers. I picked up great tips for jump-starting writer's block and warnings of pitfalls."

This year's MWW had plenty of stars—but they were homegrown ones. Wendy Kitts is a successful journalist, Valerie Sherrard has many books and awards to her credit. Carla Gunn, Riel Nason, Deborah Carr, Linda Hall, Bob Mersereau and Kelly Cooper are all well-known outside the area. You could search the country and not find better qualified mentors.

I know the key to learning to write is to write. But I also know writing groups, writing workshops and creative writing classes help in many ways. For one thing, they make it seem possible to be a writer. In Wendy Kitts' course, I became convinced that if my husband's pension plan failed, I could live by freelancing.

I attended Linda Hall's workshop, "Putting it All Together: Getting Ready to Publish." I haven't published a novel for nearly 20 years although I have written seven in that time. I must be out of date, I thought. Boy, am I! What used to be called self-publishing or vanity publishing, much frowned upon, is now called indie publishing, taking a cue from musicians who record their own music and sell it on iTunes. Linda said that if you decide to publish your own book as an eBook, be sure to hire a professional editor and book cover designer. She gave wise advice on writing a query letter to publishers or agents, and about marketing your own work using Facebook and Twitter, among other outlets.

One of the students, Terry Armstrong, had already published an eBook, which has sold 6,000 copies. He had indeed been smart about the process—hired the editor and book cover designer.

In the olden days, students came to the MWW accompanied by their manuscripts for a week. They could even stay in residence with a meal plan. This made for camaraderie and the forging of friendships. Several of this year's instructors had attended as students. Riel Nason and Ian LeTourneau had come in 2004. Lately, the emphasis has been on one-day "how-to" courses. This year two-day and three-day workshops were also offered, but didn't attract enough students to let them run.

I was pleased to hear the three writers on the "Ideas to Publication" panel say they got their start by writing for the *Telegraph-Journal*. Carla Gunn had written personal essays for the *New Brunswick Reader*. I have a special fondness for the *Reader* because, for the first year and a half of its existence, I wrote profiles of craftspeople and provided the cover illustrations. I wish *Salon* had room for personal essays.

Most of the week I felt like Rip Van Winkle, waking up after having been asleep for 20 years. The world of publishing has changed drastically. But listening to Carla, I could hear my younger self—the same interest in the writing process rather than the finished book, the same method of starting with a scene rather than with a concept.

Historic trivia: both the Maritime Writers' Workshop and the Writers' Federation of New Brunswick started off their lives without an apostrophe.

Salon, August 4, 2012

Of Goodridge and graves

Bob Gibbs and I were reminiscing about our mutual friend, the poet Betty (Elizabeth) Brewster, who died recently.[4] The subject of her empty tomb in the Poets' Corner section of Fredericton's Forest Hill Cemetery came up — Betty had bought a plot and a tombstone, planning to be buried there, but she converted to Judaism, and was buried in a Jewish cemetery, in Saskatoon.

Bob was reminded of the interment of the ashes of Goodridge MacDonald in the Poets' Corner. MacDonald was one of the Roberts clan whose two most famous members, poets Charles G. D. Roberts and Bliss Carman, are also buried there.

I wasn't present at the Goodridge MacDonald service, but I heard the story told many times by my husband and others, a memorable event. I am sorry I missed it. I did attend the burial of Alden Nowlan in the Poets' Corner in 1983, another memorable event, but a personal and sad ceremony.

Goodridge MacDonald lived in Montreal, a member of a group of poets that included Louis Dudek and Ronald Everson. MacDonald died and was cremated in January 1967, but his ashes weren't buried. When Dorothy Livesay came to Fredericton as writer-in-residence[5] at the university, Everson asked her to take charge of the ashes and have them buried in the Roberts' plot.

The ashes arrived in a jelly jar. Dorothy put the jar in a coffee can and spruced it up by wrapping cloth around it. She made all the arrangements. Before the ceremony, she went to the cemetery to check that all had been done as she had asked. Two men were there digging another grave. She said they laughed when she called out, "Where's my hole?"

---

4   Elizabeth Brewster died on December 26, 2012
5   1966-67

The ceremony for MacDonald's ashes took place on that windswept hill overlooking the Saint John River on a blustery November afternoon, in 1967, dark clouds lowering, cold rain spattering intermittently. Livesay had enlisted the help of the UNB English department to provide mourners. During the ceremony, some of the professors read poems by MacDonald. On MacDonald's various Internet biographies, it's mentioned that some of his poems were read by Canadian and American poets. It took me some time to clue in that "U.S. readers" meant Bill Bauer and John Zanes.

It's still remembered, at least by Gibbs and me, that Zanes asked, "Where have these ashes been all this while? Gathering dust, so to speak?"

The presiding Anglican priest was concerned how the can would be lowered into the hole with dignity. He didn't want to just drop it in. Someone improvised by tying a rope around the can.

Just as the ceremony was about to begin, a group of students in Sunday-go-to-meeting clothes, cold, wet and exhausted, appeared at the bottom of the hill. Led by their teacher Ted Jones, they had walked in the rain from the George Street High School. Ted said that Dorothy Livesay came up to them, warmly greeted them, delighted at their attendance. She said, "What a wonderful gesture." Later, to thank them, she sent the school a copy of her recently published book of poems.

Bob remembers, "at the climax of the ceremony, the sky, dark and brooding till then, broke and a shaft of sunlight (as if arranged for a Hollywood movie) lit the tableau," including the presiding priest standing over the hole, "impressively tall in his flowing garb." This made the occasion even more memorable.

At the time of the burial, my husband and I had only lived in Fredericton for two years. He was enchanted with its exotic ways, and the interment epitomized this for him.

I phoned Ted Jones to get his memories of the event. We got talking about Elizabeth Brewster. He said that her poetry was perfect for teaching to high schoolers. He had seen her name and birth date on her tombstone and thought, she must be dead. He was surprised to see her obituary in *The Daily Gleaner*. He suggested that, in the spring, he and I make a pilgrimage to the Poets' Corner.

Charles Roberts' siblings—Theodore Goodridge Roberts, William Carman Roberts and Jane Elizabeth Gostwycke Roberts—also were writers. Other writers in the clan include Elizabeth Roberts MacDonald and Dorothy Roberts. Dorothy Roberts' brother, the artist Goodridge Roberts, was UNB's first artist-in-residence. He was also a writer. They all were proud that Ralph Waldo Emerson was an ancestor.

Brian Bartlett is compiling *The Essential Dorothy Roberts*, another in The Porcupine's Quill series. He writes, "At her best she was a very good poet—I think a wonderful 49-page pick of her work can be made." Bartlett also edited *The Essential Robert Gibbs*.

Salon, January 12, 2013

Writing waypoints

This past winter I've been editing my new novel. This is the first time in my 46 years of writing fiction that I've enjoyed the process, felt as if I were at least a little in command. I attribute this to the brilliance of Bethany Gibson, a freelance editor I hired to look at the manuscript. Under her tutelage, I'm able to stay close to the main character and the essential structure, yet still have an objective view of how to work out the problems.

I knew I needed an editor because the main character, Faith, is closer to me than any other characters I've written. She's an invented character—not me—but her situation is mine—widowhood. The novel takes place over the course of two years, but there are more flashbacks than I have used before. The editor asked, "Are we meant to see the span of years covered in the book as those it takes Faith to get through a period of mourning/grief?" It's an important question, but one I hadn't considered.

Writers have to figure out how best to edit their work. Some writers realize they are wordy and take out adjectives. My problem in this novel is the opposite. I needed to add details, explanations, make connections clearer. Quite a few of the scenes seemed to be unnecessary, but I trust my imagination and know they should be there, but why? Since I don't know, I have to figure out what point they are making. I'm surprised at how quickly I can get back into the rhythm of the prose, reinhabit the character.

I've mentioned before that I learned invaluable lessons from studying the work of Malcolm Lowry. I imitated the rhythm of the ending sentence of his short story "The Forest Path to the Spring" for the final sentence of my novel *Samara the Wholehearted*. English professor Sherrill Grace studied Lowry's manuscripts and found he didn't take out words, but layered a sentence with more and more details. "Even individual sentences illustrate the way he added phrase after phrase, adjective after adjective to his initial idea as if to probe, develop, and expand every nuance of meaning.... His imagination continually discovered new connections and unexplored resemblances among words, images and events. Symbols, allusions, motifs, were constantly inserted."

This process of discovering "new connections and unexplored resemblances" works for me, not only in writing novels, but in writing non-fiction. I found this out when I began to write "State of the Art" seven years ago. I write a sentence, and pretty soon I'm exploring what it means. In the movement from one paragraph to the next, I discover something I hadn't thought before. A memory of a quotation or anecdote flashes into my mind. I move paragraphs around and must make the transitions between the new paragraph arrangement more explicit.

When I'm trying to recall an event in my life, I use certain waypoints, such as, "That was before Bill's mother died." I can go back further—"That's when we lived on Strawberry Hill"—when I was ages eight to ten. When I'm writing a novel, these waypoints are imagined, so they can get mixed up. I have Faith, the main character, convert her dining room into her study one time and then forget and have her do the same thing a year later.

The novelist Joan Clark told me she learned much about the structure of time in fiction from studying Alice Munro's stories.

I've had to think about the proportion between scene and summary in a novel. I've never had a creative writing course, but I've read many how-to books. The first rule of writing fiction is "show, don't tell." Show in a scene, tell in a summary. My editor very often had the criticism that I was being too general: "Specificity is crucial to engagement with a piece of writing."

So far, I've written four new scenes and made many other scenes more substantial. How could I have succumbed to this temptation of telling after all these years? Was it because I was using the novel to make sense of what had befallen me, my widowhood?

Many writers use fiction to help them make sense of the world or impose order.

I've never before contemplated this: can a scene remembered by the character, a flashback, be as vivid to a reader as a scene set in the present time of the novel?

One thing Bethany Gibson didn't point out to me was my overuse of the word "strange." It was strange how often I used the word. I am writing about a widow, drawing on my own experience, and yes, most everything was strange for the first two years.

Salon, April 6, 2013

Footnotes to the book

It's common to joke that our deceased loved ones may be looking down on us, approving our actions. Or alternately, "rolling in their graves." If Elizabeth Brewster were looking down on the group assembled at UNB's Alumni Building for her perfect memorial service, she must have been awfully pleased.

Arranged by Carolyn Gammon, the memorial service was in keeping with Elizabeth's own personality and her literary output: straightforward but eloquent. Carolyn is the daughter of Elizabeth's old friends and co-founders of *The Fiddlehead*, Francis and the late Don Gammon. Francis was prevailed upon to read one of her own poems.

Serendipity had reared its lovely head because Carolyn discovered that day that the room we were in had been furnished by Elizabeth's 1946 class, with the class photo hanging on one wall. The room is my favourite at UNB with its view of the river and its butternut panelling.

The service was just long enough—an hour—and each participant spoke movingly, but simply, of Elizabeth's life. Many of her relatives were there—nieces, nephews. Her nephew Dwight Brewster had come from Victoria, B.C., to speak for the family. Carol Morrell, a colleague at the University of Saskatchewan and also a UNB graduate, spoke of Elizabeth's life there, with quotations from other colleagues.

Elizabeth's old friend Robert Gibbs read some of her poems. He gave us a tidbit of literary history. He had suggested the subject of Elizabeth's book, *Footnotes to the Book of Job*, in a phone conversation. She was worried that no plan for a new book had come to her. Robert suggested that with her recent conversion to Judaism, she write "footnotes to Job."

Some poets write individual poems until they get enough for a book, but Betty, as we called her, thought in terms of a book from the beginning.

Former UNB professor Israel Unger read the mourner's Kaddish in both its original Aramaic and in English. I had never heard Aramaic spoken aloud. I'm sure that Betty, looking down, appreciated the ancient language.

That evening, more serendipity for me, the second Fiction Writers Circle was held in the Fredericton Public Library's River Room, also a lovely space with its view of the river. Five writers of fiction read from their work for a few minutes, discussed their methods, experience and answered questions. Corey Redekop, author of the successful comic zombie novel *Husk*, moderated. Librarian Leslie Cockburn announced that Corey will be the library's next writer-in-residence.

The writers were suitably various, representing popular fiction, memoir, and literary fiction: Deni Y. Béchard (*Cures for Hunger*), Christine Eddie (*The Douglas Notebooks*), Cameron Gunn (*Ben & Me*), Allan Donaldson (*The Case Against Owen Williams*), and Darlene Ryan (*Pieces of Me*). The first two are Quebec writers recently published by Goose Lane, the next three Fredericton writers.

Darlene Ryan writes young adult novels published by Orca. Young adult is the hottest fiction genre in publishing. Several New Brunswickers write them, Valerie Sherrard for example. Under pseudonyms, Darlene also writes two series, one published by Obsidian called A Magical Cats Mystery, in which two cats are the detectives. She also wrote a fascinating story of the process she went through to adopt a daughter from China.

Darlene told me that I had given her good advice at the Maritime Writers' Workshop. Every time I hear a published writer say that they attended my baby, the workshop, my heart swells a bit, the way it does when my child or grandchild does something good. It makes all the effort seem worthwhile.

Cameron Gunn read an entertaining story told by a dog. Two cats with magical powers and a dog who can write make a good trio.

I've raved about Allan Donaldson's novel *Maclean*. When asked if he used parts of his own life in his fiction, Allan said no. But really, even though he was a young man when he left Woodstock, the town obviously forms the core of his imagination. He writes so convincingly that I believe every word.

When I attend such events, I'm envious of the writers who can say such things as "I wanted to get inside the head of so and so" or "I wanted to explore the concept of existentialism," as if they were in command. This time I was comforted by Christine Eddie who writes as I do. She writes a sentence, then another one, never knowing what comes next. If she lived here, we could become kindred spirits. I regretted not buying Christine's book. Westminster Books' owner Janet North was there selling them. Putting out my light that night, I once again thanked my lucky stars I had unaccountably landed in New Brunswick, this hotbed of literature.

Salon, May 4, 2013

Doting on Davies

About 50 poetry lovers attended the launch of Lynn Davies' *how the gods pour tea* at Westminster Books in Fredericton. Many local poets were there: Ian LeTourneau, Mike Pacey, Ross Leckie, Travis Lane, Diane Reid, Michael deBeyer, Sharon McCartney, as well as prose writers Gerry Beirne, Jean Dohaney, Ana Watts, Jo-Anne Elder, Rhona Sawlor, Gwen Martin, Anna Mae Snider, Wayne Curtis, David Watts and Goose Lane editors Suzanne Alexander and Colleen Kitts. I obviously have missed some. I suppose there were closet poets there, too — me, for instance. A disaster would have wiped out the Fredericton literary community.

Davies gave an excellent reading — just the right length of time, with a nice structure, beginning with a poem about picking strawberries and ending with one about making strawberry jam.

A mutual friend informally reviewed the book: "What I love about her poetry is that there is no (BS) in it." In "On My Knees at the Strawberry U-Pick," the woman picking strawberries overhears sentences, phrases from the other pickers, words that invoke stories. The dialogue between "the steady plunk of berries in the box" and these few words finally opens out into a full-blown contemplation of infinity. In the poem, Davies manages to contain the whole strawberry-picking community and a meditation on life and death: a tour de force. With not a word of BS.

"November" begins, "The trees are spent, their green / energy gone, as if *this is it, this / is all we've ever needed*." It is true, isn't it? Although we humans miss the green leaves, the trees themselves seem perfectly happy and healthy without them.

One poem expresses sadness poignantly without being literal or pathetic in any sense. "That summer the far field grew wild, / the daisies a freshet through forty shades / of green and the wind's wake. *Delphiniums* / I said *stand up on your own*." The poet chides the flowers for not standing up straight. Later in the poem, she writes, "If the ground was hot / I didn't notice, me in my thick-soled boots / and heavy-socked heart." The word "heart" coming after "heavy-socked" is completely unexpected, but so exactly right.

The book is published under the new Goose Lane Editions imprint, icehouse poetry. Serendipitously, two days after Davies' launch, I was sitting in that very ice house, portraying myself as a historical artifact. I probably should have borrowed a bonnet from King's Landing. Various historical buildings in Fredericton were open to visitors on that day, and Lauren Caines at UNB had asked me to host McCord Hall with her.

In 1963, David McCord offered to pay for the renovation of the UNB ice house, because it was about to be torn down. He thought it was too fine a building for such a fate. Four years later, Kent Thompson began to host a writers' group there on Tuesday nights. We called ourselves the Tuesday Night Group or the McCord Hall writers. Later, Alden Nowlan, writing about us in the *Telegraph-Journal*, christened us the "Ice House Gang." Lauren and I didn't have many visitors, but one was Lance Caesar who had sat in the ice house in the '90s for an MA creative writing class.

I had brought some of the books that had their first airing on Tuesday nights. Lauren went to get us coffee, and while I was alone there, I picked up David Adams Richards' *The Coming of Winter* and read the first page out loud, reprising the evening the teenage Richards hitchhiked down from Newcastle to read us the first two pages of his manuscript, already using his unique cadence. "Blood had dried to his hands by mid-morning, thin streaks of blood on his fingers, and knuckles. He cradled his rifle, walking slowly over wet gully leaves, his jacket opened, his blond hair in sweaty knots. The stench of a headless yearling partridge, foot-strung and dangling, a splatter of its dried blood on his pants." We all knew we were in the presence of something special.

On a related subject, the executive board of the Writers' Federation of New Brunswick recently held an all-day session. I hadn't been to a board meeting for quite a while. I'm not strictly necessary, because, as the honourary president, I can't vote, but I was awfully delighted with how lively the organization has become.

Movers and shakers abound on the executive. Plans were being made for several exciting new programs, soon to be revealed. This year's annual fall meeting will be held Oct. 17 and 18 in Bathurst at Danny's Inn. The Port of Belledune is sponsoring a dinner. I love that a port is supporting us. Andy Flanagan is organizing the event. Douglas Arthur Brown will give a workshop on electronic publishing. Along with other writers, Lynn Davies will be reading from *how the gods pour tea*.

Salon, October 12, 2013

A richly creative life

Phyllis Rose, musing on why she compiles biographies, wrote, "Since ultimately what we all want most is to have our time on Earth prove to be valuable, we examine writers' lives to learn how to turn whatever happens to us into something useful or beautiful."

This made me think of Kent Thompson. He is full of creative energy and joie de vivre. He was grateful to the University of New Brunswick because it gave him a chance to do all he had ever wanted: teach creative writing, edit a literary magazine and write. He turned *The Fiddlehead* from a modestly printed, thin poetry magazine into a glossy one, added editorial essays and fiction from up-and-coming Canadian writers. Kent invented the MA creative writing degree — not an MFA, usually considered a terminal degree, but a regular master's with a thesis that combined the student's own poetry or fiction with an essay about the process of writing it.

Kent often went to Toronto to persuade journalists that exciting things were happening in Fredericton, the "Dublin" of Canada as he dubbed it. He was one of the founders of The Writers' Union of Canada. He wrote to Oberon Press to tell them about the young David Adams Richards. He and his wife Michaele hosted salon-type parties where artists, musicians and writers mingled. Bruno Bobak celebrated these with his painting *Kent's Punch*. Kent began the McCord Hall writers' group (a.k.a. the Ice House Gang).

During all this, he wrote: poetry, essays, history, film scripts and fiction. Several of his radio plays were produced. He was a regular on national CBC.

I became caught up in his enthusiasm and soon my husband was too. As Bill said, Kent was generous-spirited, wanting his writer friends and students to be successful. He's about my age and still writing. An exemplar.

This reminded me of the book *Old Woman at Play*. In old age, Adele Wiseman's mother began to make wonderfully inventive dolls, inspiring Adele to write one of the best books I've read about the creative impulse. She wrote, "Teachers can only teach what they know. But the creative urge teases us to what we don't quite know yet, toward different ways of knowing."

And this reminded me of my friend Dawn Watson. Like Thompson, Dawn has fashioned for herself a richly creative life. Recently, she received bad medical news. She writes, "But the important thing is that I'm happy and peaceful." I think her creative life is one of the reasons she can find this peace.

Christmas is her prime creative season. She decorates three trees. She's been making buildings for a miniature village, including a country church lighted from inside. This year she's working on a store with the shopkeeper living over it. One Christmas Day, Bill looked out our front window and saw a shotgun shell attached to a belt hanging from a tree: "a cartridge in a bare tree." For the next 11 days, something mysteriously appeared for this spoof on "The Twelve Days of Christmas."

"Five stolen things" included discarded house numerals from our basement. For "three wrench men" the tools were decorated with clothes. We enlisted friends to help us find the culprit but never did. All was revealed in the end.

Dawn fashions deep friendships with the students she tutors in literacy. Her imaginative essay on this teaching was a standout in *Breaking the Word Barrier*. Every spring, she makes a fairy garden from moss and figurines. She wrote a column in *The Gleaner*, "My Kind of Town," and performs at storyteller festivals.

Dawn and I met at McCord Hall, where I heard the beginning of her novel about the creative urge. For more than 30 years, she has been working on this fiction about a stained-glass artist. "One-third of the way down the piece, a range of pale mauve to rich purple slump glass rose upwards and outwards. He had never seen such slump glass formed on such angular molds. Set against these hills was a living green tree. The sky, pieced in the tones of morning, was leaded with graceful bird wings. A stream of crushed glass cascaded through the closely leaded grass. The tree moved in the wind, the clouds scudded, the mountains hurt. Then he saw the woman behind the tree. He'd missed the small beige face, the green draped dress, the straw basket."

Dawn's house is also a canvas for her creative urge with several assemblages by her good friend, the late Selma Brody and a gorgeous painting by Toby Graser.

I've known other people with this drive toward the full creative life. I've written about Peter Thomas, Kathy Hooper and George Fry. Their lives become works of art in themselves.

Salon, November 16, 2013

I shouldn't complain

I came across the following sentence from an Emily Dickinson letter: "Home is the definition of God."

As a good trope should do, this analogy cuts several ways. Because I cherish my home, I can imagine God to have its best attributes: love, friends, art, books, the walnut table my father made us. Going the other way, it would be good if Bill and I had created a home that mirrors our conception of God.

It also reminds me; I shouldn't complain about my disability — it will after all be fixed eventually.

The most important reason I shouldn't complain is I don't have to hobble out to see artists; they come to visit me. All I have to do is make them a cup of good coffee or inferior tea. Nowadays, they even go out to the kitchen to make their own tea.

In the last few weeks, novelists have come to talk about writing or read to me from their work: Linda McNutt, Sassi Grace, Pam Fulton. The eight members of my writers' group have met here for many years. Stephen May brought me a new painting with which to fall in love, *Margaret's Apple Pie*. Gail Fenderson showed me her latest stained-glass work on her iPad.

Poets Travis Lane and Brian Bartlett read me their new poems or talk about poetry. Karen Estabrooks Gordon brings along her newest work. Potter and photographer Bonnie Massey and her husband, fine furniture maker Jack Massey, bear a gift of ornamental silver grass. Photographer and furniture maker Jack Oudemans comes by with food from the market. Peggy Hawkes, maker of paper and other crafts, wife of poet Robert Hawkes, arrives with an apple pie. Poet Robert Gibbs brings his sister visiting from England.

Writer Chuck Bowie has promised to visit.

I'm counting my blessings as I write this. To have ended up in Fredericton was so improbably fortunate I can hardly believe it was just dumb luck.

Fredericton was my husband's idea—I had never heard of the city, scarcely heard of Canada. To have built our house in this blessed Hill Brothers neighborhood was serendipitous. Was Bill being led by some higher power in both accounts? That doesn't seem probable either.

Novelist Dale Estey suggested my house should become a museum because of all the writers and artists who have been here most of the contemporary writers of New Brunswick have: Greg Cook, Ross Leckie…

No, I can't go there—too many to mention. I should make a list of those who haven't been here and invite them: Mark Jarman, Beth Powning, Corey Redekop and Carla Gunn come to mind. My house might make the Guinness World Records as having had the most New Brunswick writers in it.

And not only New Brunswick writers, the writers from other parts of Canada have been here.

The League of Canadian Poets had a party here at their annual national meeting. Michael Ondaatje taught my daughter how to play chopsticks on our piano. Kent Thompson brought his college friend Carol Shields. Joan Clark talked about writing and offered to read my children's book. Eleanor Wachtel has been here to talk about Fredericton writers. Dorothy Livesay had too much to drink in our basement recreation room.

I wish I had kept a journal.

Hugh Hood's conversation was so interesting that I kept coming out of the kitchen to listen, letting the milk for the cream sauce boil over three times, damaging the stove so badly we had to buy a new one. John Metcalf and Billy Valgardson were here when they taught at the Maritime Writers' Workshop. The house has held two launches of David Adams Richards' novels, two of Joe Sherman's poetry, one for Ann Copeland stories. I can picture Alden Nowlan sitting like Buddha in our huge leather chair.

Here, in this house, some people met to plan the Writers' Federation of New Brunswick—Ann Brennan, Mary-Jane Losier among others. A few months ago, the executive of the Writers' Federation met here with Ann's daughter Rayanne in charge. In this living room Mary Lund convinced me that the Maritime Writers' Workshop was a workable idea. Around the walnut table, writers congregated to collate and staple New Brunswick Chapbooks hot off the Provincial Artisan press.

Bill was the star attraction because he was a marvelous conversationalist, witty and kind. Poet Yvonne Trainer said she fondly remembers my meatloaf, but I know that she loved Bill more.

On the bookcase, in the dining area, four shelves contain the books of my friends and acquaintances. I just counted: 360.

Has there ever been a home as fortunate as 252 Stanley St.?

Salon, December 14, 2013.

Odd Fellows

Allison Calvern came to call, bearing cookies. She's the impresario behind Odd Sundays at Molly's, "Fredericton's longest-running, semi-monthly, poetry-reading series." I could add "most-hyphenated."

I described to my son my dilemma, that circumstances prevented my going to events I could write about in "State of the Art." Why don't you invite people in and write about them, he said. He mentioned his friends Julie Scriver, Bob Mersereau and Steve Peacock. As it turned out, Allison was coming anyway, although she demurred that she was not worth being written about. She is wrong about that. I'll invite the others too. I've been neglecting the art of music, and Bob and Steve, experts on the subject, would fill the gap.

Next October, Odd Sundays at Molly's will celebrate its 10th anniversary. About the odd name, Allison said, "I wanted the title to do some work on its own," namely to tell where and when. What's missing is the time, 2 p.m.

Allison was so impressed with Fredericton as a rich source of poetry that she thought the town needed a regular event for presenting the work. She chose an "interesting" venue, and this surely describes Molly's Coffee House with its multitude of artifacts, including a full-sized red sleigh. Here, across from Officer's Square, there's plenty of free parking on Sundays. You can get a meal—specialties are pea soup and shepherd's pie—or just coffee or beer.

Allison invites two writers to give readings—20 minutes each. An open set of three minutes for anyone in the audience is followed by a book draw. The whole event lasts a little over an hour, Allison makes a poster for it, sends out reminding emails and includes it in the Fredericton Arts Alliance weekly newsletter of cultural happenings.

The audience has faithful regulars. These have become Allison's friends—Virginia Bjerkelund, Travis Lane and Roger Moore, to name three. A few months ago, when regular Gerry Kemp died, a big hole opened up.

Allison says she especially likes the open set, always producing a surprise. Teenagers might read for the first time, trepidation in their voices. It's a good venue for beginners, because the audience, nearly all writers themselves, radiate encouragement and energy. "The people who come are there because they love poetry."

As well, the readers—invited and open set alike—have a palpable affection for their own work; not false pride, just affection. The small size of the room forces people to sit close together, creating a connection between the reader and the audience. I have read there several times and agree—the atmosphere is special. The people are there because they cherish the word.

The invited readers are usually from Fredericton, but occasionally someone from out of town shows up—Saint John, Moncton, even Halifax. UNB writers-in-residence are invited to read—stars like John Barton and Erin Mouré.

Allison also runs a publishing firm, Poppy Press. She fashions the books herself, small volumes printed on handsome paper in a stylish computer font and then lovingly hand sewn. Robert Hawkes' *Sentinels* is one, Betty Ponder's family memoir *Little Sparrows Fall* is another.

When I ask Allison if she writes (a rhetorical question because I have read two of her very good stories and several poems), she modestly says, "a little bit." After more of my probing, she admits her work has been on the short list for a CBC prize, second or third for the Writers' Federation of New Brunswick and other prizes, has received a creative writing award from UNB and has won her $250 and ballet tickets. She and her husband, George DeMille, are active in the Unitarian Fellowship.

She told me a wonderful anecdote about Robert Chalmers, the obstetrician. He and she were taking a painting course from Pat Badani. "[Robert] had been doodling with a small piece of charcoal and, laying it down along its short length, he swished it around making a doughnut shape on the paper." He turned to Allison and asked if she knew what that was. "A cervix," she answered. "How in the world would you know that?" he asked, surprised. "I happen to own one."

This is one of her published poems, "here is a rock face":

> shaggy with moss.
> see how it cradles a back
> that leans against it;
> see how the lichens
> frill their green and daring skirts
> around a resting head.
> here. touch the cleft.
> rim these craggy earth lips
> breathing their hoary breaths.
> plunge your hand inside,
> your face.
> breathe the ancient birth breath
> released for you,
> fearsome comfort
> for your small and brittle sorrows.

Salon, January 25, 2014

Chapter and Verse

Travis Lane suggested I write about the New Brunswick Chapbooks.

By 1967, it had become customary for poets to be published for the first time in the chapbook format. A chapbook is a small, paper-covered, stapled volume. Its name derived from chapman, which was a peddler who sold pamphlet-like books.

No one in New Brunswick was making chapbooks for individual Fredericton poets, although, later, Fred Cogswell began to publish them in his Fiddlehead Poetry Books.

At the time, Kent Thompson and Dorothy Livesay began a weekly writers' group which eventually settled down to meeting on Tuesday nights in the renovated ice house, McCord Hall, at UNB Fredericton. The assembled writers, variously named "Tuesday Night,"/"McCord Hall"/"Ice House Gang," decided we should have a chapbook series. They posed the little red hen's question: But who will be the editor? Having no experience with editing or publishing, not being a poet, only having lived in New Brunswick a few years, I accepted the group's request that I be the editor. Fools rush in where angels fear to tread has been my life-long motto.

Publishing a chapbook enabled poets to apply for membership in the League of Canadian Poets, gave them a name for submitting poetry to major publishers and magazines.

I'd never seen a chapbook before I became the editor of one. We determined to make it a series, because, as my husband advised, libraries would want to buy the whole set. This proved to be true not only for libraries but for individual collectors. I was surprised that some American universities, Harvard University for example, ordered them. How did they find out about the series? We printed runs of 250 and sold them for 60 cents. The enterprise was self-sustaining, not needing public money.

A Great Cloud of Witnessing

I went to Marjory Donaldson and Bruno Bobak at the UNB Art Centre for help with the cover. Together they designed a handsome one, as you might expect from two such fine artists. The design featured a silkscreened band of different colours with the title, author and number embedded in it. Marjory did the silk-screening herself for quite a few years. She and Bruno gave us black and white drawings for the cover illustrations, as did other artists: Mary Pacey, Peggy Hawkes, Brigid Toole Grant (a drawing of my daughter), Bernice Kristmanson, among others.

The group decided who would be published first, in 1968: Robert Gibbs, Kent Thompson and William Bauer, who were members, and Robert Cockburn. To say that I was editor and publisher gives me an important sounding title for what I really did: find someone to type the poems; take them to Provincial Artisans, which printed them offset; get the covers printed with the drawings the artists provided; bring them to Marjory to silkscreen; collate and staple the whole; mail the orders, and scout out places to sell them locally. On several occasions, we had a collating and stapling party, round and round our dining table. Later, my three kids could be cajoled into collating and stapling.

There were glitches: I misspelled Marjory's and Noreen Hood's names in the credits. I brought M. Travis Lane her typed poems for proofreading and received an alarmed phone call. The typist had typed them as if they were prose.

I think of one block of three poets as "the Urchins"; students Brian Bartlett, Michael Pacey and David Adams Richards. They had started a magazine, called *Urchin*. Their books were Bartlett's *Brother's Insomnia*, No. 15, Pacey's *Anonymous Mesdemoiselles*, No. 16, and Richards' *Small Heroics*, No. 17. The three, as nearly everyone in the series did, went on to publish other books. The Urchins are nearing 60, but I still think of them as boys.

Near the end of the life of the chapbooks, we experimented with publishing a play, David Etheridge's... *Left in Slow Motion* and a book of short stories, Kent Thompson's *Shotgun and Other Stories*. Chapbooks in other provinces became more sophisticated in their printing and binding, and we had to follow suit. This necessitated asking the Canada Council for money, filling out forms, obeying rules. I enlisted the help of Dale Estey and Jo Anne Claus. Eventually the project became too complicated and petered out in 1981.

We published 18 poets, in a total of 25 books. Many of the poets became my friends and still keep in touch, visiting me when they come to town. When the late beloved Joseph Sherman, of *No. 7 Birthday*, became editor of *ArtsAtlantic*, he asked me to write for the magazine, thus beginning my career in art journalism.

The whole enterprise was satisfying. I was pleased to read this sentence in Kent's entry in the St. Thomas University's online New Brunswick Literary Encyclopedia: "Thompson's favourite works are a series of his poems under the title *A Band of My Ancestors* (1975) and his collection of nine short stories, *Shotgun and Other Stories* (1979)."

Salon, April 5, 2014

The new *Fiddlehead* is full of New Brunswick content

The Summer Poetry issue of *The Fiddlehead* is chock-a-block full of interesting New Brunswick content, while still remaining true to its tradition of being an international magazine. Six of the contributors live in the U.S. and 14 live in other parts of Canada. When Fred Cogswell turned the student publication *Fiddlehead* into a major literary magazine, he included poets from all over. One of these poets was from New Jersey, Louis Ginsberg, father of Allen. This current issue reminded me of those old magazines because three of its poems, two by Oromocto poet Shane Neilson and one by Saint John poet Anne Compton, were printed sideways. One of Cogswell's stable of poets also wrote these long-lined poems that had to be printed that way. I can't remember her name. I'll ask Bob Gibbs, longtime *Fiddlehead* editor.

The magazine pays tribute to two poets: one American, Rae Amantrout, and the other Canadian, M. Travis Lane. I was a trifle disappointed in the essay on Lane by Shane Neilson because he focused on the fact that she is not well-known. In one of the three pages of his essay he speculates on the reasons—she is a woman and lives in New Brunswick. I wish the value of our artists was not rated by their fame in Upper Canada. Or their celebrity in the world at large. Otherwise, Michael Jackson would be the greatest artist who ever lived.

To be so valued in her own home space that *The Fiddlehead* editors devote much of its poetry issue to her tells you what immense value they place on her poetry and her high standing in the literary world. Most people conversant in Canadian literature know Lane's work and admire it.

Neilson makes a good case for the special significance of Lane's long poems. "I wish I had triple the space to include a longer work, for her long poems demonstrate her strange brilliance."

What is great about the Lane section of the magazine is that Neilson has selected 19 poems from all phases of her career, a "retrospective" of her poetry. I've been re-reading these poems, trying to figure out what movement there has been. I think her poetry becomes more personal, but her voice is consistent over the years. What she does so luminously well is transform the everyday into mystery. On the surface, no everyday exists, all is sanctified, but scratch the surface, and the common life appears. In "Last Picnic (for my grandmother)," she writes, "Twilight billows like a fog / around us on our separate liths / like crones, the weird Ward women, so alike / same voice, same face, same distances." She transforms a family picnic into a scene from *Macbeth*. "Lith"—what a great word to use; it converts the rocks the women are sitting on into a primeval temple. Another aspect of the magazine that pleased me is the dramatic cover with a photo of a black tulip by Saint John artist James Wilson. Fredericton poet Ian LeTourneau is in charge of the design of the magazine.

Patricia Young has written a delightful review of a "stunning collection of poems," Lynn Davies' *how the gods pour tea*. "With each poem the reader is more deeply immersed in this vibrant, living, breathing world of plant life and changing seasons.... Deeply experienced and finely wrought, Davies' poems are a pleasure to savour." It's a good review not only in the sense of favourable, but in the sense of thoughtful; it goes into individual poems thoroughly—it's two and a half pages long. Young is a good poet herself, having received many accolades. She was writer in residence at UNB in 2008.

Michael Pacey has two poems in the issue. "Lightbulb" begins, "Icon of pure idea. Screwed into a sphere of permanence / skin-thin, fragile as eggshell, yet suffused / in an even light—a Platonic corona identical / to the thinking mind's delicate glow." Frequent *Salon* contributor Anne Compton is represented by four poems. The long-lined one, "Ice Storm: Solstice to New Year's," has these lines, "The church has no power. I hold a flashlight to Isaiah, read the first words—*The people walking / in darkness have seen a great light*—wait for the collective gasp. Some sniggering."

A Great Cloud of Witnessing

Many people in New Brunswick came to know and admire Jan Zwicky when she and her partner Don McKay taught at the university. At first they lived in a farmhouse on the edge of Base Gagetown. One of her poems is titled, "Nocturne, Upper Gagetown, 21 August 1991."

> We're playing Casino in the living room
> when a glass bursts in the kitchen.
> The army is banging away again:
> tiny shards in the butter, a pebble
> like a doll's eye in the coffee pot.

Bob Gibbs couldn't remember the long-lined poet's name either, but he went to a great deal of trouble to find it: deLancey Torrie. Thank you, Bob.

Salon, August 9, 2014

Changing the way we think about beauty

I've been reading John O'Donohue's *Beauty: The Invisible Embrace*, recommended to me by Freeman Patterson. I'm reading at a snail's pace, sitting out on my back porch with a mug of coffee, the breeze soughing in the trees, studying the book in perfect contentment.

When I came across these words: "Beauty cannot be forced. It alone decides when it will come and sometimes it is the last thing we expect and the very last to arrive." I immediately thought of two such unexpected moments.

In March of 1953 my carless date asked Bill Bauer to pick me up. As I slipped into the front seat, I looked up at him, and he was smiling down on me. At that moment I was in love. I know that sounds silly, but it's true — love at first sight. Fifty-seven years later our daughter, our youngest son and I were holding vigil over Bill in the hospital's palliative care unit. A nurse had phoned late at night to tell me that the end was near, and I should come early in the morning. Bill appeared to be unconscious, not just asleep. We took turns holding his hand, whispering our love in his ear. After about two hours a nurse came in, looked at him, and said, "He's gone." She went to get a stethoscope to verify this. When it was confirmed, she said we could stay as long as we wanted.

Very soon after she left, a knock came on the door, and a woman opened it. She stood in the doorway and said, "Isn't he calm this morning? Much better than I saw him yesterday." I hadn't seen this woman before but surmised that she was a doctor. She came in and flopped down in a chair and repeated how calm he was, how peaceful. I suddenly realized that the doctor didn't know Bill was dead. "He's dead you know," I said. She leapt up, the strangest expression on her face, and fled, closing the door behind her. The three of us looked at each other, surprised and bewildered, and then simultaneously we began to laugh, great hearty belly laughs.

When we stopped, my son said, "What must people be thinking? Our father has just died and here we are laughing." No man has ever been more deeply loved than Bill was, by me and by our children. And yet at his death, we laughed. Who would have expected such a moment of pure delight to appear at such a time?

In between March 1953 and June 2010, our family shared many belly laughs. At Bill's reading of his comic poetry, belly laughs indicated how much the audience enjoyed it. My daughter's belly laugh is notorious. Her weeping is just as intense, and plenty of that occurred after her father's death. O'Donohue writes, "Though beauty is autonomous, there seem to be occasions when human presence can become congruent with her will." The doctor's presence was that. "In creative work no amount of force or mechanical management can guarantee beauty. Suddenly without expecting it, beauty is there." In a few passages in my writing, I seem to have become congruent with the will of beauty. In one of them, in *Samara the Wholehearted*, the main character is giving someone a bath. If I wrote like that always, I thought to myself, I would be a great writer.

Beauty: The Invisible Embrace has completely changed the way I think about beauty. The book has been instrumental in integrating my metaphysics in a profound way. Beauty, Truth, the Good remain separate but are becoming assimilated. I'd always known that our laughing right after Bill's death was good, true, but I hadn't realized what a thing of beauty it was.

Later I read that beauty "does not restrict its visitations only to those whom fortune and circumstances favour. Indeed, it is often the whispers and glimpses of beauty which enable people to endure on desperate frontiers. Even, and perhaps especially, in the bleakest times, we can still discover and awaken beauty; these are precisely the times when we need it most." Comedy is as precious as tragedy, its flip side.

One of my favourite books is Sarah Orne Jewett's *The Country of the Pointed Firs*. In it a woman collects herbs to sell to her neighbours.

I wanted to know about these herbs, so I started a garden: comfrey, elecampane, angelica, tansy. Twice the garden had to be torn up, and I put it back, but the third time I gave up in despair. Unexpectedly, to my delight, many of the herbs came back and still flourish on the margins of the property. Each is a thing of beauty, although not conventionally pretty. I have always known that "beautiful" is not synonymous with "pretty." But I'm beginning to understand the difference more deeply.

Salon, September 27, 2014

The Prat sisters' bindery

The late Dr. Mary Ella Milham was a lover of libraries far and wide, a true scholar. In 1987 when she retired as an emerita from the classics department of the University of New Brunswick, she established the Milham Trust Fund for the purchase of books about New Brunswick and about the art of books. In her honour, the Harriet Irving Library established the Milham lecture series. For the 17th lecture in the series, Dr. Gwen Davies, herself a UNB professor emerita and dedicated scholar, spoke on "Designing Beautiful Books: Bliss Carman and the Prat Sisters in 1890s Bohemian New York." Dr. Davies had written before about the Prat sisters' interest in book binderies—"The Elephant and the Primrose: The Prat Sisters in New York"—in the *Journal of Pre-Raphaelite Studies*. Because the subject was somewhat esoteric, I thought few people would attend. Was I ever wrong! The staff members of the library, including its interim director Leslie Balcolm, kept lugging in chairs until the room was stuffed. I wasn't surprised however to see David Brewer, the book designer and printer, in attendance. He had produced a broadsheet of a poem by Carman to commemorate his 150th birthday.

John Carman Wilcox, a descendant of Charlotte, one of the four Prat sisters, recently donated to the library a collection of 40 volumes of poetry and prose, most of which were inscribed to Minnie Sophia Prat by her fiancé Goodridge Bliss Roberts and his cousin Bliss Carman.

I won't even try in my 800 words to reconstruct the illustrated talk because it was too wonderfully full of fascinating information. For example, poets Ezra Pound and Wallace Stevens were influenced by Carman and Roberts. Bliss and Charles were dubbed "The Angora School of Poets" because they, along with their friends Richard Hovey and Rochard Le Gallienne, wore their hair long.

Even after her fiancé's death, Minnie continued to be a member of the Roberts/Carman coterie. When he died, Goodridge was studying at King's College in Windsor, NS, where Charles was a professor. Minnie lived nearby in Wolfville. By the late 1890's Charles had immigrated to New York City where Bliss was already established. They encouraged Minnie to follow them. She came in 1897, apprenticing to Evelyn Nordhoff at her book bindery, the Elephant. After Mary Prat joined Minnie, the sisters established their own bindery, the Primrose. The custom was that a book in plain paper covers would be given as a gift. The recipient would then take the gift to a book binder to be re-covered. I have a collection of leather-bound books inherited from my father. Had the contents been re-covered this way? I can't tell. Small chapbooks of poetry, including Carman's and Roberts', were routinely re-covered. Because I edited the New Brunswick Chapbooks, I've long been interested in the chapbook movement, but didn't know of this Maritime connection.

Carman, Roberts and the Prat sisters were attracted to the Arts and Crafts movement, especially to William Morris. Among his many interests, Morris was obsessed with book design.

In 1900, Minnie won two prestigious prizes for her bookbinding, but she died in 1901 from typhus, so never got to profit from the honours. May recruited her sister Annie, who was studying at the Art Institute of Chicago, to help her. Eventually, May returned home to Nova Scotia where she maintained the bindery. She trained her niece, Miriam Wilcox, the daughter of Charlotte Prat Wilcox, in the binding of books in the tradition of Minnie and, among others, May Morris, William's daughter. The Nova Scotia provincial archives has a collection of the Prat bound books.

The sisters were also influenced by a friend of William Morris, Thomas James Cobden-Sanderson, because Evelyn Nordhoff had studied with him. Cobden-Sanderson was in the news recently when his type font, Dove, was rescued from the Thames River. Before his death, he had thrown its pieces in the water so that his partner could not have them. This got me thinking about typefaces. I discovered that I've been using Calibri Light, the default font of my new computer. Previously I'd used Times New Roman, which I now see looks heavy on the screen although not when printed. Calibri, I learned, was designed especially to look good on the screen as well as in print. Years ago, when we first could choose our computer font, my husband printed all of them out and chose Courier New.

As an aside, Dr. Davies told us that the Marshland Inn in Sackville has a room with original Morris wallpaper. I've always wanted a room done in Morris-designed paper. I regularly sit in church under the stained-glass window designed by the Burne-Jones and Morris company. Dr. Davies' delightful lecture has got my old brain percolating. I hope she gives it in other venues.

Salon, March 28, 2015

A Sunday of rich music and saying farewell to a poetry-reading host

One Sunday morning our minister, Ellen Beairsto, announced that during the offering our music director Steven Peacock would play his new guitar, a "2009 Manuel Contreras based luthier." He joined a verse of Gershwin's "Summertime" with José Luis Merlin's "Aire de estilo."

Steve is an accomplished classical guitarist with a profound knowledge of music. We know we're lucky to have him. I listened carefully, trying to perceive if I could hear an enhancement. Maybe I was fooling myself, but I believe I did hear a richer, fuller tone. The ushers were so enthralled they forgot to take the collection. This was hastily remedied.

The piano and the guitar are the most democratic of musical instruments. Many people have taught themselves to play the piano or guitar, both instruments more likely to be easily available, both handed down from one generation to the next. My father taught himself to play the guitar in the early '30s, and later taught my brother and me to sing along with him. I've been hearing the sound of the guitar ever since I was in the womb.

On that Sunday too, Allison Calvern hosted her last "Odd Sundays at Molly's" after 11 years. She is moving to Ottawa to be near her children, so we can't be sad. She did announce that her poetry-reading venue will persevere under the auspices of Kathy Mac, David Watts, and Sherry Coffey.

It was fitting that her last event was a good one. Shane Neilson gave a powerful reading from his new book, *On Shaving Off His Face*, reflections on pain. Neilson is a physician, so you expect him to know about the subject, but he ended with a tour de force poem about his own pain when his son was ill. "I said, don't let him die. And I, I / I will, I will change and become like the sky…"

The last poem in the book has a strong feeling of form. I looked it up — I think it is a villanelle, like Dylan Thomas' "Do Not Go Gentle into That Good Night." "I've watched you die, and die again, in dreams. / My son, they say in dreams we meet, / That promise met, and one cry. I rhyme in dreams // meant not for me. But not you either!…"

It is a complex book, not only with poems, but with accounts of a fictional medical conference, paragraphs of prose, and quotations about a subject we all feel is important. I got the book just before this column was to be submitted, so obviously I will have to have time to read it carefully and deal with it again.

Neilson is a fan — you could even call him a groupie — of the poetry of M. Travis Lane. He announced the imminent arrival of a book about Lane's work, a big book he said — 200 pages — put out by Frog Hollow Press where he is an editor. His anthology of young and underappreciated New Brunswick poets, including Calvern, is also forthcoming. Although he lives in Ontario, he is from Oromocto, went to the University of New Brunswick, comes back for the university's Poetry Weekend in October, and obviously loves the place.

Also on the docket was a young Riverview poet, Danny Jacobs. He read poems from his first book *Songs That Remind Us of Factories* as well as some new poems, including one on the Gunningsville Bridge, a worthy subject for the discriminations of poetry.

Many poets are naturalists, taking long walks, knowing the Latin names for flora and fauna, identifying birds from their songs, distinguishing between different kinds of ferns. Slightly tongue-in-cheek is the section in Jacob's book titled "Domestic Entomology" with 11 poems, including "Musca domestica" (a.k.a. housefly) and "Culex pipiens" (a.k.a. mosquito). In "Chalybion californicum" he writes: "

> One look
> then getimoff
> getimoff flinch,
> a movie walk-on
> stunned by your own iridescent
> illusive blue-
> quick flash
> of spacecraft turtle wax.

Of course, I had to look this up — the common name is wasp. Getimoff, getimoff.

The kind of synchronicity I love: while I was writing this, a friend emailed me a poem with the line "A nest of wasps buzzing beneath the shingles."

Jacobs nails it in his hymn to potatoes.

> Plump geezer mugs, grubby monks,
>   cosmic eggs for dirt universes,
> there's tired wisdom in your waiting—
>
> hushed dust doldrums before hands
>   go medieval, plop you in pots,
> bifurcate your calm lumped bodies
>
> and salt the post-op.

Quintessential New Brunswick.

A recent post on Facebook named the most overused adjectives in art reviews: exuberant, engaging, exhilarating, oracular, legendary, miraculous, luminous, profound and breath-taking. The critic Brian Bartlett wrote that he shuddered when he read this list. I shuddered too because I had used "breath-taking" recently and

A Great Cloud of Witnessing

used "profound" in the first paragraph here. I didn't change profound because I couldn't think of another word that incorporates technical knowledge with loving appreciation and deep understanding.

Salon, July 18, 2015

Introducing our cultural laureate

In 2015, the City of Fredericton called for applications for the position of a cultural laureate and, in January, a committee met several times to select one. On Monday, Feb. 8, at a regular meeting of city council, the choice was announced.

Anyone involved in Fredericton's literary scene won't have to be introduced to Ian LeTourneau. He enthusiastically attends every book launch, poetry reading, Odd Sundays event, often accompanied by his charming wife and delightful son. But for those who don't know him, let me introduce you to the first Fredericton cultural laureate.

LeTourneau is an accomplished poet with two volumes of poetry, *Defining Range* and *Terminal Moraine* published by prestigious presses: Gaspereau and Thistledown. He's an editor of *The Fiddlehead* and Goose Lane Editions. He's been involved in the Writers' Federation of New Brunswick, the University of New Brunswick Poetry Weekend and the Writers' Union of Canada. He talks on the CBC about local books. You might say that he has been the unofficial poet laureate.

LeTourneau is an experienced instructor, so when he says he would like to conduct workshops at the library for adults and children, I know he can. He's full of ideas about the position: taking people on walks through Odell Park, talking to groups about the importance of arts and creativity, making use of the regular media and the social media.

Although he was born and raised in Dalhousie, he received his BA and his MA from the University of New Brunswick and lives here on the north side of the river. He writes that his vision for his two-year mandate is "to celebrate, engage and inspire." One of his duties will be to compose poems to commemorate various city events.

Here are some lines from his "A Cubist View of the Saint John River."

> Stasis. This morning, the concrete piers
> of the old train bridge transform the river
>
> into a factory of ice:
> a Duchamp, nude and mechanical.
>
> Gliding over the current,
> the river's thin integument cracks.

I had to look up integument — an outer protective layer, hence the ice. I like the image.

I was looking forward to attending Ryan Griffith's play, *Returning Fire*, described by Theatre New Brunswick as "a unique theatre experience told almost entirely through text messaging." Right up until the end I was going to risk the storm, but at last good sense prevailed. The play would work like this: I bought a ticket and then all afternoon I would get text messages from the three actors who were texting each other to arrange a meeting place. At 7:30 p.m., they would finally agree on a place to meet, and I, along with the others in the audience, would join them some place downtown. When I confessed to Ilkay Silk that I couldn't remember how to use my so-called smart phone, she invited me to her place where she also would be getting the text messages. I phoned Bell Aliant to make sure my phone was smart enough to receive such messages. I phoned my grandson to go over details. I was ready and felt "with it." But it snowed and snowed and police said stay off the roads, and finally I decided I shouldn't risk life and especially limbs. In the last week, three of my friends — able young men — have fallen on the ice.

I was especially eager to see *Returning Fire* because I've seen several of Griffith's plays. A couple of years ago I wrote, "He's one of New Brunswick's most talented young playwrights."

But by the next day, the roads and sidewalks were cleared enough for me and my passenger Travis Lane to get to Westminster Books to attend the launch of Shari Andrews' *First Thin Line*, her sixth book of poetry, a handsome volume published by Oberon Press. Fellow poet Lynn Davies gave an excellent introduction to Andrews' reading. I was surprised when I got the volume home to see that many of the pieces were prose poems. When she was reading them to us, I was picturing them as poem poems.

As preface to her reading, she explained that the book explored women's identity. Davies pointed out how often Andrews gives details of the clothes the women wear and the jobs they do. An announcement of the opening of a boarding house in 1838 by Mrs. Atherton inspired these lines from a prose poem: "You wore your funeral suit, navy-blue serge, buttons covered in the same heavy fabric. The row of buttons and your spine were like book ends keeping you upright, when your heart beats too fast, when your hands trembled as you and your accounts were examined by the bank manager."

Riverview's Danny Jacobs has won the grand prize in *PRISM International*'s 2015 creative non-fiction contest with his piece, "Ghostly Transmissions from John D. Rockefeller." I've written about Jacobs' poetry, so I'm eager to read his essay.

Salon, February 15, 2016

Why is it that our province is the last to have a provincial book awards?

A dream has been realized. On April 27, the very first New Brunswick Book Awards in English will be presented at the Atlantic Book Awards Gala as part of the Frye Festival. The possibility of creating these awards has been talked about for years, various stabs have been made at it, but now it is a reality.

New Brunswick's Acadian community has the annual Prix littéraire Antonine-Maillet-Acadie Vie, founded in 1998. Two literary awards are associated with Nova Scotia: the East Coast Literary Awards and the Atlantic Book Awards. I find it a little confusing that Nova Scotia has two groups of awards. Both are open to all books from the Atlantic provinces. The Thomas Raddall Atlantic Fiction Award has twice been won by David Adams Richards, once by Herb Curtis and once by M.T. Dohaney.

Another first is that this will be the first time the Atlantic Book Awards Gala is held in New Brunswick.

The awards are being co-sponsored by the Writers' Federation of New Brunswick and *The Fiddlehead* under chairpersons Rayanne Brennan, former president of the federation, and Ian LeTourneau, secretary of *The Fiddlehead*. Also on the awards committee is Rosalyn Hyslop, a federation director and co-chair of Saint John's Fog Lit Festival, and Ross Leckie, editor of *The Fiddlehead*, professor of English at the University of New Brunswick, and organizer of its poetry weekend.

The shortlist of the nominees for poetry are Phillip Crymble for *Not Even Laughter*, M. Travis Lane for *Crossover* and Michael Pacey for *Electric Affinities*. Lane's book was also on the shortlist for the Governor General's Literary Award for poetry.

The nominees for fiction are R.W. Gray for *Entropic*, Mark Anthony Jarman for *Knife Party at the Hotel Europa*, and Beth Powning for *A Measure of Light*.

The nominees for non-fiction are Nicholas Guitard for *The Lost Wilderness*, Donald Savoie for *What is Government Good At?* and David Sullivan for *Boss Gibson: Lumber King of New Brunswick*.

An innovation for these awards is that self-published books are eligible. When LeTourneau was asked on the CBC how the committee found the books to be considered, he said they sent out notices to all the publishers to ask them to submit books. I asked him how self-published *Boss Gibson: Lumber King of New Brunswick* was discovered, and he said he heard Sullivan being interviewed on the radio, the book sounded interesting, so LeTourneau himself submitted it. The committee asked the Writers' Federation to put out a notice to its members to submit self-published books. The Writers' Union of Canada has recently established a policy whereby writers of self-published books will be considered for membership. The literary world is turning.

LeTourneau was recently named the first cultural laureate of Fredericton. At his induction, he said that two of his dreams are to have a literary festival created in Fredericton and to have the New Brunswick Book Awards ceremony come to it one year. Moncton has the Frye Festival, established in 2000, now well-known across Canada. Saint John has the newer but successful Fog Lit Festival. In the past, the Maritime Writers' Workshop served as a literary festival with readings every night and lectures during the day, both open to the public. The annual University of New Brunswick Poetry Weekend in October has a festival-like atmosphere. The Alden Nowlan Literary Festival was held for four years on a weekend from 2001.

I've mentioned several of the books in this space. I even bragged a little that Michael Pacey's *Electric Affinities* was dedicated to me.

A Great Cloud of Witnessing

Why is it that our province is the last one to have provincial book awards? Part of the reason is financial. None of these award winners will receive any money.[6] The other provincial awards bring money with them. The Thomas Raddall prize winner receives $25,000. Other prizes are smaller—$200 or $300. The Prix littéraire Antonine-Maillet-Acadie Vie winner receives $4,000.

I will speculate—perhaps wildly—that part of the reason may be a hesitation to blow our own horns. If this is so, I wonder why. Selective migration? Our sports heroes come back home when their careers are done, but they don't swagger around. If I found myself at an event with Matt Stairs, I would feel free to introduce myself and shake his hand. David Adams Richards is one of the most famous living Canadian writers, but he too came home and does not swagger around. Maybe this is a ridiculous generalization, but New Brunswickers seem to be gifted with humility.

I love the story our former premier and former Canadian ambassador to the United States Frank McKenna told about living in the embassy in Washington. He had to get used to not taking his dishes out to the kitchen after a meal.

The books up for awards are not inferior books. They have been highly reviewed. They would hold their own in any province's book awards competition.

Salon, March 12, 2016

---

[6] The organizers managed to fundraise and award $500 prizes in each category.

Large crowd of writers honoured

Writers wake up about this time of year from their winter hibernation at their desks, which must explain why in the period of one week, they gathered together for three events. On May 24, the second annual New Brunswick Book Awards ceremony drew a large crowd of writers, publishers and their friends to the University of New Brunswick's Memorial Hall. The Fiddlehead Poetry Prize was given to M. Travis Lane for her monumental work, *The Witch of the Inner Wood*, a collection of her long poems gathered by Shane Neilson. Poets usually get by with slim volumes. A 377-page hardbound book is reserved for the best of them. The Mrs. Dunster's Award for Fiction was given to Kerry Lee Powell for *Willem de Kooning's Paintbrush*. The book has won or been nominated for four other prizes. The non-fiction prize was given to Bobbi-Jean MacKinnon for *Shadow of a Doubt*. A highlight of the evening was the children's book prize, awarded to Jennifer McGrath for her *The Snow Knows*. Sisters Colleen Kitts-Goguen and Wendy Kitts sponsored the award in honour of their mother Alice Kitts. Wendy read the citation, and although she didn't break down, her voice was full of emotion. Two of the four winners were published by Goose Lane Editions. The book award project is a joint venture of *The Fiddlehead* magazine and the Writers' Federation of New Brunswick.

David Adams Richards gave the keynote address[7]: several people have commented to me on how good a speech it was. It was in the form of a memoir whose theme was his hitchhiking to Fredericton from Newcastle when he was seventeen to read his poetry and fiction to those he thought would appreciate them. His friends thought he was crazy, and his mother worried when he was hitchhiking home on January nights. I'd never been on the road to Newcastle at that time and so I didn't really understand the dangers he'd faced until I heard his accounts of the trip. My second winter here, however, I took my three children and my

---

7   This keynote, "Strange Comfort," was later published in *The Fiddlehead* No. 274 (Winter 2018), pp. 5-8.

friend's three sliding. I had to carry the two littlest ones back up the hill to the car, and on the way I realized, terrified, that I might not have the strength. I never underestimated the dangers of a New Brunswick winter again.

Last weekend in Saint John the Writers' Federation held its annual general meeting, with readings, workshops, the awarding of the literary competition prizes and the usual warm camaraderie. M. Travis Lane and I received bouquets, she being the past Honourary President and I being the present one. This is a little strange because we are both originally Americans who came with our husbands to Fredericton and embraced New Brunswick with a passion.

As I sat there and heard people of all ages read from their work, I was content. Many of the writers said they had always wanted to write but began after they retired. They seemed happy with what they had produced, fiction and memoirs mostly but also a few poems. I was happy for the many young—under retirement age—writers. About 450,000 Anglophones reside in the province, and the federation has about 350 members. Most of the writers I know don't belong so—extrapolating—I'm surprised by the percentage of New Brunswickers who write. How could this be? I was on the founding committee of the organization and often get annoyed—why does my baby have to live on such a pittance?

The winner of the Kyle memorial fiction prize was the young fisherman Orry O'Neil from Salmon Beach with the first story he'd ever written. I've been around long enough to know that people who put their minds to writing by working hard, crafting many drafts, enlisting the help of an editor, reading widely in the genre they want to create can produce a good manuscript. But some people just do have the gift.

When someone takes good care of your baby, you appreciate it immensely. That's why I feel grateful to the executive directors over the years, Anna Mae Snider for one, who shepherded it at the beginning and for many years; Gwen Martin who worked four times the hours she was getting paid for to bring it back from near collapse; and Cathy Fynn who recently has sustained it. The evening literary soirée was dedicated to Rosi Jory, much beloved of the federation, she an exemplar of the warm camaraderie.

Last Thursday at the public library, "Word Feast" announced its program for the Fredericton literary festival to be held in September. Under the leadership of Fredericton's cultural laureate, this first festival will include readings in the schools, a Saturday for children at the Beaverbrook Art Gallery, noon-time speakers at various restaurants, lectures, music, workshops, book tables, ending with a gala Odd Sunday of readings by the members of all the writing groups in Fredericton.

Salon, June 3, 2017

The literary life

I've been overwhelmed lately with literary life, listening to writers and accumulating many books. First there was the weeklong Word Feast and then the University of New Brunswick's Poetry Weekend. More of this latter event next Saturday.

Fredericton's first literary festival, Word Feast, was a success, exceeding its founders hopes in the numbers attending, in adhering to its budget, and in the enthusiasm at the various proceedings. Because I was on the committee, I attended most of the events, and hosted two, so I know whereof I speak.

A highlight of the festival was the ceremony giving Robert Gibbs the first Community Impact Award, "recognizing a substantial contribution to Fredericton's literary community." Gibbs' own work is masterful indeed—his poetry, his fiction, his non-fiction. Poet and critic Brian Bartlett writes in the Word Feast program, "The poetry of Robert Gibbs plumbs depths of insight and imagination with an appealing mix of the casual and the polished, the idiomatic and the freshly turned. His strongest poems are among the most distinctive written in Canada during the past half a century."

Introducing Gibbs, Michael Pacey gave an erudite explication of his poetry: "To place the poetry of Robert Gibbs in the realist tradition of Fred Cogswell and Alden Nowlan is to do his work a disservice—in the sense that his poems display equal affinities with New Brunswick metaphysicals Alfie Bailey and M. Travis Lane. Yes, his work frequently focuses on sensuous delight and quotidian detail, but it also foregrounds language, especially wit and inventiveness in the use of language." Jeremy Gilmer wrote, "It was an amazing, complex, rich and deeply engaging talk."

Gibbs has always been generous with his time and energy, agreeing to comment on the manuscripts of many poets before they send their poems off for publication; they all value his scrutiny. He's long been an editor of *The Fiddlehead* and a beloved professor of creative writing. His humility, and indeed the whole way he lives his life, have been an inspiration for me.

Another highlight was the grand turnout of dozens of local writers for "Odd Sunday." David Watts inspired this idea — asking seven writers' groups in the city to send its members to read in the Chickadee room of the public library. Lucille Caseley's splendid poetry, usually hidden, was uncovered there.

An innovation — and this must be a first for a literary festival — was to hold an event in the Forest Hill cemetery, with readings of the work of the poets buried there. Jane Tims, the organizer, is already adding items for next year. I just found out about two more poets buried there.

Fredericton comes late to the literary festival game. Fog Lit in Saint John just held its fifth festival. The Northrup Frye Festival was founded 17 years ago. The pre-eminent Canadian literary festival, Harbourfront International in Toronto, has been going for 43 years. Ian LeTourneau, appointed two years ago by the City Council to the first Cultural Laureateship, wanted a way to leave a legacy of his term. The festival was his vision, and although run entirely by volunteers, he assured that it be packed full to the brim with activities. A member of the Fredericton committee, Keith Helmuth, publisher of Chapel Street Editions out of Woodstock, latched onto the idea and ran a Word Feast festival for the upper Saint John River Valley. I hope the two can be fully meshed next year.

At the King Street Ale House, Don McKay gave one of the best readings I've ever heard. He's a powerful reader, paradoxically because he gives himself no airs. It helps that his poems are full of wit. His prose piece had me laughing hard, the kind of laugh that empties worries and pessimisms.

During the week, events were held in the schools, and on Saturday morning a grand event for kids occurred at the Beaverbrook Art

Gallery. Zach Hapeman was in charge of the children's programs, but he also was present everywhere else, especially setting up microphones. His getting the mics to work so well for the readings was miraculous.

If you wonder how I survived a week of so much activity, one reason was that because many events were held in restaurants I ate well. My literary life of the last 50 years was flashing before me, inspiring and energizing me. Jo-Anne Elder wrote, "The festival really perked me up." Many others made similar comments.

I did have to miss the launch of Wayne Curtis and Heather Browne's books of short stories at Westminster, coinciding as it did with a festival activity, but they both kindly gave me copies. Wayne said 35 people attended.

A few weeks ago, I wondered why three murals of Fred Ross had disappeared. I said I was going to start a conspiracy theory. Carol Taylor wrote to tell me that Ross' portrait of G. Forbes Elliot had also disappeared.

Salon, October 7, 2017

A bolt of poetry among grey clouds

Poetry Weekend at the University of New Brunswick is a two-day marathon reading by 60 poets in six groups of ten. The weekend was initiated by Ross Leckie 14 years ago for his friends and students, but it has by word of mouth become known all over Canada. Most of the audience consists of the poets doing the readings and their partners. I find it enormously enlightening: what makes a good poem, what a lousy one.

A certain uniformity did amuse me. Most of the poets dressed in black, carried a bottle of water to the podium even though they were only going to read two poems, announced that the poem "is called:" before they gave its title, as if the poem had given itself the title. Many of the lesser poets read in the "poetry-reading" cadence that sounds like a monk's chant. I wondered if they heard that cadence in their mind's ear when they were creating the poem.

At one of the sessions, I began to have an unearthly feeling, as if I were living in a world consisting entirely of words — words that had nothing to do with reality.

The poetry-reading cadence has the effect — on me at least — of making the poetry seem unfelt. Inauthentic. I know this isn't true because often before the poet began to read the work, he or she would vividly describe the experience that prompted the poem. The use of the f word would snap me out of my hypnotised state. I fear that one day the word will become so common that it will cease to be the snapper it is.

Why do I attend these sessions? Sometimes in the winter there will be many days of grey changeless weather and then comes a massive storm or a hot sunlit day. So too into these mind-numbing words comes a bolt of lightning.

The performance of a work should convey to the audience that the poet believes in the words they are spouting. Satire doesn't work well off the page. Making fun of someone or something else doesn't, but making fun of yourself works beautifully. Jenna Albert read a crack-of-thunder poem about an embarrassing situation — she admitted that reading it took courage. Madeline Bassnett is at a firing range in San Francisco shooting with a "ladies hand gun" but her male partner has a Glock. *Glock*.

I notice that poems about mothers often feature unlovely details, but about grandparents the poet inevitably uses happy details.

One of the six sessions was particularly electric. Almost every poet in the session got me holding my breath. Ross Leckie's public persona was so charmingly humble, self-deprecating, but then he read, modestly but beautifully, his well-wrought thoughtful poems. This is what poetry should be, I think. Carol Steel did likewise.

Halfway through that session Sue Sinclair read poems so superb that I thought, I'm going to write a poem. A couple of lines formed in my head. I bought her latest book, *Heaven's Thieves*. I'm reading it slowly, several poems at a time. "A caribou lopes slantwise / across the scree belly of the mountain. / The choir of its antlers sits upright." When Leckie retires next year, Sinclair will become the czar of creative writing at the university, the editor of *The Fiddlehead*, and the general poetic inspiration for the province. She certainly inspired me. Even though she had been in Fredericton as a graduate student and then as the writer-in-residence, I think I hadn't heard her read before. She recently completed a PhD at the University of Toronto in philosophy, writing about beauty and ethics.

I was told several times that many of the poets were influenced by John Ashbery. I don't remember having read anything by him. Had Bill read him? Do I have a book of his poetry? Ashbery recently died at age 90.

The Friday night launch of Goose Lane Editions' *Collected Poems of Alden Nowlan*—all 700 pages of it—kicked off Poetry Weekend. It's the "Collected" not the "Complete" because although it contains every poem that Nowlan published in his short life, it doesn't have the unpublished ones.

The editor, Brian Bartlett, says that another volume could be made of the poems now languishing in manuscript in the University of Calgary archives. The volume has been meticulously edited by Bartlett with an erudite introductory essay. On pages 17-21 Bartlett discusses the placement of words in Nowlan's poems—illuminating. A must for a new poet.

He sent out word before the launch that anyone could read their favourite Nowlan poem at the event; 24 responded from all over—Toronto, Halifax, Alma, Woodstock—to pay homage. He sprung a surprise—Nowlan himself read. Everyone's favourite, "He Sits Down on the Floor of a School for the Retarded," was lovingly delivered by Allan Cooper to end the evening. Not a dry eye in the hall.

Salon, October 14, 2017

About the Cover Painting

"Nancy's Living Room with Nancy:"
oil on canvas, 25 ¼ x 32 ¼ inches; 2022

Two years ago, acclaimed artist Stephen May looked from my hall toward my front window and said, "This would make a good painting." He arrived the next afternoon with drop cloth, easel, canvas, and oils. He painted from 1 to 4 and this miracle was born.

Recently he said, "It doesn't happen very often that I know before I start that it's going to be a good painting, but it did this time."

This painting is perfect for the cover of this book because on those walls hang works by many local artists — David McKay, Philip Iverson, Karen Estabrooks, among others. On that leather couch, lively discussions have been held with writers from near and far — Brian Bartlett, Michael Pacey, Hugh Hood, Carol Shields, Dale Estey, and countless others.

Oberon Press launches were held in this room for the books of David Adams Richards, Joseph Sherman, and Ann Copeland. For twenty years a writers' group has met here.

A few years ago, on his first visit, John Leroux — historian of architecture and currently curator at the Beaverbrook Art Gallery — sat in that blue chair and exclaimed, "You have a Mid-Century Modern house," and explained the room's characteristics.

Stephen May's painting now hangs on the wall of this room.

Nancy Bauer
October 2024

About the Author

Nancy Bauer is the author of five novels, including *Samara the Wholehearted* and *Wise-Ears*, three published by Goose Lane Editions and two by Oberon Press. Her collection of short stories, *Hammering at the Door*, will be published in 2025 by Chapel Street Editions.

She has been an instructor in the English Department at the University of New Brunswick, teaching courses in creative writing, the literature of Atlantic Canada, and English as a second language. She was a writer in residence at Bemidji State University in Minnesota, Mount Saint Vincent University in Nova Scotia, and the University of New Brunswick. She has been an instructor at over 30 writers' workshops in the Maritimes.

Nancy was an organizer and founding board member of the Maritime Writers' Workshop, the Writers' Federation of New Brunswick, and the Word Feast Literary Festival in Fredericton. She received the Alden Nowlan Award for Excellence in the Literary Arts in 1999, a Canadian Senate Medal in 2017, and Community Impact Award in 2020. She has been an active member of the Wilmot United Church, serving on its communications committee and as chair of the Wilmot Writers' Group.

Her 37-year career as an arts journalist is detailed in the editor's introduction to this book. Nancy has written the following about how it all came to pass:

> When the poet Joseph Sherman became editor of *ArtsAtlantic*, he asked me to write about art in New Brunswick. I knew very little about art and had never written articles about anything like this. My first assignment was to write about David Silverberg's engravings. I learned then that as a result of my education at Mount Holyoke College, I could educate myself. I hope the arts journalism that was the result

of this discovery still communicates the excitement of my ongoing engagement with this kind of creative writing. I've conducted many interviews, attended innumerable book launches, symphony concerts, craft fairs, and art openings. I've communed with several hundred mesmerizing creators. The richness of culture in the Maritime provinces still boggles my mind.

About the Editor

Ian LeTourneau is a poet, editor, and publisher based in Fredericton, NB. He is the author of two collections of poetry, *Terminal Moraine* (Thistledown Press, 2008) and *Metadata from a Changing Climate* (Gaspereau Press, forthcoming 2025). By day he is the managing editor of *The Fiddlehead* and *Studies in Canadian Literature* at the University of New Brunswick, and by night he is publisher of chapbooks at Emergency Flash Mob Press.

Index

Symbols

252 Stanley St. 201

A

Abbey Theatre 79
Aberdeen Cultural Centre 45, 143
Acadia 43–47
Acadian artist 36, 42, 45, 64
Acadian Association of Professional Artists in New Brunswick 42
Acadian culture 42
Acadian moment 43
Acadian New Brunswickers 65
Acadians 43–44, 64
Access Copyright 158
Acorn, Milton 83
Agee, James 102
Albert County 56
Albert, Jenna 234
Alden Nowlan Festival 68
Alden (Rick Merrill) 169
Allen, Sandra 33
Allpress, Pam 27
Alma 235
Amantrout, Rae 208
Amazon [online store] 85, 91–92
Amphibian (Carla Gunn) 155
Anderson, Mia 52
Anderson, Vivienne 74
Andrews, Shari 68, 223
Angel Gabriel [ship] 24
anglophone arts community 64
Anonymous Mesdemoiselles (Michael Pacey) 206
Ans, Tom 163
Anthony Powell 91
Anthropocene Epoch 110
Apollinaire's Bookshoppe 94
Aramaic 191
Armstrong, Terry 182
Art Gallery of Ontario 45
Arts and Crafts movement 215
ArtsAtlantic i, 26, 38, 61, 64, 70, 74, 80, 135, 142–143, 148, 151, 207, 239
ArtsNB 129
Ashbery, John 234
Ashfield, Keith 157
Atkinson, Carolyn 131
The Atlantic Advocate 4, 7
Atlantic Book Awards Gala 224
Atlantic Canada 82–83, 239
Atlantic Canada's 100 Greatest Books (Nimbus Press) 128
Atlantic provinces 70, 74, 143, 224
The Atlantic Provinces Book Review 74, 77, 135
At the Back of the North Wind (George MacDonald) 56
The Attic Owl 92
Atwood, Margaret 158
Auden, W. H. 57, 152
Avalon Peninsula 109
Ayala, Francisco 115

B

Back Roads to Far Towns (Basho) 180
Badani, Bernie 33
Bailey, Alfred G. 20–25, 57, 80, 119, 164, 230
Bailey, Loring 21
Balcolm, Leslie 214
ballet companies 88
Ball, John 170
A Band of My Ancestors (Kent Thompson) 207
Bangor 92
Baptist 23, 143
The Baptist Church 12
Barry, Sebastian 132
Barthes, Roland 46
Bartibog 6
Bartlett, Andrew 33
Bartlett, Brian i, 27, 29, 32, 58, 97, 104, 130–131, 150, 160, 186, 199, 206, 219, 230, 235, 237
Barton, John 155, 203
Basho 180

Bateson, Mary Catherine 132
Bauer, Tommy 136
Bauer, William [Bill] i, 18, 27, 28, 29, 31–32, 185, 206, 211
Bay du Vin 6
Bayley, John 137
Beairsto, Ellen 217
Beaulieu, Roland 34, 39
Beauty: The Invisible Embrace (John O'Donohue) 211–212
Beaverbrook Art Gallery iii, 40, 61, 70–71, 75, 98, 112–113, 132, 134, 153, 158–159, 172, 229, 231–232, 237
Lord Beaverbrook 23
Beaverbrook Residence 57
Beaverbrook Scholar 57
Béchard, Deni Y. 191
Behan, Brendan 7
Being Charlie (Brian Bartlett) 131
Beirne, Gerry 193
Bellisle Bay 73
Bemidji State University i, 239
Ben and Me (Cameron Gunn) 155, 191
Benjamin Books 91, 93
Bertin, Johanna 164
Bertrand, Anne 88
Betts, John 180
Betts, Rolene 178, 180
The Bible 12, 29
Bick, Julie 92
Big Sevogle 6
bilingual 64–66, 128
Birney, Earle 59
Birthday (Joseph Sherman) 207
Bishop, Elizabeth 62
Bishop Medley 80
Bjerkelund, Virginia 203
Black Box Theatre 175–177
Black Horse Tavern 6
Blackmore, R. D. 11
Black River Bridge 6
Blake, William 14
Bleak House (Charles Dickens) 132
Bliss Carman Poetry Society 22, 57
Blithe Spirit (Noel Coward) 171
Blood Ties (David Adams Richards) 5–8, 29

Blue Interior (Molly Lamb Bobak) 153
Blythe, Will 102
Bobak, Bruno 75, 80, 94, 119, 134, 196, 206
Bobak, Molly Lamb iii, 70, 134, 151, 152
Bonnard, Pierre 152
Book Inn 155
Bookmark [bookstore] 91
book reviews 73, 76–78
The Book Room 93
Books in Canada 19
Book*hug [BookThug] 94
Borders Books 91–92
Borges, Jorge Luis 139
Boss Gibson: Lumber King of New Brunswick (David Sullivan) 225
Boston Globe 92
Boston, Stephen 33
Bowie, Chuck 199
Bowman, Judy 121
The Box of Delights (John Masefield) 56
Bradbury, Elspeth 80
Bradbury, Ray 80
Bradley, Michael 104
Brautigan, Richard 50
Brave New Words 50
Breaking the Word Barrier: Stories of Adults Learning to Read (Marilyn Lerch and Angela Ranson) 125
Brebner, Mary 154–155, 155
Brennan, Ann 52, 125, 154, 165, 201
Brennan, Rayanne 125, 155, 165, 201, 224
Brewer, David 214
Brewster, Dwight 190
Brewster, Elizabeth iii, 17, 22, 32, 184, 186, 190
The Bricklin: An Automotive Fantasy (Ledoux & Cole) 171
British Columbia 140
Brittain, Miller 75, 80, 128
Brizendine, Louann 115
Brody, Selma 33, 198
Broken Jaw Press 66
Brother's Insomnia (Brian Bartlett) 206
Brown, Douglas Arthur 195
Browne, Heather 68, 232

Index

Browning, Elizabeth Barrett 180
browsing 86, 91
Brunswick String Quartet 135
Buddhism 51
Buddhist 51
Burke, Edmund 12
Burnaby, Frederick 24
Burne-Jones and Morris company 216
Burns, Bob 33
Burns, Rick 33, 36, 64, 71, 79, 124
businessization of the arts world 88
Butcher, Evelyn 155
Butler, Edith 47
Butlin, Ron 27
Button, Marshall 176

C

Caecilia [typeface] 85
Caesar, Lance 194
Caines, Lauren 194
Caissie, Judy 164
Call It Sleep (Henry Roth) 148
Calvern, Allison 66, 202, 217
Calvino, Italo 139
Cambridge University 56–57
The Cameraman (Bill Gaston) 50
Cameron, Elspeth 52
Cameron, Marian 33
Campbell, Ted 80
Campfire Girls 12
Campobello Island 176
Canada 1, 4–5, 13, 15, 17, 18–19, 23, 25–26, 32, 48, 52, 70, 74, 82, 88, 91, 93, 134, 155, 178, 196, 200, 208, 225, 230, 233
Canada Council of the Arts 5, 41, 42, 59, 74, 90, 94, 104, 159, 172, 207
Canadian Army 71
Canadian Art 132
Canadian Broadcasting Corporation [CBC] 28, 44, 54, 59, 73, 196, 203, 221, 225
CBC Literary Competition 59
CBC radio 73
CBC TV 73
Canadian Forestry corps 12

The Canadian Forum 5
Canadian Historical Association Regional History Award 82
Canadian literature 3, 13, 208
Canadian music 173
Canadians 69
Canadian Senate Medal 239
The Canterbury Tales (Geoffrey Chaucer) 164
Carman, Bliss 20–22, 57, 79, 119, 184, 214
Carman-Roberts years 20
Carnegie Foundation 21
Caron, Rodolphe 39
Carr, Deborah 155, 182
The Case Against Owen Williams (Allan Donaldson) 155
Caseley, Lucille 231
Catedral de Santiago de Compostela 113
Cattley [Professor R.E.D.] 57
Centre Communautaire 64
Centreville 11
Cezanne, Paul 152
Chalmers, Robert 204
Change in a Razor-backed Season (Michael deBeyer) 98
chapbook movement 215
Chapbooks, New Brunswick 201
Chapel Street Editions 231, 239
Chapters [bookstore chain] 91–92
Charette, Luc 64, 129, 143
Charlotte Street Arts Centre 65, 68, 71
Chaucer, Geoffrey 164
Chestnut Canoe factory 124
Chestnut Complex 124
Chevalier des Arts et Lettres 42
Chiasson, Herménégilde 42–47, 65, 72, 125, 134, 143
Chocolate River poets 61
Christian Scientist 56
Christina Sabat Memorial Lecture i
A Christmas Carol (Charles Dickens) 170
Clark, Joan 140, 188, 200
Clark, Peter D. 95
Claus, Jo Anne 7, 74, 172, 207
Clayden, Gerry 104
Clayden, Leta 104

245

Cobden-Sanderson, Thomas James 215
Cockburn, Leslie 191
Cockburn, Robert 206
Coffey, Sherry 217
Cogswell, Fred 3, 10, 22, 24, 67, 83–84, 170, 205, 208, 230
Colbert, François 88
Cole, Allen 171
Coleridge, Samuel Taylor 146
Collected Poems of Alden Nowlan 235
Collicutt, Carol 124
Collins, Billy 89
Colson, Ted 27
Comeau, Louise 157
The Coming of Winter (David Adams Richards) 3–8, 194
Community Impact Award 230, 239
Composing a Life (Mary Catherine Bateson) 132
Condon, Tom 71, 154
The Conflict of European and Eastern Algonkian Culture, 1504-1700 (Alfred G. Bailey) 23
Connelly, Karen 78
Cook, Greg 103, 129, 200
Cooper, Allan 154, 235
Cooper, Kelly 164, 182
Copeland, Ann 18, 32, 51, 141, 201, 237
Corey, John 152
Cormier, René 38
Corn Hill Nursery 163
Costco 92
Costello, Ralph 55
Coulter, Claire 146
The Country of the Pointed Firs (Sarah Orne Jewett) 212
Coward, Noel 171
Crane, Stephen 12
Crawford, Terry 18, 32
Creaghan, Laurence 33
Creasy, Sir Edward 11
creation grant 90
The Creative Habit (Twyla Tharp) 106
Creative Moments in the Culture of the Maritime Provinces (Alfred G. Bailey) 20
Cronin, Ray 74

Crossover (M. Travis Lane) 224
Crymble, Phillip 224
Cultural Development Branch 35, 36, 38
cultural laureate 221–223, 225, 229, 231
Cultural Laureateship 231
Culture and Nationality (Alfred G. Bailey) 20
curating 47, 70, 153
A Cure for All Diseases (Peter Thomas) 84
Cures for Hunger (Deni Y. Béchard) 191
Curtis, Wayne 95, 121, 154–155, 193, 232

D

The Daily Gleaner 29, 74, 130, 172, 186, 197
Dalhousie [New Brunswick] 221
Dalhousie University 79
Dali, Salvador 112–114
Dalkey Archives 91
Dance Fredericton 48
Dancers at Night (David Adams Richards) 5, 9
A Dance to the Music of Time (Anthony Powell) 91
Daniel Deronda (George Eliot) 117
Daniells, Roy 21
Dashner, Jordan 171
Davies, Gwen 214
Davies, Lynn 98, 193, 195, 209, 223
D'Avray, Marshall 21
Dawes, David 33
Dawes, Kwame 58
A Death in the Family (James Agee) 102
The Death of Little Simon (David Adams Richards) 8
deBeyer, Michael 98, 193
Defining Range (Ian LeTourneau) 221
Deichmann, Erica 80
Deichmann, Kjeld 80
DeMille, George 203
Dennis, Bruce 38
Department of History at UNB 22
deportation 43
DesRochers, Alfred 12
de Staël, Nicolas 152

Index

deVigny, Alfred 13
Dickens, Charles 12, 170
Dickinson, Emily 199
Different Minds: Living with Alzheimer Disease (Lorna Drew) 138
Doctorow, E. L. 172
Doerr, Harriet 117
Dohaney, M.T. 67, 138, 193, 224
The Dollar Woman (Walter Learning and Alden Nowlan) 175
Donaldson, Allan 67, 122, 155, 191–192
Donaldson, Marjory 80, 94, 134, 206
The Douglas Notebooks (Christine Eddie) 191
Dove [typeface] 215
Drew, Lorna 138
Dudek, Louis 184
Duguay, Calixe 47
Duguay, Guy 143
Duncan, Sara 25
Duplacey, James 173

E

East Centreville 10
East Coast Literary Awards 224
e-books 85
The Eclectic Reading Club [ECR] 178–180
Eddie, Christine 191–192
Ediacara Hills 109
Ediacaran Period 109–110
Edmundston 121
ekphrastic poetry 70
Elder, Jo-Anne 127–128, 193, 232
Eldridge, Keith 165
Electric Affinities (Michael Pacey) 224
Elephant [bindery] 215
Eliot, George 92, 117
Eliot, T. S. 22, 57
Elliot, G. Forbes 232
Emergency Flash Mob Press 241
Emerson, Ralph Waldo 21, 107, 186
English 23, 36, 40, 43, 44, 47, 64, 66, 72, 83, 86, 127, 128–129, 134, 191, 224, 239
Entropic (R.W. Gray) 225

ERC tradition [The Eclectic Reading Club] 179
Espresso Book Machine 155
The Essential Dorothy Roberts (Brian Bartlett) 186
The Essential Haiku: Versions of Basho, Buson, and Issa (Robert Hass) 131
The Essential Robert Gibbs (Brian Bartlett) 186
Estabrooks, Karen 199, 237
Estey, Dale 27, 30, 40, 52, 94, 140, 200, 207, 237
Estok, Michael 28, 148
Eternal Life: A New Vision (John Shelby Spong) 132
Etheridge, David 206
Evans, Valerie 154
Everson, Ronald 184
Ewing, Juliana 131

F

Façade 64
Falkenstein, Len 145–147
Farnon, Jeffrey 12
Fawcett, Brian 62
The Female Brain (Louann Brizendine) 115
Fenderson, Gail 199
Ferrari, Leo 6, 138, 170
The Fever (Wallace Shawn) 146
Fiction Writers Circle 191
Fiddlehead Poetry Books 13, 83
The Fiddlehead Poetry Prize 227
The Fiddlehead 13, 22, 24, 57, 71, 82–83, 109, 139, 148–150, 190, 196, 208, 221, 224, 227, 231, 234, 241
Fifteen Decisive Battles of the World (Sir Edward Creasy) 11
First Step (Michael Pacey) 160
First Thin Line (Shari Andrews) 223
Fitch, Sheree 48, 52, 140, 154–155, 173, 181
Flanagan, Andy 195
Flat Earth Society 6, 104, 149
Flemming, Aida 29
Flora, Write this Down (Nancy Bauer) i

247

Florenceville 125
Fog Lit [Saint John literay festival] 224, 225, 231
Footnotes to the Book of Job (Elizabeth Brewster) 190
Ford's Mill 121
Forest Hill Cemetery 184, 231
Forrestall, Anne Cheverie 27
Forum 87 34, 37
"The Four Johns" 51
francophone arts community 64
Frankenstein: The Man Who Became God (Walter Learning and Alden Nowlan) 175
Fraser, Ray 6, 75, 104, 128
Fredericton i–ii, 1, 3–4, 9, 17–19, 20–26, 31, 34, 38, 48, 50, 52, 54, 58, 61, 64–65, 68, 70–71, 74, 79, 83, 91–92, 94, 97, 113, 121–122, 124, 130, 133–134, 145, 152, 155, 157–158, 168, 173–174, 181, 184–185, 191–194, 196, 200, 202–203, 205, 209, 221, 225, 227–231, 234
Fredericton literary festival [Word Feast] 229, 239
Fredericton Playhouse 124, 175
Fredericton Public Library 61, 173
French 13, 36, 40, 42, 44, 66, 72, 83, 127, 128–129, 156
French Canadians 43
French terroir tradition 13
Freud, Sigmund 57
Frog Hollow Press 91, 218
Frost, Robert 57, 89, 150
Frye Festival 224–225, 231
Fry, George 140, 142, 171, 198
Fry, Molly 177
Fugitive Pieces (Anne Michaels) 132
Fulton, Pam 199
Fynn, Cathy 229

G

Galerie d'art Louise-et-Reuben-Cohen 129
Gallant, Yvon 64
Gallery 78 118, 134, 143, 151
Gallery Connexion ii, 41, 64, 71, 79, 94, 124–126, 132
Gambino, Jose 113
Gammon, Carolyn 190
Gaspereau Press 66, 241
Gaston, Bill 48, 134, 162
Gaston, Dede 48–49
Gautreau, Kim 121
Gibbs, Donald 137
Gibbs, Robert (Bob) i, 19, 22, 26–28, 32, 51, 53–59, 63, 80, 107, 119, 122, 132, 137, 140, 143, 148–149, 160, 162, 169, 184, 186, 190, 199, 206, 208, 210, 230
Gibson, Bethany 187–189
Gildiner, Catherine 132
Gillies, Jane 164
Gilmer, Jeremy 230
Gimli [Manitoba] 95
Ginsberg, Allen 208
Ginsberg, Louis 208
Ginsberg, Morris 22
Glencross, Charlotte 71
Globe and Mail 62, 77, 133, 158
Goggin, Kathie 154, 164
Golden Age of Acadian art 43
Gool, Réshard 83
Goose Lane Editions i, 58, 66, 75, 83, 88, 123, 125, 134, 139, 173, 191, 193–194, 221, 227, 235, 239
Gould, Roy 121
government funding of the arts 36
Governor-General's Award 25, 52, 82, 139
Grace, Sassimint 181, 199
Grace, Sherrill 106, 187
Grady, Jeanine 33
Graff, Terry 112
Grant, Brigid Toole 206
Graser, Toby 129, 198
Gray, R.W. 225
Green, Joseph 19
The Green Party 157, 159
Grenon, Barry 164
Griffith, Ryan 222
Guggenheim Foundation 104
Guitard, Nicholas 225
Gunn, Cameron 155, 191–192

Index

Gunn, Carla 155, 182–183, 200
Gunningsville Bridge 218

H

Hadfield, Ann 179
haikus (Lin Yutang) 13
Haliburton-Howe era 20
Halifax 20, 45, 50, 67, 91, 93, 203, 235
Hall, Linda 182
Hall's Bookstore 18
Hammock, Janet 156
Hampton 80
Hannah, Don 170
Hapeman, Zach 232
Harbourfront International [literary festival] 61, 65, 231
Hardy, Anne 17
Hardy, Thomas 12
Hare, Madeline 106
Harkins High School 6
Harlequin 89, 173
Harper, Stephen 157–158
Harriet Irving Library 118, 154, 214
Harvor, Beth 19
Harysym, Sally 33
Hass, Robert 131
Hatfield, Richard 34, 135, 157, 171
Hatt, Rick 33
Hawkes, Peggy 199, 206
Hawkes, Robert 160, 199, 203
Heath Steele Mines 6
Heaven's Thieves (Sue Sinclair) 234
Heiti, Matthew 146
Helmuth, Keith 231
Helwig, David 140
Heraclitus 97
Hess, Harry 109
Hess, Paul 27
Hide and Go Sell (Chris Nyarady) 170, 171
Hill Brothers neighborhood 200
Hill, Grace Livingston 12–13
Hill, Rev. James 178
Hockey New Brunswick 122
Hocking, W. E. 91
Holy Grail Across the Atlantic (Michael Bradley) 104
Home: Chronicle of a North Country Life (Beth Powning) 179
Hood, Hugh 32, 132, 200, 237
Hood, Noreen 206
Hooper, Kathy 129, 198
Hopkins, Gerard Manley 57
Houle, Jennifer 164
Hovey, Richard 214
how the gods pour tea 193–195, 209
Huggan, Isabel 52
Humphrey, Jack 80
Husk (Corey Redekop) 191
Hyslop, Rosalyn 224

I

I am Danielle Steele (Bill Gaston) 50
Ice House i, 3, 58, 79
Ice House Gang 5, 26–27, 79–80, 149, 194, 205
icehouse poetry [Goose Lane Editions] 194
The Imperialist (Sara Duncan) 25
Imperial Theatre 71
The Incredible Murder of Cardinal Tosca (Walter Learning and Alden Nowlan) 175
independent bookstores 91
Ingram, Anne 74
inky poet 160–162
International Women's Day 115
internet 73, 91, 93, 95, 133, 185
Iris and her Friends (John Bayley) 137
Irving, Daphne 143
I've Always Felt Sorry for Decimals (Robert Gibbs) 19, 28, 54
Iverson, Philip 237

J

Jablanczy, Alex 27
Jacobs, Danny 218, 223
James, Henry 100, 118
Jarman, Mark Anthony 200, 225
Jesus' "hard sayings" 176
The Jesus Sayings (Rex Weyler) 132

249

Johnson, Brian 124
Johnston, Wayne 106, 134
Jones, Ted 185–186
Jory, Rosi 229
Journal of Pre-Raphaelite Studies 214
"Journey Without Words" (Alfred G. Bailey) 25
Judaism 184, 190
jury 34, 38–40, 74, 89, 129, 172

K

Kaddish 191
Kashetsky, Joseph 148
Kay, Alan 135
Keenan, Leona 27
Keeping Watch (Laurie King) 101
Kemp, Gerry 203
Kent County 121
Kent's Punch (Bruno Bobak) 119, 196
Kerouac, Jack 44, 179
Kerslake, Susan 18, 32
Kindle 85–87
Kindness Club 29
King, Laurie 101
Kingswood Park 124
Kinsella, W. P. 51
Kipling, Rudyard 136
Kirkbride, Ralph 130
Kitts, Alice 227
Kitts-Goguen, Colleen 227
Kitts, Wendy 181–182, 227
Klinck, Carl F. 13
Knife Party at the Hotel Europa (Mark Anthony Jarman) 225
Knox, Kelly 163
Kowolik, Leopold 118
Kristmanson, Bernice 206
Kroeber, A.L. 23
Kyle memorial fiction prize 228

L

La Bohème 131
L'Acadie, L'Acadie (Pierre Pierrot) 44
The Landscape of Craft (George Fry) 142
Lane, M. Travis i, 21, 53, 63, 67, 70, 94, 129, 148, 153, 160, 193, 199, 203, 205–206, 208, 218, 223–224, 227–228, 230
Langland, William 11
Lanteigne, André 39
Laubach Literacy 125
Lauzon, Lutia 79
Layton, Irving 52
The League of Canadian Poets 17, 68, 200, 205
Learning, Walter 31, 149, 175
Leckie, Ross 66, 148, 193, 200, 224, 233–234
Ledoux, Paul 171
Lee, Laurie 179
Left in Slow Motion (David Etheridge) 206
Legalian, Richard 12
Le Gallienne, Rochard 214
Lemond, Ed 121
Lerch, Marilyn 121, 125, 155, 165
Leroux, John 80, 124, 135, 237
LeTourneau, Ian iii, 155, 173, 182, 193, 209, 221, 224, 231, 241
Levesque, Roger 34
The Liberal Party 159
Lieutenant Governor 65, 72, 128
Lieutenant-Governor's Award for High Achievement in English Literary Arts 128
Lieutenant-Governor's Award for High Achievement in the Arts 128
Lieutenant-Governor's Award for High Achievement in the Visual Arts 128
Lightning Demand Press 155
Lindquist, Vernon 77
Lingeman, Dan 33
Lin Yutang 13
Literary History of Canada (Carl F. Klinck) 13
Little Sparrows Fall (Betty Ponder) 203
Livesay, Dorothy 26, 58, 184–185, 200, 205
Lives of Short Duration (David Adams Richards) 9–10, 18
Lochhead, Douglas 83–84
Loneliness of the Long Distance Runner

Index

(Alan Sillitoe) 9
Long Ago Far Away (Wayne Curtis) 155
"The Loop" (Alexander MacLeod) 164
Lorca, Federico 113
L'Ordres des Francophone d'Amerique 42
Lords of Shouting (Joseph Sherman) 18
Losier, Cynthia 128
Losier, Mary Jane 52, 154
Lost Land of Moses: The Age of Discovery on New Brunswick's Salmon Rivers (Peter Thomas) 82
A Lost Tale (Dale Estey) 30
The Lost Wilderness (Nicholas Guitard) 225
Lowry, Malcolm 9, 106, 187
Lund, Mary 181, 201
Lynch, Allan 164

M

Macaulay, Warren 146
MacDonald, Elizabeth Roberts 186
MacDonald, George 56
MacDonald, Goodridge 184–185
Mac, Kathy 217
MacKinnon, Bobbi-Jean 227
Macklem, Michael 4, 17
Maclean (Allan Donaldson) 192
MacLennan, Hugh 52
MacLeod, Alexander 164
MacLeod, Alistair 173
MacQuarries 55
Mailer, Colin 36
Maillet, Antonine 43
The Maine Alliance of Writers and Publishers 95
Maine books 95
Manitoba 95
Manitoba Arts Council 34
Margaret's Apple Pie (Stephen May) 199
Margison, Pam 27
The Maritimes 3, 17–18, 43, 46, 61, 155, 239
Maritime Writers' Workshop (MWW) i, 18, 32, 48, 51, 69, 79, 89, 139–140, 149, 154, 181–183, 191, 201, 225, 239

Marshland Inn 216
Martin, Gwen 123, 193, 228
Masefield, John 56
Massey, Bonnie 138, 199
Massey, Jack 199
The Master (Colm Toibin) 100
Matamoros, Santiago 113
Maxfield, John 33
Maxfield, Margaret 33
May, Stephen iii, 129, 132, 139, 152, 199, 237
McAdam 61
McCain exhibition 46
McCain, Marion 46
McCain, Wallace 167
McCartney, Sharon 173, 193
McCord, David 194
McCord Hall i, 3, 26, 27, 30, 32, 33, 148, 149, 154, 194, 196, 197, 205
McDorman, Betty Ann 33
McFarland, Scott 132
McIntyre, Peggy 6
McKay, David 143, 237
McKay, Don 109, 210, 231
McKeen, Randy 158
McKenna, Frank 34, 226
McLaggan, Katherine 119
McNair, J. B. 22
McNutt, Linda 199
The Meaning of God in Human Experience (W. E. Hocking) 91
A Measure of Light (Beth Powning) 225
Merrill, Rick 149, 169
Mersereau, Bob 173, 182, 202
Metadata from a Changing Climate (Ian LeTourneau) 241
Michaels, Anne 132
Middlemarch (George Eliot) 117
Milham lecture 214
Milham, Mary Ella 168, 214
Milham Trust Fund 214
Miller, Elizabeth 113
Miltown 136
Ministry of Tourism, Recreation, and Heritage 34
Minnesota i
Miramichi 6–7, 9, 18, 61, 121, 128

Miramichi Lightning (Alfred G. Bailey) 24
Miramichi River 95, 154
Mistaken Point 109
Molly's Coffee House 202
Moncton 42, 44–47, 61, 64–65, 92, 121, 129, 133–134, 143, 180, 203, 225
Monet, Claude 132
Montreal 5, 30, 43, 47, 50, 65, 184
Moore, Marianne 62
Moore, Roger 203
Morell, Jim 35
Morgan, John 145
morphic resonance 108
Morrell, Carol 190
Morris, Grace 121
Morris, May 215
Morris wallpaper 216
Morris, William 215
Mount Allison University 30, 41–42, 122, 143, 156
Mount Holyoke College i, 239
Mouré, Erin 203
A Mouth Organ for Angels (Robert Gibbs) 33, 55
Mrs. Dunster's Award for Fiction 227
Muchacha en la ventana (Salvador Dali) 114
Munro, Alice 167, 188
Murdoch, Iris 137
The Mystery of the Silver Staircase (Robert Gibbs) 56

N

Nadeau, Sylvie 38
Nahamee of the Squamish 59
The Narrative Voice (John Metcalf) 1
Nashwaak 53
Nason, Riel 182
National Film Board 44–45
National Library 42
National Poetry Week 68
Neilson, Shane 208, 217, 227
Ness, Adam Scott 157
Netrebko, Anna 131
New Brunswick i–iii, 12–13, 17, 21–23, 34–36, 42–47, 53, 61, 67–69, 74, 82–83, 86, 149–150, 154, 157, 159, 160, 163, 175–177, 192, 205, 208, 219, 224, 228
New Brunswick Arts Award 42
New Brunswick Arts Board i, 34–35, 38–41, 67, 84, 90, 135
New Brunswick Arts Branch 72
New Brunswick Arts Policy Advisory Committee 34
New Brunswick Book Awards iii, 224–225, 227
New Brunswick Chapbooks 2, 32, 79–80, 94–96, 148, 149, 201, 205–207, 215
New Brunswick College of Craft and Design 71, 72, 79, 133, 177
New Brunswicker 17, 29, 36, 65, 68–69, 126, 134, 169, 176, 191, 226, 228
New Brunswick Foundation of the Arts 88
New Brunswick Literary Encyclopedia (Tony Tremblay) 207
New Brunswick Reader i–ii, 65, 74, 142, 183
New Brunswick Youth Orchestra 134
New Carlisle 47
Newcastle 6, 9, 194, 227
Newcastle Library 6
Newcastle Opera House 5
New Democratic Party [NDP] 157
Newfoundland 67, 109, 140
New Ross 104–105
Newsweek 85
The New Yorker 89
The New York Times Book Review 78
The New York Times 31, 73, 92
Nicholas, Graydon 127
Nimbus Press 128
non-New Brunswickers 69
Nordhoff, Evelyn 215
Norma Epstein Award 5
North America 52, 65
North American 24
North, Janet 192
North of Jesus' Beans (Bill Gaston) 50–51
Northrup Frye Festival 65, 231
Northumberland Street 83

Index

NotaBle Acts Theatre Festival 147, 149, 169
Not Even Laughter (Phillip Crymble) 224
Nova Scotia 19, 62, 66, 67, 105, 122, 215, 224, 239
Nowlan, Alden iii, 6–7, 9, 19, 27, 36, 54, 57, 59, 68, 75, 83, 103, 118, 128, 149, 152, 157, 169–170, 175, 184, 194, 201, 225, 230, 235, 239
Nowlan, Claudine 103–104, 118, 149, 169, 175
Nowlan, Johnnie 103
Nowlan, Michael 67
Nyarady, Chris 170

O

Oberon-Maritime association 17
Oberon Press 3, 5, 17, 28, 32, 54, 71, 196, 223, 237, 239
obituary 166–168, 186
Obsidian 191
Odd Sundays 160, 202, 217, 221, 229, 231
Odell, Jonathan 21
Odell Park 145, 169, 221
O'Donohue, John 211
Officer in the Order of Canada 25
Officer's Square 202
oldest reading club in Canada [Eclectic Reading Club] 178
The Old Testament 12
Old Woman at Play (Adele Wiseman) 197
Oliver, Michael Brian 33, 148
Oliver Twist (Charles Dickens) 56
On and Off the Shelf (Marcel-Romain Thériault) 128
Ondaatje, Michael iii, 200
One Heart, One Way (Greg Cook) 103
O'Neill, Robbie 169–170
O'Neill, Tip 61
O'Neil, Orry 228
One Step Inside (David Adams Richards) 4
One (Thibodeau and Elder) 127
"the only genius I've ever known" (Kent Thompson) 29

On Shaving Off His Face (Shane Neilson) 217
Ontario Arts Council 5
On the Road (Jack Kerouac) 179
Orca 191
Order of Canada 70
"Orion" (Charles G. D. Roberts) 80
Oudemans, Nel 75
Ouellet, Danielle 143
"Out of Place" (essays) 83
Owens Art Gallery 41
The Owl's Nest 92, 101
Oxford University 21

P

Pacey, Desmond 22, 30
Pacey, Michael i, 27, 29–30, 97, 130, 160–161, 206, 209, 224–225, 230, 237
Page, P. K. 80
Palgrave's *Golden Treasury* 11
Parkin, George R. 21
Passing Ceremony (Helen Weinzweig) 139
Pataki, Inge 118
Paths to Literacy (Goose Lane Editions) 123
Patterson, Freeman 73, 80, 211
Patterson, Jack 33
Patterson, Mike 33
PBS [Public Broadcasting Service] 131
Peacock, Steve 202
Pelletier, Cathie 52, 141
Pentecostal 56, 133
Peter Buckland [gallery] 134
Pieces of Me (Darlene Ryan) 191
Pierrot, Pierre 44
Pittman, Al 6, 104
Plains of Abraham 47
Plato 57
Pluto's Ghost (Sheree Fitch) 155
Poetry Weekend [University of New Brunswick] 221, 225
Poets' Corner [Forest Hill Cemetery] 184–186
Poet's Corner of Canada 26
Pogo 110

Policy Secretariat 35
Pollard, Dawn 33
Pompman and Hutchie stories (Robert Gibbs) 28
Ponder, Betty 203
Poppy Press 66, 203
The Porcupine's Quill 186
post-avant 62
post-modernism 33
Pound, Ezra 214
Powell, Kerry Lee 227
Powning, Beth 163–164, 179, 200, 225
Powning, Peter 75
Prat, Annie 215
Prat, Charlotte [Wilcox] 214
Prat, Mary 215
Prat, May 215
Prat, Minnie Sophia 214
Prat sisters 214–216
Premier's Advisory Committee on the Arts 36, 38
Pressfield, Steven 106
Price, Reynolds 136
Primrose [bindery] 215
Prince Edward Island 70, 143
Prince, Heather Browne 58
print 73, 86, 91, 94, 216
PRISM International's 2015 creative non-fiction contest 223
Prix littéraire Antonine-Maillet-Acadie Vie 224, 226
Professional Writers of Canada 68
The Progressive Conservative Party [New Brunswick] 157
Proterozoic era 109
Prouty, William 122
Provincial Artisans 94, 206
Provincial Pride 38
Pugh, Anthony 74, 172
Purdy, Al 121

Q

Quebec 42–43, 47, 65, 157, 191
Quill and Quire 132

R

radio 31, 44, 47, 73, 136, 196, 225
Ranson, Angela 125
Raspberry Vinegar (Joan Fern Shaw) 140
Redekop, Corey 191, 200
Reid, Diane 155, 164, 193
Reminiscences of Bliss Carman (Charles G.D. Roberts) 21
Resisting the Anomie (Kwame Dawes) 58
Returning Fire (Ryan Griffith) 222
Reynolds, Neil i, 142
Richards, Buck 57
Richards, David Adams i, 3–5, 17, 27, 29, 33, 36, 83, 154, 164, 194, 196, 201, 206, 224, 226, 227, 237
Richer, Shawna 61
Rick Burns Gallery 124
A Ride to Khiva (Frederick Burnaby) 24
Rigelhof, T. J. 77
Rio, Nela 112–114, 160
Robbe-Grillet, Alain 139
Roberts, Charles G.D. 20–24, 79–80, 119, 143, 184, 186, 214–215
Roberts, Dorothy 186
Roberts, Goodridge Bliss 214
Roberts, Jane Elizabeth Gostwycke 186
Roberts, Theodore Goodridge 186
Roberts, William Carman 186
Robichaud, Gabrielle Savoie 45
Robinson, E.A. 12
Rodriguez, Elizabeth 148
Rosenblatt, Roger 172
Rosenfeld, Roslyn 64
Rose, Phyllis 196
Ross, Fred 148, 232
Rossignol, Rino Morin 128
Ross, Malcolm 79
Ross, Veronica 19
Rothesay 91
Roth, Henry 148
Ruet, Karen 129–130, 172
Ruhm, Christopher 95
Ruskin, John 21
Ryan, Darlene 191

Index

S

Sabat, Christina 74, 172
Sackville 61, 141, 156, 216
Saint Denis 97
Saint James 113
Saint John 28, 54–55, 61, 80, 92, 121, 133–134, 142, 178, 203, 208–209, 224–225, 228, 231
Saint John River 146, 152, 181, 185, 222
Saint John River Valley 127, 231
Saint Thomas University 5–6, 112, 138, 148, 169, 175, 207
Salmon Run Auction 124
Salon ii, 61, 74, 80, 124, 152, 155, 172, 183, 209
Saltwater Sounds 121
Samara the Wholehearted (Nancy Bauer) 77, 187, 212, 239
samizdat 96
Sanctuary: The Story of Naturalist Mary Majka (Deborah Carr) 155
Santiago El Grande (Salvador Dali) 112–113
Saskatchewan Writers' Guild 122
Saul, John Ralston i
Saunders, Barbara 26
Saunders, Doug 133
Savoie, Donald 225
Savoie, Jacques 45
Savoie, Roméo 45, 128
Sawlor, Rhona 69, 193
Schama, Simon 111
Schofield, Nancy 129
Scott, Andy 158–159
Scottish Pretender 6
Scott, Sir Walter 12
Scott, Stephen 103–104, 118
Scriver, Julie 129, 139, 145, 202
The Sea Captain's Wife (Beth Powning) 163
The Secret Scriptures (Sebastian Barry) 132
self-employed artists 159
self-published books 95, 225
self-publishing 182
Sentinels (Robert Hawkes) 203
serendipity 91, 124, 190, 191
Seul on est (Thibodeau and Elder) 127
Seventh Day Adventist 56
Shacking Up (Kent Thompson) 18–19
Shadbolt, Jack 152
Shadow of a Doubt (Bobbi-Jean MacKinnon) 227
Shamata, Michael 40
Shambhala meditation 49
Shampers Bluff 80
Shaw, Alvin 118
Shaw, Joan Fern 52, 140
Shawn, Wallace 146
Sheldrake, Rupert 108
Sherman, Francis 79
Sherman, Joseph (Joe) i, iii, 17, 26, 27, 30, 51, 58, 63, 70, 80, 135, 142, 161, 201, 207, 237, 239
Sherrard, Valerie 181–182, 191
Shields, Carol 200, 237
Shklovsky, Viktor 91, 145
Shotgun and Other Stories (Kent Thompson) 1, 207
Silk, Ilkay 38, 177, 222
Sillitoe, Alan 9
Silverberg, David 142, 239
Simpson, Jeffrey 157
Sinclair, Sue 234
Singleton, Jo 33
Singleton, Martin 33
Six Great Russian Novels 4
Skretkowicz, Victor 33
Slade Lecture 21
Small Heroics (David Adams Richards) 206
Small Press Fair 94
Smart, Tom 134
Smith, Kay 51, 80
Smythe Street 83
Snider, Anna Mae 132, 193, 228
Snider, Meredith 124
The Snow Knows (Jennifer McGrath) 227
Snow, Michael 45
Songs That Remind Us of Factories (Danny Jacobs) 218
Sony Reader 85
Sorbonne 42
Soviet Union [USSR] 4, 96

255

Spong, John Shelby 132
Spray, Carole 26
Springhaven (R. D. Blackmore) 12
Starbucks 92, 118
"State of the Art" iii, 188
Stevens, Wallace 57, 214
Stewart, Jim 104
Stewart, John 6
St. Martin's Press 30
St. Mary's University 50
Stones for Ibarra (Harriet Doerr) 117
St. Onge, Audrey 36
The Story of Bobby O'Malley (Wayne Johnston) 106
Stout, Patricia 164
Strangers from a Secret Land (Peter Thomas) 82
Strike/Slip (Don McKay) 109
St. Simon 42
Studies in Canadian Literature 241
The Stunted Strong (Fred Cogswell) 12
suicide 49–50, 76
Sullivan, David 225
SUNY at Rochester 42
Sussex 61, 163, 165
Sussex Artists' Co-op 163
The Sussex Literary Initiatives and Cultural Events [SLICE] 163–165
Sutton, Carol 180
Sutton, William 180
symphonies 88
Symphony New Brunswick 71, 134
synchronicity 91, 219

T

Tall Lives (Bill Gaston) 50
Tantric tradition 51
Taylor, Carol 232
Taylor, Michael 8, 82
Teale, Edwin Way 179
The Telegraph-Journal i, 55, 59, 61
Terminal Moraine (Ian LeTourneau) 221, 241
Tharp, Twyla 106
Theatre L'Escauotte 44
Theatre New Brunswick 31, 36, 40–41, 50, 175, 222
Thériault, Marcel-Romain 128
Thibodeau, Serge Patrice 127
Thistledown Press 221, 241
Thomas, Dylan 9, 22, 89, 218
Thomas, Helen 83, 101
Thomas, Peter 35, 58, 82, 101, 198
The Thomas Raddall Atlantic Fiction Award 224, 226
Thompson, Hugh 169
Thompson, Kent 1, 2, 18, 26, 27, 28, 58, 68, 71, 79, 139, 149, 154, 194, 196, 200, 205, 206, 207
Thompson, Lee 121, 123, 125, 155, 165
Thompson, Michaele 71, 196
Thorpe, Michael 122
Tibetan Buddhism 51
Timmins, John 33, 139
Tims, Jane 231
Toibin, Colm 100
The Tongue Still Dances (Robert Gibbs) 54
Too Close to the Falls (Catherine Gildiner) 132
Toronto 21, 23, 47, 50, 61, 65, 77, 140, 196, 231, 235
Torrie, deLancey 210
Towers 56
Toynbee, Arnold 22
Trainer, Yvonne 27, 59, 201
transplanted unilingual American 65
Travis, Jesse 157
Tremblay, Tony 148
Trinity Church [Saint John] 178
Trinity [gallery] 134
Trungpa, Chogyam 51
Tuesday Night Group i, 26–27, 31–33, 194
Turner, Dean 179
TV 31, 44, 73, 170

U

UNB Art Centre 206
UNB Elderhostel 52
UNB English Department i, 49, 119, 170, 239

Index

UNB's Alumni Building 190
UNB writer-in-residence 155, 157
Underhill, Doug 154
Under the Greenwood Tree (Thomas Hardy) 12
Unitarian Fellowship 115, 203
United States 26, 32, 52, 91, 95, 226
Université de Moncton 129
University of Edinburgh 13
University of Maine 77
University of Moncton 42, 64
University of New Brunswick [UNB] i, 3, 13, 20–23, 26, 29, 48–49, 52, 54, 57, 59, 68, 71, 78, 79, 83, 104, 109, 133, 134, 139, 149, 154, 168, 169–171, 181, 185, 190, 194, 196, 203, 205, 209, 214, 218, 221–222, 224–225, 227, 230, 233, 239, 241
University of Toronto 234
University of Toronto Press 82
Unsnarling String (William Bauer) 155
Updike, John 119
Urchin [Bartlett, Pacey, Richards] 206
Urquhart, Jane 51

V

Valgardson, William 51, 140
Vancouver 50
Vancouver Writers' Festival 61
Van Den Hoonaard, Debbie 127
Van Den Hoonaard, Will 127
Venerable 61
Vermeer (toutes les photo du film) (Herménégilde Chiasson) 46
Giambattista Vico 14
Vic the Bookseller 92, 95
A View from the Roof (Helen Weinzweig) 139
The Vision of Piers Plowman (William Langland) 11
Vuillard, Édouard 152

W

Wachtel, Eleanor 200
Wales 5, 32, 82

Walking to Idaho (David Wojcik) 170
The Wanton Troopers (Alden Nowlan) 169
The War of Art (Steven Pressfield) 106
The Watchmaker's Table (Brian Bartlett) 97
Watson, Dawn 154, 197
Watts, Ana 193
Watts, David 193, 217, 231
The Way Home (Elizabeth Brewster) 18
Weinzweig, Helen 32–33, 48, 139
Welch, Liliane 32, 156
Welsh Arts Council Non-fiction Prize 82
The Welsher (Peter Thomas) 84
Wermuth, Nicholas 33
West, David 33
Westminster [Westminster Bookmark] 91, 132, 192, 193, 223, 232
Weyler, Rex 132
What is Government Good At? (Donald Savoie) 225
When Things Get Back to Normal (M.T. Dohaney) 138
Where to Eat in Canada (Anne Hardy) 19
Whitelaw, Marjory 18, 32
White, Lewis 176
White Madness (Alden Nowlan / Robert Gibbs) 59
Whitman, Walt 24–25
Whitney, Lee 165
Wilbur, Richard 160
Wilcox, Charlotte Prat 215
Wilcox, John Carman 214
Wilcox, Miriam 215
The Wildflowers of Canada (Molly Lamb Bobak) 152
Willem de Kooning's Paintbrush (Kerry Lee Powell) 227
Williams, William Carlos 57, 152
Wilmot United Church 239
Wilmot Writers' Group 239
Wilson, James 130, 209
Wise-Ears (Nancy Bauer) 28, 32, 148, 239
Wiseman, Adele 197
The Witch of the Inner Wood (M. Travis Lane) 227
Wojcik, David 170
Wolf Moon 138

257

Wolf Tree Group 61
Woodcock, George 49
Woodstock 160, 192, 231, 235
Woozles 91
Word Feast [Fredericton literary festival] 229–231, 239
Words on Water 121
WordSpring 123
World Pond Hockey Tournament 88
World Wide Web 73, 91
writer's block 49, 89, 181
The Writers' Federation of New Brunswick i, 25, 40, 67–69, 71, 79, 121–123, 125–126, 135, 149, 154–155, 163–165, 183, 195, 201, 203, 221, 224–225, 227–229, 239
Writers' Federation of Nova Scotia 122
The Writers' Union of Canada 68, 71, 158, 196, 221, 225
Writing on the Wall iii, 70, 98, 112, 153
www.ronsilliman.blogspot.com 62
Wynne-Jones, Tim 52

Y

Yard Sale (Bill Gaston) 50
Yeats, William Butler. 79, 131
Yerxa, Tim 124
young adult novels 191
Young, Patricia 209
Yuge Designs [Bostra and Comando] 124

Z

Zanes, John 185
Zwicky, Jan 210